YOUR **AUTHENTIC** SELF

YOUR **AUTHENTIC** SELF

BE YOURSELF AT WORK

Ric Giardina

BEYOND
WORDS
Publishing

Beyond Words Publishing, Inc.
20827 N.W. Cornell Road, Suite 500
Hillsboro, Oregon 97124-9808
503-531-8700
1-800-284-9673

Editor: Julie Steigerwaldt
Proofreader: Marvin Moore
Design: Big-Giant
Composition: William H. Brunson Typography Services

Printed in the United States of America
Distributed to the book trade by Publishers Group West

Library of Congress Cataloging-in-Publication Data
Giardina, Ric
    Your authentic self : be yourself at work / Ric Giardina.
        p. cm.
    ISBN 1-58270-075-3   ISBN 978-1-58270-075-5
    1. Personality and occupation.   2. Self-actualization (Psychology)
    3. Spiritual life.   4. Vocational guidance.   I. Title.

BF698.9.O3 G5   2002
158—dc21

                                              2001056554

The corporate mission of Beyond Words Publishing, Inc.:
    Inspire to Integrity

This book is dedicated to the following people, each of whom has taught me a great deal about business and about the importance of being authentic in the workplace. Some taught me by example; others taught me by blessed adversity. Some I watched and emulated; others I watched while making efforts to do exactly the opposite of what they did. These are the heroes and antiheroes of my own story of authenticity in business, each one of whom has taught me valuable lessons:

Frederick R. Adler, Esq.	Thomas R. Lavelle, Esq.
Wally "Famous" Amos	John Lockley, Esq.
Michele Andreetta	Henry C. Montgomery
Craig R. Barrett	Stephen P. Nachtsheim
L. Owen Brown	Michael Rothschild
Dennis L. Carter	Seymour I. Rubinstein
Chérie Carter-Scott	Lynn Stewart
F. Thomas Dunlap, Jr., Esq.	Joseph J. Sweeney, Esq.
Carlene Ellis	Theodore Vian, Esq.
Philip J. Galanti, Jr.	Kay A. Warden
Andrew S. Grove	David C. Weeks
H. Glen Haney	Phyllis K. Wilkendorf
Harold E. Hughes, Jr.	Leon Williams

CONTENTS

ACKNOWLEDGMENTS

It now amazes me that only one name or two appears on the cover of a book as though it springs forth from one or two people working independently. Those who participate in the process of writing, editing, designing, publishing, marketing, and distributing a book—and most notably the author—know that dozens of people contribute to its completion. That process begins with the first person who listens to a would-be author's ramblings and then is wise or foolish enough to encourage him.

My own *complete* list of acknowledgments would be endless. Multitudes of friends and acquaintances, as well as clients in business and government and participants in conferences, workshops, and classrooms, have listened to me talk about these ideas and my plans for this book and convinced me of the value of putting these concepts into writing. Instead, what I offer is, at best, an incomplete list, but my heartfelt gratitude is expressed to everyone who has had any part whatsoever in the creation of this book.

Hal Zina Bennett was the first to urge me to put my workplace experiences into writing. He edited the first draft and persuaded me to permit him to show it to a publisher he believed was an ideal candidate to publish the book. If that were not enough, he then acted as my agent in securing the publishing contract. I am and always will be grateful for his talents and expertise, his mentoring and encouragement, and most of all, his friendship.

Hal was absolutely correct about that publisher. From the first, it was clear to me that Richard Cohn and Cindy Black created an extraordinary place when they founded Beyond Words. I can only thank them for taking on this book and me. I have been impressed by the heart-centered vision, integrity, and creativity of the entire staff as we have moved through the various stages of editing, design, and publication. My special thanks to Jenefer Angell for making the acquisition process uncomplicated, to Sylvia Hayse for her incredible efforts on the book's behalf in both the national and international arenas, and to Adrianna Sloan for making the process of marketing—normally the bane of authors everywhere—a fun, exciting, and fruitful adventure.

Authors explain concepts in words, and editors make sure that readers can understand those words and translate them into usable concepts. Many of the ideas in this book would have been lost to understanding without the keen eye and excellent editing work of Julie Steigerwaldt, to whom I owe a great deal. Proofreader Marvin Moore surprised me time and time again with his insightful suggestions that went far beyond correcting punctuation, word usage, and sentence structure.

I had no idea that public relations could be so much fun! At least I didn't until Cindy Black introduced me to Tammy Richards, who handled PR for this book with aplomb and a remarkable sense of humor. She has been both a delight to get to know and a joy to work with.

Many others who contributed to the successful completion of this book may not even be aware of their contributions. In that group, I include Jan Jarnagin and Orlan Friedli of Sierra Properties for finding me the perfect cabin in the Sierra Nevada where I wrote the vast majority of this book; my Aunt Vi, who keeps telling me what a great kid I was and what a fine man I turned out to be; Kimberly Williams for being the perfect focal partner for the last three years and for keeping me honest with respect to my goals; and Helen McIntyre for the prayer and spiritual support she has continuously given to me and Spirit Employed.

There is no way I can adequately thank my wife, Betsy, for the gifts of love and support she has given me all our life together—but most especially since that day not so many years ago when we walked along the Pacific coast in Seascape and I told her I was considering leaving my job to move in a new direction. Her consent was immediate, and her faith has never wavered. More than simply allowing me to take the time necessary for solitude, reflection, and writing, she has unselfishly urged me to do so.

Beginning with the event when she was barely two years old that started the process which led to this book, our daughter, Annalisa, has continued to be a source of some of the most important lessons in my life. She has been at one and the same time a tender and a persistent teacher. I am filled with love, gratitude, and awe.

INTRODUCTION

I do not know the man so bold
He dare in lonely Place
That awful stranger Consciousness
Deliberately to face—.

—Emily Dickinson

A WAKE-UP CALL

It had been a typical day at work. I had spent most of the day in meetings or dealing with the many kinds of problems that are continuously presented in a global corporation with tens of thousands of employees and tens of billions of dollars in revenue. As usual, I had arrived at the office at 6:00 A.M. so there would be time to contact some of my colleagues in Europe before their business day was over. I needed to respond immediately by phone to several voice-mail and e-mail messages that had been left for me during the California night. I stayed at work until nearly 7:00 P.M. to complete a few lingering items that were now in danger of becoming emergencies, to talk with employees working on my projects in Asia, where it was already late morning of the next day, and to make an attempt to plan tomorrow's activities.

As I drove home through the Silicon Valley traffic, work and workplace issues continued to occupy my mind. New ideas as well as things forgotten and needing attention flashed like a kaleidoscope in my consciousness. Before I lost some of these thoughts, I used the car phone to leave messages for staff members, vendors, customers, and even myself on the ubiquitous voice-mail systems.

People would arrive at work the next morning to find my instructions, suggestions, requests, and demands waiting for them, giving their own days early starts toward spinning out of control, much as mine always did.

As I arrived home and stepped through the door, Annalisa, my two-year-old daughter, raced around the corner from the family room, her eager face beaming with joy over Daddy's homecoming.

But Daddy was still "at the office."

I don't know what I said or even how I said it, but whatever it was, it stopped her in her tracks. The words I said, or perhaps more precisely, how I said them, made her understand that something was not quite right. This wasn't the warm and tender, fun-loving Daddy she knew. Something was different. Something was *wrong*.

Annalisa immediately began to cry. I don't think I will ever forget the image of that curly-headed kid standing about four feet from me with her face contorted in anguish, fear, and confusion. Tears rolled down her cheeks. That stopped me in *my* tracks.

While I was standing there immobilized for what seemed like minutes but was probably only a few seconds, my wife, Betsy, came in from the kitchen, where she had heard the entire exchange. She swept Annalisa up in her arms and comforted her by saying, "Don't worry, honey. Daddy will be all right. It's just that he's still in work mode."

The truth of her words struck me with powerful force. I *was* still in work mode, but what did that mean? If there was a way of being that could be identified as my work mode, then what other mode or modes did I have? It was an in-your-face way of forcing me to ask, who am I *really*?

During that time of my life, work had an ordered feeling about it. My workplace—and my part in it—was like a well-oiled although overly stressed machine. I was good at my job and responsibilities, and the benefits and promotions that come with good performance were making their way to me at an accelerated pace. The cogs and wheels of my activities in one of the world's most important companies clicked and turned in time with the rhythm of the belief that organizations are machines in which we have roles of greater or lesser importance. As I moved up the corporate ladder, my role seemed to be one of increasing importance, so the rhythmic clicking and turning was especially loud and seemingly significant.

What I didn't realize at the time, however, was how much of *myself* I had given up in the process of fitting into this mechanized world.

LESSONS IN AN OUTER-CENTERED REALITY

The unfortunate thing is that this "giving up of ourselves" comes only too easily. It is the result of training we have received from our earliest years. This is true in many cultures, but it is particularly true in the culture of the West. Our system trains us early in our lives to accept an "outer-centered" reality as opposed to developing an "inner-centered" reality.

Early on we develop the ability to determine what those in authority want from us—whether it's our parents, our teachers, or other caregivers. We learn how best to provide it. This is an outer-centered way of being. In contrast, an inner-centered reality means checking in with ourselves to determine what *we* want and then following that inner guidance.

Growing up, we quickly learn what behaviors are acceptable to Mom and Dad and the older siblings, or Grandma and Grandpa, or Aunt Dorothy, or Mom's best friend. We are molded from the beginning with a stream of warnings, admonitions, and threats—and in some unfortunate circumstances with physical punishment—against making choices that displease those around us who are certain they know what is in our "best interests"—or theirs. Consider that the word heard most commonly by toddlers is "No!"

Outer-centered reality training continues in preschool, kindergarten, and on through grammar school. As it does, we refine the ability to determine what those in authority want from us, and we mold our behavior and ourselves accordingly. This training picks up speed in high school and adds an almost malicious element—the promise of future reward, perhaps acceptance to the "right" college or university, good grades, a degree, or a good job. Those who do well are those who are best able to determine what is wanted by those in charge and then show themselves capable of providing it.

THE WORK EXPERIENCE

By the time we arrive at our first jobs, we are well steeped in the elements of an outer-centered reality, and on-the-job performance continues to reinforce the concept. Our careers seem to flourish to the extent that we are able to continue to give our employers what they want, generally unquestioningly.

The "company" man or woman gets the promotion, the title, the salary and benefits. And just what does being a "company woman" or "company man" mean? For far too many, it means that one day you discover that what the company wants from you is not consistent with what *you* want from you, but you do what the company wants anyway!

This habitual putting work before self creates stress of almost incalculable measure. Eighty percent of American workers report themselves suffering from work-related and stress-induced exhaustion, insomnia, depression, muscle pain, and ulcers. Stress-related claims in the United States have increased by 300 percent since the early 1980s. The American Medical Association has reported that approximately 40 percent of all heart attacks occur between the times of 8:00 A.M. and 9:00 A.M. on Mondays.[1] And the American Heart Association reports that arrhythmia is more pronounced, even in retired people, on Monday mornings than at any other time. Apparently, the body remembers when it's time to go into work mode.

This is not intended as an indictment of capitalism or of the education system. It is, however, intended to expose an unfortunate and, I believe, unnecessary by-product of those systems. And that exposure is an attempt to raise awareness and develop an antidote for those who are feeling the effects and stresses of living a life at work that is not truly their own in the mistaken belief that this is the road to success and happiness.

ARE SPIRITUALITY AND WORK COMPATIBLE?

During the past twenty years and at the same time that many of us have been living lives of outer-centered reality in our workplaces, there has been a rebirth of interest in the spiritual aspects of life, especially in the personal arena. People everywhere are exploring spiritual values and looking at what these values mean in terms of their everyday lives. This movement consists of varied approaches: reading books; creating and attending support groups; listening to audiotapes; attending meditative and spiritual retreats, workshops, and classes; and participating in communities such as traditional churches and non-traditional spiritual centers.

Unfortunately, this search for fulfillment and meaning has not extended to the workplace, even though the themes we are seeking in spiritual studies can have a dramatic impact on our lives both inside and outside work. Most have looked outside their workplaces to find the meaning and sense of community that their work environments lack, largely because they have no expectation that any spiritual fulfillment or authentic sense of self can be found there.

When the readers of these books and the students of these spiritually based classes arrive at work, they do not feel they have the freedom to express what they have learned. They do not feel capable of applying their new insights and practices to their work environments—largely because of their well-established habit of applying outer-centered reality. Again, we slip into work mode, separating work from our interests in spiritual development.

The belief that our workplaces exist somehow outside the realm of our "real" lives is further exacerbated by the fear running rampant as a result of the changing nature of the workplace. In an increasingly competitive environment, most companies have become so focused on the tasks of making sales, getting product out the door, and increasing profits for Wall Street that any behaviors which do not appear to directly support these goals are suspect. In our outer-centered workplaces, employees quickly learn to eliminate behaviors that do not directly contribute to the bottom line because these are not what those in authority want.

In most companies, it is acceptable to speak about corporate values that provide guidelines for group behavior in support of corporate objectives but not to talk about personal values that provide fundamental guidelines for individuals. This is because of the mistaken belief that discussing values related to spirit, divinity, higher power, or the connection between all living things will somehow divert focus from the organization's goals. What is most interesting in light of this is the fact that, as most every organizational-development professional knows, organizational goals that align with the personal goals of the workers assigned to achieve them have a significantly better chance of being reached.

When people come to work without their spiritual values, attitudes, and behaviors, they are leaving behind their *authentic* selves. Thus, today's workplaces are filled with people who live two lives: an "on-the-job" life and an authentic life. Just as I was, many are unaware of this schism. Others who are aware may believe that they are effectively traversing these waters and may find out too late that it has taken its toll in the form of broken marriages, estranged children, and poor health. Either way, this split negatively affects an individual, an individual's performance, and, ironically, the organization that this system is intended to serve.

Work in the modern world isn't getting easier. We all know this. Downsizing, reengineering, and mergers have resulted in employees working longer hours to achieve expanded goals with fewer resources and fewer rewards. As far back as 1991, the average American worked roughly two hundred *more* hours per year—the equivalent of one month—to maintain the same standard of living that was enjoyed in 1973.[2] The shakeout in the high-tech "dot.com" industry that began in the fall and winter of 2000–2001 and the general economic downturn that resulted from the September 11 terrorist attacks on the United States have only intensified the problem for many, increasing their fears and inducing them to do whatever it takes—at whatever personal cost—to ensure they are not one of the casualties.

The outcome of this general tone is that most workers have created an even greater imbalance between their work and their personal lives and selves. For many, the line between one's "work life" and one's "personal life" has blurred all but to the point of invisibility. Many have lost track of which of their two lives is the "real" one.

A PERSONAL JOURNEY

This confusion is precisely what I saw with such clarity that day when I had to face my daughter's tears. On the one hand, I saw myself as a spiritually centered human being seeking to express gratitude, love, and the unlimited joy of life. On the other hand, I was being everything my company wanted me to be, which for the most part left no room for me to express what was closest to my heart. I saw that the person I was in the workplace was very different from the person I was outside of work. And my work-mode mentality was slipping over into my life as a parent, husband, and friend.

I was living *two* lives, one an appropriate "corporate" life and the other a more authentic, spiritually oriented life. To deal with this internal inconsistency, I had effectively become two people: Corporate Ric and Authentic Ric. But as my business life required more and more of my time, Corporate Ric had to stay around for longer periods. It was getting more difficult to revert back to Authentic Ric when I wanted or needed to.

As painful as it was for both of us, my daughter's horror at her initial inter-action with Daddy in full-blown Corporate Ric mode was a gift of the greatest value that started me down the path of taking a closer look at what was happening in my own life. I began to carefully observe my behavior at work and in the rest of my life. I began seeing just how separate these two lives really were. Returning home from the office each day, I could actually feel the moment when I would shed "work mode" and move into "authentic mode." I became conscious of how difficult it was for me to relate to Betsy and Annalisa in a meaningful way when I first got home and how long it took before I became my true self.

I began to notice that my manner—even my voice and my body—would instantly shift when I was in one mode and some element from the other mode would intrude. These "intrusions" occurred when someone from my family or a personal friend called me at the office or when I was interrupted by some business emergency at home during my permitted "authentic" time. I began seeing, too, that I was not alone. Co-workers and staff members seemed to be facing some of the same issues. Friends were no more comfortable in chance workplace meetings with me than I was with them. I wasn't the only one who whispered into the telephone to speak with loved ones during the business day, as though being overheard in an intimate or loving discussion would blow our corporate "covers" and expose us as human beings.

A NEW PATH

I knew I had to make a change. I decided to consciously work to have Authentic Ric make regular appearances at my office. It was difficult at first and somehow felt unnatural. Initially, I was unable to stay in authentic mode for very long. This was undoubtedly due to my training that outer-centered reality was the appropriate way to be in the workplace. It had become my natural habit to keep my corporate mode in place for the full business day—and unintentionally to take it home at night. Initially, breaking this habit was harder than I had expected.

But there was help available. Support came from some very surprising sources. First, I discovered that my Authentic Self—the caring, compassionate, committed, and loving individual—had roots in the spiritual traditions I had studied most of my life. These traditions had begun with my upbringing in a dutiful Catholic family, were expanded during four years of required theology and philosophy courses in a variety of disciplines at a Jesuit university, and culminated in a personal search through the mysticism of both the East and the West. I quietly began applying to the workplace the timeless principles that had succeeded everywhere else in my life.

Second, positive reinforcement for this change was immediate and strong, and it came from the highest levels in the corporation. My on-the-job performance soared and the company began rewarding me in spectacular ways. My relationships with my peers and other executives as well as with my staff, vendors, and customers completely transformed. I found myself increasingly in demand as a manager, as an employee, and—all too rare in the context of the workplace—as a friend, advisor, and confidant.

More importantly, I no longer felt a schism between my Authentic Self and some artificially created corporate self. I felt more integrated, happier, and more comfortable in both my home and work environments.

I had found my footing on a new path.

THE AUTHENTICITY ADVANTAGE

There are advantages to being in touch with your Authentic Self, and those advantages can serve you and your employer exceedingly well. The Authentic

Self, often also called the Inner Self, Spirit, or the Soul, is the true source of creativity, innovation, and intuition. It is the place from which spring self-esteem, compassion, understanding, insight, and even forgiveness.

When we separate ourselves from our authentic selves in an attempt to be more focused on our corporate or organizational responsibilities, we lose much of the competitive edge that is unique to us alone. We lose touch with our intuitive abilities, our creativity loses elasticity, and the wonder of insight into dealing with complex issues is replaced by hackneyed solutions that have not worked before and will not work now.

We give up much when we give up our authentic selves to fit in better in the workplace. Our employers and our society lose a great deal as well. They lose us—who we really are—at our best.

You will find that having magnificent results by simply being who you are is a lot easier than having satisfactory results trying to be someone you aren't. It is always easier to ride a horse in the direction it is going!

WHAT THIS BOOK CAN DO FOR YOU

Many of the tools and techniques in this book come from humanistic and spiritual traditions that reach far into the past. Some are new. A few are modern versions of ancient practices, approaches, and principles. Some are quite practical; others verge on the mystical. All are based on fundamental spiritual principles of nearly every religion. These tools have the power to revitalize your experience of work and provide you with access to your own brand of authenticity.

You do not need to utilize all the tools at once. In fact, it is perhaps a better use of this book to look upon it as a reference work rather than as something read once and then set aside. Consider trusting your inner guidance enough to pick one of the tools or techniques that speaks to you, read about it, and then begin to consciously apply it in your workplace for some period of time—a day, a week, a month. See what results you get and, if you like them, develop the tool into your own personal habit. Then choose another, and another, and another.

No matter how bizarre one of the approaches might seem to you, give it at least one try. If it works for you—great! You have another tool or technique on your side. If it doesn't work for you, just discard it. In the end, any one of these tools applied consciously, habitually, and daily to your workplace has the power to transform your experience of work and your entire life along with it.

THE 360-DEGREE ARC OF AUTHENTICITY

This book is based on two very simple principles: first, that we are 100 percent responsible for our own responses to what happens to us; and second, that we have the power of choice to transform our experience of the world around us at any time and in any circumstances. Life is a series of choices from which real consequences flow, both those we are happy with and those we are not. Too often, after we make our choices, the consequences of those choices weigh on us, and we forget that what we now find so burdensome is the product of the choices we made. We may feel victimized, when all we really need do is choose again. You've built what you have in your life by the choices you've made up until now, and you will build your future life by the choices you make today and will make tomorrow.

What I mean by the 360-Degree Arc of Authenticity is that you can completely transform your experience of work—and in reality your entire life—by *consciously* creating a circle of authenticity around yourself in your workplace. You do this by being fully present to each event in your workday, whether you perceive the event as good or bad. You do this by being fully present with each and every person with whom you interact in the course of your workday, again notwithstanding any judgments you may have about the person. You create the 360-Degree Arc of Authenticity by consciously looking at what you can do to make the situation better or the relationship more meaningful *right now*.

Creating your 360-Degree Arc of Authenticity is not always an easy task. My own experience is that the habit of living an outer-centered reality is a hard one to break. But this habit can be broken! As I said earlier, the rewards for being authentic are swift and dramatic, so there is immediate and considerable reinforcement for your efforts. As you realize what a difference you are making in your own life and in the lives of others by initially developing even small portions of your 360-Degree Arc of Authenticity, you will start actively seeking more opportunities to do so.

This book will show you how.

PART I

Being Authentic with Yourself

1

Seek Life Balance

*Live a balanced life—learn some and think some and draw and
paint and sing and dance and play and work every day some.*

—Robert Fulghum

There seems to be a general consensus, particularly in today's stress-filled work
environment, that we all need a good dose of Life Balance. But far too many
people approach Life Balance as if it were just another thing to add to their
"to do" list, something that will require an allocation of their time and financial
resources. Worse yet, some people approach Life Balance as if there was a
single personal recipe that will produce for them a life of perpetual equilibrium
and happiness. And then there are those who are in pursuit of *the* magic potion,
the single one-size-fits-all equation. They are convinced that life will at last be
much better—indeed, *perfect*—when they can grasp that equation and make it
their own.

For years I have been teaching courses about the role of balance in our lives.
One of the first things I tell people is that *there is no such thing as Life Balance.*
However, that does not mean we should stop seeking it. One source of content-
ment in the misunderstood area of Life Balance comes from our relentless

pursuit of it—even when we know that it will never quite be found. There is value in living the life of a Parsifal; while he never actually found the Holy Grail that he sought, he still exhibited many of the graces anticipated with its possession solely from his determined search for it.

There is much to learn about oneself and about one's Authentic Self from our search for balance. For one thing, we must recognize that the Authentic Self *is* balanced. It is a natural balance of the physical, mental, emotional, and spiritual elements that make up each one of us. Do not interpret this to mean that an even split of 25 percent for each of the four elements is advisable; there will be times when one or another of these four elements will require more of our attention than the others because of circumstances or an individual preference. Overall, however, a balanced life is one that includes equal attention to one's physical, mental, emotional, and spiritual needs. Another thing to realize about authenticity and Life Balance is that the search is a two-way street. In much the same way that striving to express the Authentic Self will naturally result in a more balanced approach to life, working toward a more balanced approach to life will result in a greater expression of the Authentic Self.

Most of the people dealing with Life Balance issues whom I counsel find themselves wrestling with the balance between work and just about everything else. And, for most, the scales definitely tip toward the work side. In my thirty-plus years of working for others, I have noticed one thing consistent with all employers, whether large enterprises or small, corporations, government agencies, the armed services, or not-for-profit organizations: the more you give, the more they take. There is nothing wrong or draconian about this. It is simply a fact of life, and few of us understand it or have learned to deal with it effectively. Someone has to draw the line, and that someone will *never* be your employer. That someone has to be *you*!

The only solution is for each of us to take stock of what we are actually doing with our time, examine that information to determine how it fits in with how we want to spend our time, and then make adjustments to bring our realities more in line with our desires and expectations. There's an ancient Chinese saying that applies here: "If we don't change our direction soon, we will end up where we are headed." This is valuable advice, but only so long as we stop long enough to orient ourselves—where do we stand now, where do we want to go, and where might we be headed?

Maintaining Life Balance is not unlike rocket navigation. Rocket navigation is usually based on inertial guidance with internal gyroscopes used to detect changes in the position and direction of the rocket. Traveling from point A to point B in space is almost never in a straight line or at a constant velocity because of the many influences on the body in motion. By use of a memory system in a computer it is possible to determine the rocket's position anywhere along a predetermined trajectory. By changing attitude—the rotation about one or more of the axes—and firing a small jet or rocket motor, the path of the rocket's trajectory can be corrected. Preprogrammed computers, both on the ground and in larger spacecraft, monitor the rocket—where it is, where it was, and where it is supposed to be going.

Such navigation systems are not based on determining a specific course at the beginning of the journey and then maintaining it. Instead, they depend on knowing when the vehicle is *off-course* and making frequent course corrections. During the flight of a rocket, it can be off-course as much as 90 percent of the time, aligning with its correct course only momentarily. The rocket keeps moving toward its destination only by the navigational system's ability to recognize each error and make what is usually an exaggerated course correction.

Just so with Life Balance. We are most likely to be off-course to some degree most of the time, but with constant monitoring we can arrive with near pinpoint accuracy at a predetermined destination. So if we were to model our inner navigational system for maintaining Life Balance after a rocket's system, what would that look like? It would mean doing the things that are truly important to us rather than responding primarily to the constant demands of the external world—whether those are the demands of our families, our friends, our work situations, or others. However, like the rocket's navigational system, such an approach requires constant and vigilant monitoring and self-correction—even overcorrection.

A good place to start is with a diagnostic tool I have used successfully in my own life as well as in my seminars for many years. It consists of comparing what we *say* is important in our lives with what we are actually doing with our time. The process is simple: Draw a circle and divide it into pie slices—each slice representing an important area of your life, according to your own judgment. Adjust the sizes of each slice according to how you would like to be spending your time. For example, maybe you'd like the biggest slice to be the time you spend with your family. Perhaps you'd like the next largest slice to be the time you spend doing volunteer work in your community. After that might come a smaller slice that represents the time you'd like to spend at work. Then there would be a number of smaller slices that represent the time you'd like to be spending reading, taking classes, hiking in nature, and so on.

Once you've completed the pie chart of how you ideally would spend your time, make a second chart that indicates where you are actually spending your time now. Compare your two charts. What do you notice?

Most people discover a significant disparity between what they say is important to them and what they are doing with their time. I am still surprised by the number of people who are truly shocked by the information this simple diagnostic tool gives them. It would seem that far too many of us use some sort of mental legerdemain to prevent ourselves from seeing the truth about our life situations.

Once you begin to see and understand the disparity, you can begin to determine what kinds of course corrections you need to make—just like a rocket's navigational system. If from the pie-chart exercise you find an area of your life that is out of balance, come up with a written plan to make a course correction. First, specifically list the steps you will take to change the amount of your time and attention this particular area receives—whether an increase or a decrease. Second, commit to completion dates for each step. Third, after a reasonable period of time (usually not less than one month or more than three), repeat the pie-chart exercise. Reevaluate and design another plan. Continue to diagnose your Life Balance and make appropriate course corrections on a regular basis. It is best to make these changes in tiny increments, as adjustments in one area can have repercussions that affect your entire lifestyle. Making changes in one area only and then letting your daily life settle down before implementing additional changes helps to minimize or even eliminate unpleasant surprises.

It is important to note also that there is no one-size-fits-all solution to creating and then maintaining Life Balance. Indeed, what one needs to do to maintain a semblance of Life Balance over the course of an entire lifetime will change—not just from year to year, but if you are consciously applying yourself to the process, probably from month to month or even from one day to the next.

You won't necessarily know right away what you will need to take on or let go of in your efforts to capture Life Balance in your daily activities. This is where your Authentic Self can provide you with valuable information. It can help you answer questions such as these: What appeals to you? What gives you joy when you do it and sadness when you cannot?

In the process of asking these kinds of questions, you may find that you need to start leaving for home at a reasonable hour and leaving the office *at* the office. Perhaps you need to rediscover your family and friends. Perhaps you need to find or create an activity that is engaging—something that makes your heart sing—outside of work. Maybe you want to renew an interest in music, books, the theater, old movies, a sport, a hobby, or volunteering. It does not matter what the elements are that make up your own individual equation for Life Balance as long as they matter to you.

Only you can change the Life Balance you have created in your life. Interestingly though, you can help others in your workplace change theirs. Take an objective look at your workplace. What is it about its culture that supports people enjoying a healthy life balance? What is it about its culture that thwarts people's efforts to have a healthy life balance? Consider what you can do to make the environment friendlier toward people enjoying balanced lives, but always within the context of the organization reaching its goals. If you are in charge of the workplace or some significant portion of it, implement some changes on your own. If you are a business owner, employer, or manager, don't be the first one into work in the morning and the last one out at the end of the day. It sets a standard that your employees will feel pressured to emulate if not beat. Set a pace that expects everyone to perform to their best abilities without sacrificing their entire lives to the effort.

Talk openly in the workplace about the need for Life Balance, making it a subject of discussion and shared ideas. Most importantly, go beyond lip service and start living it.

2

Apply the Law of
Mind Action

The mind is its own place, and in itself
Can make a heaven of hell, a hell of heaven.

—John Milton

The Law of Mind Action originated thousands of years ago. As a universal principle it is timeless. One of the earliest articulations of it is "Like begets like." Another way of putting it is that *things held in the mind create after their own kind*. Whatever you focus your attention on, you will get more of it in your life. This is so because our words and our thoughts have power. The Buddha says, "The thought manifests as the word; the word manifests as the deed."

Even if you don't subscribe to the metaphysical belief that our words and thoughts actually *create* the world we experience, you must acknowledge that our thoughts and words *create our experience* of the world. And certainly they influence how the world responds to us.

Have you ever noticed how bad the traffic looks and how many people cut you off or perform other breaches of commuting etiquette when you are traveling home after a particularly bad day at the office? It always seems worse than usual, doesn't it? What you are experiencing is an example of the Law of Mind

Action in full bloom. You're upset about your day. Your mind is filled with images of the outrages that have been visited upon you. And what you get are more outrages.

And it doesn't matter whether you believe in the Law of Mind Action or not. Like gravity, it works either way. Not believing in gravity won't save you if you jump off a building. Similarly, not believing in the Law of Mind Action won't prevent it from affecting your life. Given that this is so, you might as well understand the Law of Mind Action as best you can and begin consciously directing its power toward creating the life you want.

How does this law apply to your daily life? Remember that the Law of Mind Action says that you will get more of whatever it is that you are carrying in your mind. Let's say that things are not going well for you. If this is where you hold your attention—*things are going badly*—chances are great that you are going to get more of the same. But if you want to make immediate and permanent changes, get the Law of Mind Action working for you, not against you.

One of the quickest ways to get it working for you is through cultivating gratitude. If that seems a bit of a stretch for you, let me explain. Most of us believe that we can change some *thing*, *someone*, or some *situation* if we complain about it long enough, either quietly to ourselves or vociferously to others. At some point, we think, somebody will do something about it. Even if life worked that way, this approach fails to take into account the negative effect that these thoughts have on our own happiness, our health, our performance, and our relationships with others. Ultimately, it will also have an impact on our relationship with ourself, in the form of diminished self-esteem. Worse, complaining flies in the face of the Law of Mind Action.

Gratitude, on the other hand, focuses our attention on what is positive in our lives. If we carry those positive thoughts in our mind, we will attract more of the same. The energy that surfaces through your expression of gratitude is healing and creative. It attracts solutions. Its power lies in the fact that it is a completion and a new beginning at the same time. You'll see that gratitude is the "starter" that kicks the engine of change into action. For example, you can begin to make changes by blessing your work. This isn't dependent on how good or bad your job is. It isn't dependent on how much you hate what you have to do or how much you dislike the people with whom you work. It isn't dependent on how little they are paying you. And it isn't dependent on how overworked and underappreciated you are. There is *some* aspect of your job for which you can be grateful. Find it! Focus on it. Express gratitude for it daily—constantly, if you can.

It seems we have our priorities turned around in the popular culture. We send our thank-you cards *after* we get the presents. We treat gratitude as if it were our way of rewarding the world for doing right by us. When what we want or expect to happen actually happens, then we are grateful. In the meantime we withhold our gratitude. By doing it this way, however, we lose the power of the Law of Mind Action. The irony is that as long as you are focused on what is *not working* in a situation, the likelihood of those circumstances changing is practically nonexistent.

Initially, you may not be able to be grateful for everything that happens in your life, but be grateful for whatever you can. You might consider expressing gratitude for a situation that you first believe to be negative. We've all had seemingly terrible situations in which something unexpectedly pops up to transform them into positive experiences. In those circumstances you may have found yourself being grateful not only for the transformative elements but for everything which brought you to that point.

The truth is that so much of life really is a matter of how you look at it. There is a Zen koan about a farmer in the Middle Ages in Japan who finds a wild horse. His neighbors come to congratulate him on his good fortune. "We'll see," is all the farmer has to say. Within a week, the man's son attempts to ride the horse. He is thrown, and his leg is broken. The farmer's neighbors come again, this time to express their sadness over this misfortune. "We'll see," is all the farmer has to say. Within a month, the army comes through the countryside conscripting every able-bodied young man to fight in the war. The farmer's son is left behind as unsuitable for military service because of his injured leg. Again, the farmer's neighbors come to congratulate him on his good fortune. You already know what the farmer said. In the Zen tradition this story continues with hundreds of such twists and turns.

The purpose of the Zen koan is to get us to look at how much our limited perceptions determine the value we place on an event. It was Shakespeare who first noted in *Hamlet* that "There is nothing either good or bad, but thinking makes it so." This is as true today—and in your workplace—as it was in Shakespeare's time.

Consider keeping a gratitude journal. For two weeks, write in it either first thing in the morning or last thing of the day. List everything and everyone that comes to mind for which you are thankful at that particular moment. Notice any difficult situation you find yourself in and begin focusing only on the elements of the situation for which you feel genuine gratitude. Note these elements in your journal on a daily basis. See what impact giving thanks has on your outlook and your life.

In my workshops, I begin the discussion of this section by having everyone spend a few minutes doing a silent check-in on their state of mind. I ask them to be aware of any physical comfort or discomfort and any feelings or emotions they are experiencing. After the check-in, everyone spends three minutes writing down a list of everything for which they can express genuine gratitude. Some people sit there for half a minute trying to find something. Then, when they find the first thing, the floodgates are opened, and they find it hard to stop.

After the written exercise, I ask them to do another silent check-in on their state of mind. In all the years of doing my workshops, no one has ever told me they didn't feel better in body, mind, emotions, and spirit after spending just three minutes consciously expressing gratitude. Some felt marginally better, while most experienced significant positive shifts in mood, feelings, and body sensations along with an increase in their conscious connection to whatever they viewed as their "source."

Try these exercises for yourself. A regular, daily program of expressing gratitude—and applying the Law of Mind Action—can have immediate and long-term benefits on your body, mind, emotions, and spirit.

3

⚜ ⚜ ⚜ ⚜ Develop Your Intuition

Call intuition cosmic fishing. You feel a nibble, then you've got to hook the fish.

—Buckminster Fuller

In our left-brained, the-universe-is-one-great-big-cause-and-effect-machine oriented society, intuition is less than fully appreciated. We're taught in school, from a very early age, that we have to "explain and justify" how we arrive at our answers. We are conditioned to believe that not doing this is *dangerous* anywhere, but particularly in our workplaces, where showing cause and effect is viewed as essential. As a result, the valuable wisdom of intuition is too often discarded as worthless, solely because the intuitive person's knowledge is not based in logic. We've come to a place in our evolution when we mainly understand and value only what is logical. Anything that can't be quantified with the strict rules of reason is labeled unreliable.

Intuition is not a "voice from the heavens." More likely, it will manifest itself as a feeling, a "loose" thought, or a mental picture. I believe that intuition is actually the subconscious part of ourselves which is signaling that it knows something which the conscious self does not. Another way to think about this, particularly in the context of the workplace, is that intuition is a part of your Authentic Self which has information that your Corporate Self probably wants to hear.

Will you listen?

Probably not.

In most work environments, admitting to relying on intuition or "gut feelings" is perceived as an admission of weakness. In spite of that belief, industrial giants such as Henry Ford and Andrew Carnegie as well as scientists such as Albert Einstein always paid homage to intuition as a key ingredient in their success. And Oliver Wendell Holmes pointed out that many great decisions in court, as in life, "depend on a judgment or intuition more subtle than any articulate major premise."[1] Ordinarily, though, admitting to using your intuition in the workplace signals that you have not applied sufficient reasoning to the issue. Reliance on intuition in most workplaces is generally relegated to the same end of the credibility scale where words like "emotional" and "hysterical" reside.

I am not suggesting that rational thought be abandoned. But I do insist, like Oliver Wendell Holmes, that there are situations in which reliance on rational thought *alone* is not enough. For example, when a situation is vague and there are no apparent right answers, it just may be time to rely on intuition. Sometimes you don't have enough data or sometimes you have too much data, but in either case it's important to be able to recognize when it is time to turn to intuition. Sometimes despite the application of your best cognitive abilities, you cannot see a pattern that indicates the best course of action.

Einstein counseled other scientists to honor the mysteries of life and to understand that it is often our best work which comes out of intuitive processes joined with the rational. He once said that what we would term *mysterious*, which includes intuitive knowing, is "the source of all true art and science." He put forth convincing evidence that perhaps it is time we begin supplementing our cognitive, left-brained decision-making processes with a good dose of right-brained intuition.

Everyone has some level of intuition, but just like the muscles in your body, if you fail to use your intuitive skills, they atrophy and weaken. Because of the cultural bias against intuition in the workplace, we sometimes consciously turn away from even the most insistent intuitive feelings. We then forget about those feelings in our attempts to push them down, so it is no wonder that many people think they have no intuitive skills. Just as people who live near railroad tracks tune out the sound of trains, many of us have learned to completely tune out the intuitive messages that come to us. Because intuition is in the realm of the Authentic Self, at the same time that we are avoiding or ignoring intuitive messages we are also disregarding important aspects of our Authentic Selves.

The key to harnessing the power of intuition is to be willing to start paying attention to your hunches and respecting them for the value they contain. The way to do this is to start noticing when you are getting "funny feelings" about something, whether it is that new marketing campaign, a candidate you are interviewing for a position, or just about anything else. Be careful not to discount those feelings because of your reasoning that the marketing campaign has been well thought out by experts who know more about it than you do, or that a job candidate's résumé and references look great on paper, or that you don't dare go against the prevailing consensus of opinion. There is no way that your intuition can get you to listen to its signals if you are predisposed to mistrust or ignore them. You have to begin with the willingness to become aware of the feelings associated with intuition and then trust those feelings long enough to see what will happen. At a minimum, always allow an intuitive feeling to delay a decision until you get clear on what it might mean. Many people who use their intuitive faculties in business recognize intuitive signals early on, following up either with further investigation or with a wait-and-see approach.

One tool to use in strengthening your intuitive muscle is hindsight. When something surprising happens, look to see whether you had any intuitive feelings about it before the event occurred. As you begin to see that your intuitive feelings are offering valuable "pre-event" information, you will begin to feel more comfortable about relying on them.

Another way to begin tapping into your intuition is to start playing intuitive games. For example, while waiting in front of a bank of elevators in a high-rise building, see if your intuition will guide you to the elevator that will arrive next. While waiting in a long line at the bank or the post office, let your intuition tell you which of the tellers or postal clerks will be available when it is your turn. When you are sitting in your car for any reason with traffic passing by, make an intuitive game of guessing how many of, say, the next twenty-five cars driving past you will be red. In your leisure, choose five or six ordinary playing cards out of a deck, shuffle them, and then try to intuitively predict which one will turn up as you select one and turn it over. While I am downloading my e-mail, I always make an intuitive guess as to how many messages I have. Be creative in thinking of your own intuition-based games. If you play these games regularly and keep track of your results, you'll discover that your success rate increases over time. Besides being good exercise for your intuitive muscle, these games will teach you which types of clues and signals are unique to your own style of intuiting.

Start creating space for intuition in the workplace. After carefully listening to a staff member give you his or her data-driven cognitive case for why something should or should not be done, ask him or her, "What's your gut feeling about this?" At first this question will surprise people, but as people become more comfortable about trusting their intuition, they will learn to trust it more as an integral part of decision-making. Ultimately, they will come to expect it and rely on it, at least in their dealings with you.

We should start accepting as normal the application of intuition instead of apologizing for it, hiding it, or worse, ignoring or even censoring it when it presents itself. Ignoring intuitive warnings can have disastrous consequences, as my own experience has shown.

I participated in what I have come to call the "$475 Million Intuition Lesson." Intel introduced the first Pentium[2] processor in March 1993. About a year later, Intel engineers discovered a minor software flaw in the floating-point device of the chip that caused extremely rare computation errors. The multiplication of two numbers with very specific parameters would result in a wrong answer caused by the processor making a rounding error restricted to integers twelve and thirteen places to the *right* of the decimal point—and thus not likely to be of concern to the vast majority of desktop computer users at the time.

Although several million Pentium processor–based systems were already in use worldwide, the engineers and executives determined that the best and most appropriate course of action was an in-line fix of the problem, which meant that new versions of the Pentium processor would have the flaw corrected but that there would be no recall or correction to those already in service. At the time, it was believed that desktop computers were being used exclusively for home and business use, which meant that no one would likely stumble on the error because those users generally do not require such accuracy.

But that assumption turned out to be wrong. Desktop computers had become so powerful that they had migrated to use in scientific *and* mathematical research. And so, three months after Intel's initial discovery, a mathematics professor who was using a Pentium processor–based desktop system for prime-number research contacted Intel. He had discovered the flaw!

Intel provided him with a new system without the flaw and assumed that this would be the end of it. But news of the flaw quickly spread, and the next month, *Electrical Engineering Times* ran a cover story on the flaw and CNN ran a feature story discussing it, Intel's explanation of the problem, and why the problem was statistically insignificant, and yet focusing on Intel's refusal to do anything for consumers. Within a matter of days, the Pentium-processor "FDIV" flaw had become world news, and thousands of people were contacting Intel asking for processor replacements.

At the time, I was in transition to a newly designed role as a special projects attorney. I was assigned to handle the legal but non-litigation aspects of the Pentium-processor flaw, including customer-service complaints, warranty issues, and computer-manufacturing contracts.

I began meeting daily with the FDIV Task Force, which consisted of the president and CEO and his direct reports, along with European and Asian staff members on telephone-conference hookups plus a few others with specialized expertise such as myself.

What became apparent to me from the start was that the entire team had bought into the concept that since there was no *rational* reason to replace the processors, Intel would refuse to do so unless the end-user purchaser could *prove* to Intel that its computing needs required a processor without the FDIV flaw, as the mathematics professor had done.

Previous to participating on the task force, I had co-designed the Intel Inside[3] program, which aimed to align Intel's name and products with trust, quality, and integrity. And I believed that the public perception now would be that the company was not living up to this promise. Despite the data and the pure logic proving that almost no one needed a desktop computer accurate to twelve places to the right of the decimal point, something didn't *feel* right to me about the company's position.

I discussed the issue with a few co-workers on the task force and discovered that several of them were having the same intuitive feelings as I was. But I was warned that if I brought up the subject openly at a task-force meeting, I would be doing so at my personal peril, because the CEO and a few others were adamant that nothing would force the company to replace the processors. Although my intuition continued to tell me nonstop that we were making a very big mistake, *no one* was willing to bring it up and face the apparent dire consequences for doing so.

The more the company resisted replacing the processors, the greater the external pressure became. Within four weeks of the initial task-force meeting, due to massive press, consumer, and governmental pressure, Intel's board of directors had no alternative but to reverse the company's policy and replace on request any Pentium processor affected by the flaw regardless of the user's need. At the same time, the company set aside a reserve of *$475 million* to cover the costs of the replacement program, which dramatically affected its financial results for both the quarter and the fiscal year.

Had the company been willing at least to *entertain* a discussion of the intuitive aspects of the situation, hundreds of millions of dollars would likely have been saved. What blew the entire thing out of proportion was that Intel's response was based entirely on statistics and pure logic.

This experience taught me to rely on—or at least take into account—the messages I get from my intuitive self, no matter what the prevailing winds seem to be.

You are both a rational *and* an intuitive being. When you leave out the intuitive part in your quest for success, you are using only half the skills available to you. Quite simply, neglecting your intuition is a self-imposed handicap—and you are driving away your Authentic Self with a stick. On the other hand, by regaining your ability to utilize your intuitive skills *along with your cognitive skills*, not only do you increase your chances for success in the workplace, but by the very act of using those intuitive skills, you become more authentic.

4

Find Yourself a Coach

Coaches have to watch for what they don't want to see and listen for what they don't want to hear.

—John Madden

There's a piece of advice that has stuck with me most of my life: Avoid comparing one's situation with that of others because we will always find those who are much better off than we are and those who are not. Comparisons are certain to make one crazy. On a metaphysical level, there is a blessing in the realization that there are always some who are *ahead* of us and some who are *behind*. Those who are behind give us the opportunity to be of service by coaching and sharing what we already know. Likewise, those who are ahead can provide us with insights and stories of their life experiences that can move us along our pathways and, possibly, catapult us to another level of awareness in the blink of an eye.

In chapter 26, "Mentor Someone," you'll see that you have messages for other people, the delivery of which is part of your life's mission. In exactly the same way, other people have messages for you that are part of their lifetime missions. Just as you have things to teach, there are others who have things to teach you. The world is just waiting for us to find out what we need to know. The adage, "When the student is ready, the teacher will appear," is absolutely true, so be ready!

One of the most valuable skills we can learn is how to identify and engage teachers in mutually beneficial relationships. The best way to do that is to follow your own inner guidance and intuition. If you have a good feeling about someone, try to spend a bit more time with him or her and see if that feeling expands, contracts, or disappears. If it expands, if you start discovering that you have things in common, if you notice that some deeper level of sharing is starting to take place, if you sense that there is an *invitation* of sorts, you're probably onto something, so keep with it.

When you feel strongly about your connection with a potential coach, build a long-term relationship with that person. When choosing a coach, find someone who is exhibiting skills and attributes that you want to acquire. Find someone you feel can help nurture your Authentic Self. Watch that person's behavior and how he or she interacts with other people. Most importantly, be sensitive to how that person relates to you. You won't always have all the information you might like to know about him or her, but you will find yourself acting on intuition and willing to take a risk.

When I was just out of undergraduate school and before I started law school, I worked as a research scientist with an organization in Washington D.C. whose field was in the biological sciences and which was under contract to NASA. It was an interesting place with about twenty-five employees, and for the most part, each of us was left alone to do the work required. Indeed, we were left too much alone for my taste. I looked around for someone who could serve as a coach to me and found myself drawn to the deputy executive director, whom I had met only once or twice. Acting on my intuition, I walked into his office and told him I was in need of a coach, and unless he had any objections, I thought he was it. He immediately agreed and became my first formal coach. That was over thirty years ago, and the friendship remains to this day. The lessons I learned from him and his wife have been invaluable in both my professional and personal life.

There is a wealth of information available out there for anyone willing to look for a coach and risk asking for help. Look for the channels through which this information and these lessons are coming. Expect that you will receive guidance, but don't have expectations about *where* you will find it. We would all like to receive life lessons placed neatly on silver trays with a crystal vase holding a rose and a little note in calligraphy saying, "Pay attention! This is an important life lesson!" Unfortunately, it doesn't happen that way. My experience is that the most important life lessons tend to manifest in forms that are not always pleasant or easy to take in. Some say that the most difficult lessons are difficult because they are the ones we most stubbornly resist. Your next life lesson may come directly from that homeless person you would much rather step around than engage in conversation. Don't lose valuable guidance—or a great coach—because the messenger or the manner of the message do not match your preconceived pictures of what a coach should be.

Coaching relationships can be informal or formal. Informal relationships are fueled by serendipity and happenstance. An informal coaching relationship may never even be acknowledged for what it is, but you will find that you regularly experience personal breakthroughs when you are with some particular person simply by virtue of the things he or she or even you might say when you are together. Leaps in one's self-awareness need not take a great deal of preparation, and in the right circumstances they can occur instantly, almost outside time.

Formal coaching relationships, by their nature, require a bit more organization and planning. For example, a good formal coaching relationship will include regular meetings between you and your coach and perhaps the articulation of definite agreed-upon goals to be achieved as a result of the relationship. How you and your coach design the meetings and the interaction is up to both of you. You may opt for weekly face-to-face meetings. You could elect to use a combination of face-to-face meetings and telephone or e-mail exchanges, which can work particularly well in situations where you and your coach are frequently on the road.

While coaching can come in many forms, there are a few elements that must be present for the relationship to be fruitful. First, it is important that communication between the two of you is open and honest. This means being willing to talk about *anything* that has the possibility of advancing the knowledge or the goals you have set for the coaching relationship. Second, you must give permission to your coach to tell you *whatever* it is that he or she sees about you or your behavior. A good coach will operate like a mirror, reflecting back to you what you are doing, what you are saying, and your attitudes and stances about both. That can only be done effectively if the coach has your unqualified permission; otherwise he or she will be walking on eggshells, and both of you will lose the benefit of the relationship. Third, you must be willing to give and receive honest feedback on the coaching process itself. The coach needs to know what is working for you about the relationship and what is not. You need to know what is working for the coach about the relationship and what is not. From those discussions you will find that you and your coach will come up with interesting solutions to some otherwise perplexing challenges in this process.

I was once coaching a young woman who had a bad habit of interrupting people, particularly in meetings. Worse, she did not recognize that she was doing this, although it was clear to me that other people were getting increasingly upset with her behavior. In her defense, I must add that her behavior was frequently an expression of her enthusiasm over an idea or a solution that was being presented. Nevertheless, her behavior presented a problem that could have limited her advancement in the company.

On several occasions when I attempted to discuss the matter with her, she had a hard time believing me. Because of her resistance to hearing what I had to say, I felt stuck and unable to help her with this issue. I know it would have been entirely inappropriate for me to correct her in front of others when she was exhibiting her interruptive behavior, and she denied the problem existed when I was in a position to address the problem privately. I knew that if we didn't handle this conflict in our relationship, there would be little point in my coaching her further. I discussed my conundrum with her from the perspective of how it was impacting our coaching relationship. From that discussion, we came up with the idea of a secret signal. When I noticed that she was interrupting, I would immediately work a set of uncommon words into whatever I said next.

Because she was getting feedback right on the heels of the objectionable behavior, she was able to recognize it and eventually change it. The lesson for all of us here is that if both you and your coach are committed to the relationship and the results, you and your coach will get very creative together—even when dealing with issues involving the coaching process itself.

Another important thing to remember about coaching is that, like most things in life, it has a beginning and an end. A coaching relationship that has run its course though the two participants continue to hang on for whatever reasons can become extremely uncomfortable. A great coach knows when his or her job is done and will take the initiative to change the relationship to reflect the new reality of the situation. If a strong personal relationship has developed, a long-lasting friendship can result, but there will undoubtedly come a point when it is time to eliminate the coaching aspect of the relationship or, at least, to amend it.

The best way to end a coaching relationship is to tell the truth about it—simply, openly, and compassionately. When the time has come to close the mentoring phase of a relationship, both parties are usually aware of the situation, sometimes painfully. Telling your truth about the relationship creates the best chance for the two of you to remain lifelong friends.

There is someone you probably already know who is ready, willing, and able to provide you with the coaching support you want. That support will remind you to be authentic, and it will help make you as successful as you can possibly be. Be alert to finding that person. Be willing to have that person support you in every way possible. Take active steps to secure him or her as your coach. Do everything you can to keep the coaching relationship healthy and productive, and most importantly, be open to the personal-growth possibilities which the relationship with that coach can provide you.

Here are some tips for finding the right coach: Make a list of all the people who you have considered formal or informal coaches at one time or another in your life. For each one, write down what attributes of that person attracted you to him or her in the first place and what, in the end, you think you learned or gained from the relationship. Then make a list of all the people you have in your environment who you could consider as candidates for possible formal or informal coaching relationships. For each one, write down what attributes the person has that attracts you to him or her as a possible coach and what you might stand to learn or gain from the relationship. Finally, using your intuitive sense and inner guidance, determine which coaching candidates on your list are best for you and place them in order of your excitement and interest. Approach the first candidate on your prioritized list, explain your interest, and see if he or she is agreeable to a formal mentoring relationship. If not, continue down your list until you find the person with the response you want. Set up a formal mentoring relationship for a limited period of time—perhaps three months—at the end of which you and your coach can discuss what, if anything, to change about the relationship and whether or not to continue it.

5

. . . . # Be Committed

The road to happiness lies in two simple principles: find what it is
that interests you and that you can do well, and when you find it
put your whole soul into it—every bit of energy and ambition and
natural ability you have.

—John D. Rockefeller III

If you find that your job is not feeling right to you or that you are not getting
the results you want at work, check your commitment level. Keep this principle
in mind: Your results are directly proportional to your level of commitment.

If you discover that you are no longer committed to your work to the
degree that you once were, you have two choices: either get recommitted or find
something different to which you *can* get committed. That "something different" need not mean moving to a different company or even a different job in the
same company, although it can. Recommitting can be as simple as finding
something about your present position that is exciting enough to restimulate
your commitment.

You can't fake commitment. It involves metaphysical elements that simply
cannot be counterfeited, because your Authentic Self would protest—and

loudly! Faked commitment can actually give you worse results than no commitment at all. If you have ever been in a situation where you had to fake enthusiasm, you'll know how much energy that takes. It can exhaust and depress you
because there is always a part of you that knows it's a lie.

You might believe that because you have made a decision to grit your teeth
and *make it work*—to tough it out—you are committed. But this may not be the
case at all! If you are not consciously and affirmatively committed, you are *not*
committed—it's as simple as that. Real commitment fosters total involvement,
and that's what gets the most positive results. Calling something less than your
Spirit's full commitment by another name or making believe it is something
other than it is *ain't gonna make it*, as they say. You may fool your boss, but you
can't fool yourself. You will know. Your Authentic Self will know. And your
results will reflect the true level of your commitment no matter how good a
show you put on for the rest of the world.

The reason that only a full measure of commitment will produce opti-
mum results is that only full commitment engages our authenticity. When fully
committed to our work, we can accomplish the impossible. Everyone is familiar with the story of the mother exhibiting superhuman strength by lifting a car
off her loved one following a traffic accident. That's perhaps the ultimate
measure of commitment. We have more power to produce results in our lives
than we can possibly imagine, and the key to opening the door to those possibilities is commitment.

On the morning of April 21, 1519, which was also Good Friday according
to the Catholic calendar, Hernán Cortés and his force landed their ships in what
was to become Mexico. There were eleven vessels and about 110 mariners, 553
soldiers, including thirty-two crossbow-men and thirteen harquebusiers. There
were also some two hundred Indians from the Caribbean islands and a few
Indian women to do the menial work. This was the small group whose mission
it was to conquer the vast and uncharted empire of the fierce Aztecs. In addition to facing the Aztecs, Cortés's forces had begun to mutiny and were
demanding that he return them to Spain or the Caribbean islands. In a bold
move, exhibiting his commitment to a difficult mission, Cortés burned all of the

ships on which he and his soldiers had arrived. There were now only two alternatives for the group: fight and win or fight and die. While I certainly don't sanction Cortés's decision or the actions that followed, his burning of the ships serves as an amazing and instructive story about commitment.

Are you willing to burn your ships, or do you keep something in reserve just in case your mission does not work out as you planned? If you are playing the keep-something-in-reserve game, you are less than fully committed. That gap will negatively affect your results and your authenticity.

This is not to say you shouldn't have contingency plans, that is, alternatives for dealing with unforeseen and unexpected complications. The important thing is to be willing to let go of everything—to burn your ships if that is the only way, or the best way, that you can verify your commitment. And don't confuse burning your ships with burning your bridges. These are definitely not the same thing! Burning bridges is another way of saying that you are "destroying community," and that is not what I am talking about.

What I *am* talking about is being so committed to a course of action—to your *cause*—that you will take the next step even when you are not certain there is anything to step onto. There's a scene in Steven Spielberg's film *Indiana Jones and the Last Crusade* where the hero is faced with traversing a wide and immeasurably deep chasm. He steps off the cliff in pure faith although he is unable to see the land bridge that will take him to the other side. As he puts his foot down, the land bridge appears, having been there all the time but completely camouflaged. In fact, it is the placing of his foot into what could prove to be endless space that causes the land bridge to come into view. I love this image as a metaphor for the way commitment works in our own lives. Only when we are willing to step off the cliff is it possible to discover the land bridge.

You'll have to decide for yourself what burning your ships or stepping off the cliff means to you in any particular situation. What will be required for your full commitment will vary in each situation. It is important only that you understand that *you* will know what is required of you at the appropriate time. Only you can determine if you are experiencing a level of commitment that will keep you happy at work and create success for you, your co-workers, and your employer.

Commitment is a matter of both personal *choice* and personal *metrics*. For some, commitment means something akin to sacrificing your entire life to your work. For others, it means having a deep sense of mission and purpose about what you do while continuing to have a rich and vital life beyond the workplace.

To make a true commitment to whatever you wish to change, it takes a combination of decision (*mind*), dedication (*spirit*), and action (*body*). Sometimes we think we are committed because we have made a decision to do something, but decision alone is not commitment. Here's a little riddle to illustrate what I mean: Five frogs are sitting on a log. Two decide to jump off. How many are left? Did you guess three? If you did, you're wrong. Sorry! The answer is five, because *deciding* to jump is not the same thing as *jumping*. Real commitment also requires the spirit's dedication and the body's action.

Often once these three factors are in place, it seems as though our level of commitment becomes tested, with obstacles seemingly rising out of thin air. We no sooner make a commitment to be more patient with our children than we find our patience being tried in ways we would never have thought possible. The first day after a commitment to begin a daily running program, you wake up to unseasonably cold and damp weather. Immediately after a commitment to get your finances in order and to stop making impulse purchases, the "sale of the century" is announced at your favorite store and everything you "need" is now 40 percent off.

When this seems to be happening, it is not your imagination. Our resolve does get tested as soon as we utter or even think words of commitment. My friend Les Hewitt, of Achievers International in Alberta, Canada, offers what I think is the best solution to this phenomenon. With respect to our commitments, Les says that we must adopt a "no-exceptions" policy. What this means is that you make no exceptions to following through on the action part of your commitment—period. Once you allow even one exception, the crack is in the dam, and the next exception is easier, the next easier still, and soon the action segment of your commitment triad is missing. The no-exceptions policy works, and I have successfully used it to create new personal habits that support or reflect the commitments I have made.

The no-exceptions policy can carry you quickly to what I call the "Threshold of Magic," a point crossed in the course of working on a project or taking a course of action when we are truly committed. After crossing the Threshold of Magic, obstacles may pop up unexpectedly, but they just as swiftly disappear—as if by magic. It is also the point at which we have more energy and ideas flow more freely. Johann Wolfgang Goethe had it right when he wrote,

Until one is committed
there is hesitancy, the chance to draw back,
always ineffectiveness.

Concerning all acts of initiative (and creation)
there is one elementary truth
the ignorance of which kills countless ideas
and splendid plans:

That the moment one definitely commits oneself
then Providence moves too.

All sorts of things occur to help one
that would never otherwise have occurred.

A whole stream of events issues from the decision
raising in one's favor all manner
of unforeseen incidents and meetings
and material assistance
which no man could have dreamt
would have come his way.

Sometimes when I discover that obstacles are not dissolving and that I am not experiencing some level of "extra" or "otherworldly" support, I take it as a clue that I am not as committed as I thought I was. That's the time for a round of good old-fashioned self-examination. More often than not, I find that I have mis-characterized a feeling that I *have to* do something as a genuine commitment to do it because of the circumstances in which I find myself. That mind-set never works, no matter how well disguised.

The reason commitment is important in your relationships with your co-workers and your workplace is that it carries you directly to your Authentic Self. The integration of mind, spirit, and body through decision, dedication, and action required by true commitment is the most compelling of all invitations to the Authentic Self. Indeed, it is hard to imagine someone being truly committed who is not being authentic at the same time.

If you are not experiencing a high level of commitment in your workplace, then promise yourself to find something to do that will allow you to have that level of commitment. Yes, it will benefit your employer. But more importantly, it will allow you to experience yourself in a new way and to embrace your Authentic Self.

Take a look at your work and workplace. What is your commitment level to the various aspects of them? Do you feel the level of commitment you deem necessary to your work? How about to your co-workers? If not, what's missing? If you find that your level of commitment to your work and your workplace is not what you want it to be, make a list of changes which, if they occurred, would raise your level of commitment. Make that list without regard to whether or not you believe you have the power to effect those changes.

6

Declare All
Things in Order

There is nothing either good or bad, but thinking makes it so.

—Shakespeare

We smelled the smoke about ten minutes after eleven, just as we were getting ready for bed. As we searched the house for the source of the smoke, a passerby starting banging on the door and yelling that the house was on fire. We grabbed our bathrobes, and at the very moment that we started down the two flights of stairs to the front entrance, smoke exploded from every crevice in every wall, and the house filled with the thick, black, billowing stuff. Luckily, we were able to follow the handrail down to the front door to the safety of outside.

We stood across the street from our home as the fire department bravely fought to save the material possessions that represented something of the life Betsy and I had built together. At about 4:30 the next morning, just as dawn was breaking, the fire marshal escorted us back into the house for a few minutes to show us where the fire had started in an electrical short in the wall and to see if we could retrieve some necessary items, such as our eyeglasses and wallets.

As soon as we entered, it was clear that the house was no longer habitable. Most of the walls were burned; a major section of the roof was missing, with the clear California sky showing through; ashes and soot covered every surface; and the dank, lurid smell of wet cinders permeated everything.

I remember my first words to Betsy after surveying the damage, mostly because of the shocked look on the face of the fire marshal. "I can't wait to see what good is going to come from this," I had remarked without thinking. The fire marshal's expression indicated that he was concerned I had lost my senses along with my house.

My response came out of the blue, but there was a big lesson for both Betsy and me in what might otherwise have been a disastrous event in our lives. When something—anything—happens, we have a choice. We can choose to hold it as a negative event and respond accordingly, or we can choose to hold it as a positive event and respond accordingly. We really do have a choice.

Our natural inclination is to go with the negative, sometimes even when the news is good. As I have pointed out earlier in this book, thoughts held in the mind will create after their own kind, in accordance with the Law of Mind Action. And this is true whether the thoughts are negative or positive in nature. The best way to ensure a disastrous future is to envision one. The best way to ensure a bright future is to envision one no matter what the present appearances. The process of creation goes directly from your thoughts to your reality.

It can be difficult to visualize that bright future when you are in the middle of lamentable circumstances. Even so, rather than giving in to the visions of disaster that your mind will certainly conjure up, your best alternative is to simply declare that all things are in order—or, in other words, Divine Order.

What is Divine Order? I think of it as a visceral understanding that things happen in the right order and in the right way. It means approaching life from the point of view that every event is part of a plan guided by Spirit, the Higher Self, the Soul, or God—that component within us which makes itself known through the Authentic Self.

We can develop the knowledge that everything which happens to us moves us to higher levels of consciousness and aligns us with our true spiritual selves. All of us have read stories of people afflicted with life-threatening and even terminal illnesses, such as heart disease, cancer, and AIDS, who report that being forced to deal with the illness was the greatest gift of their lifetime. *That* is recognition of the Divine Order in all things. When we recognize the Divine Order in our lives, life will be good no matter what the circumstances may appear to be.

Can you absolutely prove—even in the most egregious situations—that there is a Divine Order involved? Rarely, though years later you may be able to see it. Still, by adopting this position, you will be amazed at what happens. Doors open to you that you could not have even imagined. At the very least, take this process on faith and begin practicing it in your everyday life. Approaching life's daily annoyances this way will often reveal that there really is a higher order at work in our lives, one that we might otherwise not recognize.

Begin by noticing your immediate reaction to events that do not match your expectations. If you, like most people, have a tendency to "go negative" by envisioning dreadful outcomes, try declaring Divine Order instead, and in a short time you'll begin to notice a shift in the way you view events around you. Remind yourself often that when you are in the middle of some seeming misfortune, you cannot know for certain what the final outcome will be. Allow yourself to move into the mind-set of expecting good and, at the same time, being curious about what the nature of that good will be.

This discipline serves several linked purposes. First, it keeps the Law of Mind Action working in your favor, for if you are putting energy into worrying about an outcome you have categorized as "bad," the likelihood that you will create this outcome increases dramatically. Second, declaring Divine Order, even if you can't envision the good to come, primes the pump of your mind so as to position you to recognize and be able to take advantage of the positive opportunities when they do come along. Third, it reduces your stress level dramatically and saves wear and tear on your mind, body, spirit, and emotions. Fourth, because the Authentic Self experientially knows the truth that all things are in Divine Order, declaring Divine Order in all things does not deny the Authentic Self but rather honors it and invites it to take a more active role in your everyday life.

By this time, you may be wondering what possible good could come from one's house burning. The full answer was not apparent for almost three years, although there were other gifts to enjoy along the way. The process of rebuilding the house began almost immediately. As it turned out, we were able to rent the house next door to ours while our own home was being rebuilt, which took just about a year. Living next door to the ongoing construction work so we could keep an eye on things was certainly a gift, as were the stronger ties that grew between Betsy and me as we worked on rebuilding our home together. During the reconstruction we were able to do some remodeling and upgrading to make the house more the way we wanted it in a shorter period of time—another gift. When we bought the house, we had thought that some of the changes we wanted to make would take decades to accomplish. At the time of the fire, we had no intention of selling the house, but three years after the fire, I accepted a position at a company that was over seventy miles away. Commuting was not an option; we had to move. When we put our house on the market, we learned that it had a significantly higher sales price because of the rebuilding, which gave us the money we needed as a down payment on a home in our new neighborhood, where housing costs were more than twice as high.

The challenge for you in declaring Divine Order is that it isn't always easy to tell yourself *not* to think about the negative consequences when any fool can see that the situation you are facing is a disaster! At such a moment, you can't tell yourself to not think of that situation as a disaster. Doing so would be like the old perceptual exercise of sitting very quietly for ten minutes not thinking about a pink elephant. Of course it can't be done, because the directive to not think something pushes you into the very act of thinking it. The *only* thing that works is to replace your negative thoughts with positive thoughts—which means affirming Divine Order. To be fully effective, this response needs to become an unconscious habit. It was the development of that habit in my own life which provided me with my comment on the morning after the fire.

Stop for a minute and think back over your life. Look specifically at those seminal events that, at the time, frightened you the most—the loss of your job, the breakup of a relationship, a health challenge. Looking back, is it not possible to find substantial good which came out of that event? Even if you cannot yet identify that good, was the outcome as horrible as you fearfully imagined it would be? It could not have been the mortal blow you might have imagined—after all, you are still here or you would not be reading this book.

Declare Divine Order unceasingly. Make it a part of your rhythm—your own personal heartbeat as you go through life. Whenever your fears get triggered, immediately declare Divine Order. Declare Divine Order at every opportunity—when you drop something or when you miss a freeway exit, for example. Immediately fantasize about the divine reason that the event happened and make a game of guessing at the good which might come from it. If you find that you cannot envision a positive outcome, move into the space of curiosity by thinking, "I wonder how this is going to turn out? I know it will be wonderful, but I am curious about what that outcome will be." This approach is a lot safer than dwelling on your fears and having the Law of Mind Action manifest those fears as your reality.

It is important to develop a foundation of what I call an "Is that so?" attitude toward life's events. The following Zen koan will help explain: A master lived as a hermit in a cave on the outskirts of a medieval town. One day, he heard a clamor at the opening of the cave and, coming out, discovered the townspeople outside with anger and hatred in their eyes. Based on the testimony of the child's mother, they accused him of fathering an illegitimate child, and they demanded that he take responsibility for raising the infant. He knew his own innocence, but he responded, "Is that so?" He took the child and raised him. A decade or so later, his peace was again disturbed by a commotion outside the cave entrance. The townspeople had returned, but this time they demanded that he give them the boy since the mother had confessed the true identity of the father. "Is that so?" the master responded as he gave them the child.

The Zen master's "Is that so?" responses represent a state of mind which is so centered on Divine Order in the universe—and in the events that make up our lives—that there is no need to resist. It represents another interpretation of Jesus' suggestion that we "turn the other cheek."

Declaring Divine Order is a step beyond the mind-set of "Is that so?" because it reminds us that all things are happening for good. When we are holding life in an awareness that all things are happening for good—that every- thing is in Divine Order—we move naturally into our Authentic Selves. The Authentic Self understands that life *is* in Divine Order—there is nothing we need to do to move it into Divine Order. This simply is the truth of life. Holding your life and the world around you in the context of Divine Order creates an environment in which the Authentic Self will express itself.

7

Embrace Change

The universe is change; our life is what our thoughts make it.

—Marcus Aurelius Antoninus

There are huge numbers of books, both ancient and modern, that discuss the nature of change and how to successfully manage one's self in the process. From Lao Tzu to Marcus Aurelius, and from William Bridges to Spencer Johnson, the advice and knowledge about how best to deal with and assimilate change is varied and often contradictory. One would think that, with the quantity of material available on the subject of change, this would be one area which had long since ceased to be a problem for us. That, however, is not the case.

Change continues to be one of life's most formidable challenges for most of us. Undoubtedly, many of us get better at dealing with it over the course of our lifetimes, but like some living and evolving creature, change seems to have learned to outstrip our efforts to deal with it effectively. This is because the dynamics of change continue to, well, change.

First, the number of changes we are required to integrate into our lives on a daily basis is increasing exponentially. For example, I recently heard an estimate on Public Radio International that 90 percent of the jobs which people will be holding within the next ten years do not even exist today! The amount of change that has occurred just in the area of employment and the workplace is staggering. The changes in our personal lives, which by themselves would be overwhelming, are in addition to those in our work lives.

Second, the rate of change continues to accelerate. Think of the changes that have resulted since the adoption of the Internet as a medium for information distribution, research, marketing and sales, and personal communication. The Internet as we know it today did not even exist ten years ago. To expect anything other than continued and accelerated change in the future is foolish.

We humans have a natural tendency to resist change. Many of us get caught in habitual emotional responses to change, preferring to hold on to our comfort with the familiar rather than risk the unknown. We find an extreme example of this in the cases of battered spouses who stay with their abusers because even that seems somehow preferable to venturing into a future they cannot predict. On a less dramatic level, we've all stayed in a job long after we realized it was time to leave, simply because we weren't ready to face an uncertain future.

There is very little that can cause more stress in our lives than resisting change, yet nothing would happen without change. It is the very essence of action, and resisting it is futile. Do any of us *really* believe that we can remain effective in an active, dynamic organization without changing ourselves? No, but that doesn't seem to stop us from attempting to resist change, even though the main thing our resistance produces is struggle.

Our human reaction to change is so predictable that a science has grown up around it. Change-management theorists generally describe four phases through which the vast majority of people pass when dealing with significant changes in their lives:

Phase One: Denial. Our first response is a general refusal to recognize the evidence that the change is occurring: "This can't be happening!" Denial is natural because it provides a mechanism that protects us from being overwhelmed. It buys us a little time to let the new information sink in and to integrate what this information will demand of us. But sooner or later the truth hits home and leads to a personal response.

Phase Two: Resistance. In this phase, most of us move deep into our negative feelings about the change. We move from denial into any or all of these resistances: self-doubt, anger, depression, frustration, or anxiety. Along with that resistance we often experience the fear which arises from the uncertainty attending change. Some people never fully move through the resistance phase of a change and may find themselves handicapped or even crippled by its lasting effects, usually in the form of chronic anxiety.

Eventually, almost everyone reaches a low point in the resistance phase. The resistance phase is an uncomfortable place to be, so it is natural that after some period of time—how short or how long really depends on the individual—people begin looking around for opportunities. When they do, they move into the *exploration* phase.

Phase Three: Exploration. During this phase, people start looking at the possibilities and opportunities that the change represents rather than staying in denial or continuing to resist the change. At some point, exploration hits pay dirt, and the person's energies are again directed toward positive steps forward.

Phase Four: Commitment. In the final phase, we begin to focus on the new direction that the exploration phase has uncovered, and we embark on a journey of new experiences and new growth. The commitment phase lasts until the next change occurs, whether initiated by the individual or by outside sources, at which time the entire process starts all over again.

The journey through the four phases of change is not often a pleasant one. Because of our attachment to the past and the familiar, most of us spend altogether too much time in denial and resistance, neither of which is a comfortable place to be—physically, mentally, emotionally, or spiritually. The exploration phase can be exciting, but its creative energy is often imbued with a chaotic tinge that many find a bit unnerving.

In the commitment phase, we start to get comfortable again as we establish our new routines and return to what we would like to think of as "normal." Once again in our lives, there is nothing distracting us from a rosy future, nothing to deny, nothing to resist, nothing to explore, because our paths seem clear and unfettered. Perhaps this was the case in simpler times when the commitment phase represented a plateau of some lengthy period of time before we were faced with new changes. Usually the changes we were faced with were the so-called natural rhythms of life—the seasons, droughts, floods, births, deaths, and interpersonal dynamics. But change is inevitable, and it seems that we are no sooner getting accustomed to one new set of circumstances when we're faced with changing again. Indeed, in my consulting work in corporations, government agencies, and other organizations, the most common complaint I hear is that the next round of changes hits before people ever feel they've gotten their feet back on the ground after the last one. Most people these days seem to have barely moved out of the exploration phase before they are thrown back into phase one, denial.

Dealing with change can be daunting, but I am about to tell you everything you need to know to deal with it successfully. It does not matter to which change-management theory you subscribe. It makes no difference what discipline you choose to follow or whether you follow none at all. It is not significant if you have chosen a field in which rapid change is your daily currency or if you believe you have chosen a field that is immune to high-speed change. Your personal wealth, title and position, skills, education, experience, and ability to communicate can all work as effectively against you as they can work in your favor if you do not know and take into account the one secret of dealing with change.

The only thing that matters in dealing successfully with change is on which side of "the line" you stand. The line separates those who *welcome* change from those who *resist* change. That's all. That's it. Everything else around the dynamics of change can be traced to your attitude and your resulting approach to change. Your apparent demeanor, what you say, what actions you take in response to change will all be dictated by which side of the line you stand on.

Look back on your life and the changes that have come your way. From which side of the line do you think you have approached change? Pick out one of the most important changes from your past. Track your experiences and actions through the four phases of change to get a better idea of how you have tended to respond.

Whether you welcome change or resist it is a mind-set over which you have total and complete control. Too many people *unconsciously* resist change—they do it from habit, but with a little self-awareness, even they can convert resistance to acceptance. The effects of the Law of Mind Action are no less powerful in the area of dealing with change than elsewhere. If you are predisposed to have a hard time with change, you will get exactly what you expect. The results are different if you have a predisposition to think of changes as unlimited opportunities for your continued success.

As you might expect, when we are in denial and resistance, it is difficult for the Authentic Self to express itself. Indeed, at such moments we are usually "in our heads" rerunning conversations about what we said or think we should have said or revisiting actions we took or believe we should have taken. Creativity vanishes under those circumstances, because we are living in the past or in fantasies of the future that will never come to be. Either way, we're living in a never-never land of our mind's making. We have cut off any ability to access our intuition in favor of gnawing on the bone of our judgments about the situation and the people who we believe have caused it. It's a very dim place.

When you embrace change, you take a shortcut through the first two phases of change and quickly enter the third and fourth. You overrun denial, short-circuit resistance, and arrive at exploration in record time. You then have more time to explore and envision what the future can be for you in the changed environment and move quickly into committing to those things that excite your creativity. In short, you succeed, and you do so in record time with significantly less wear and tear on your physical, mental, emotional, and spiritual well-being.

Take a look at a change you are experiencing now. Which of the four phases of change do you think you are in at this moment? Which of your attitudes and behaviors tell you that? Determine what you can do to accelerate your movement to the next phase if you desire to do so. Next, prepare a written plan for yourself to deal with the next major change in your life. At the time of this change, force-march yourself through the four stages of change as efficiently as possible. When you are in the denial phase, write down all your thoughts of denial. Think about how you might let go of that denial and accept the truth. Do the same thing with each of the stages of resistance and exploration. Gauge your speed moving through the four stages of this planned change and compare it to your past experiences.

If you can approach change by engaging your Authentic Self beforehand, you will discover yourself automatically on the "welcoming change" side of the line. Recognize, though, that particularly during times of change it may be difficult for you to access your Authentic Self. You might feel as though you are attempting to access it in a vacuum in order to bring its power to bear on the change issues themselves, which may be the case when you are mired in the first two phases of change. Many of the tools in this book can help you move through that conundrum.

Recognize that the Authentic Self is, by its nature, an agent of change. It easily gets bored with repetition, which may be explained by the fact that it is the source of creativity and innovation. Indeed, I believe that one of the reasons so many people resist their Authentic Selves is because of their fear that the Authentic Self will cause them to do things they are afraid to do—like change. To the extent that you are succeeding in your efforts to bring your Authentic Self to bear in your workplace, you will find that, as a natural by-product, you are also more welcoming of change.

Change in all things is a part of life, and it is imperative that you understand that the organization of which you are a part is just naturally going to change because it must in order to survive and succeed. If you can welcome and embrace change, you will succeed in expressing your Authentic Self—your own personal agent of change—and gain access to its inherent knowledge, wisdom, creativity, innovation, and intuition to ensure your continued success in your changing work environment.

8

Manage Monkey Mind

No man will be found in whose mind airy notions do not sometimes tyrannize him and thus force him to hope or fear beyond the limits of sober probability.

—Samuel Johnson

You are busily working on a critical project. It is your opportunity to prove yourself capable, and you need to concentrate and do your best. But your mind—well, your mind keeps coming up with reasons why your efforts are not good enough, why you aren't good enough, and why this will be a complete and total disaster. Your worst job-related nightmares keep floating into your consciousness, preventing you from being effective with the task at hand.

Or perhaps you must make a decision. But no matter which course of action you examine, your mind offers up all sorts of reasons why that option is no good—indeed, why it would be a *terrible* alternative and why some other alternative is better; that is, until you focus on that other alternative. Then your mind moves into hyperdrive giving you reasons why *that* isn't a good choice either. Decision paralysis has got you in its grip.

Welcome to the world of *Monkey Mind*, a place many of us know only too well. The human mind is very active. For reasons that no one truly understands, our minds tend to chatter away, describing all manner of disastrous possibilities and outcomes, particularly when faced with difficult tasks or decisions.

Where does the chatter of Monkey Mind start? If you observe the inner prattle carefully, focusing on the sense and tone of what is being said, you will probably discover messages from your past—messages of your parents, siblings, teachers, and others whose criticism in your early years left indelible impressions on you. Monkey Mind tends to get strongest when we feel we have the most at stake, so it only seems logical that it would plague us the most in our workplaces. Whatever the impetus, most of us are unable to eliminate this useless chatter.

Barraged by Monkey Mind's complaints, criticisms, and doomsaying, it is no wonder that we can become paralyzed and unwilling or unable to take any action at all. Sometimes we think that more data could help. But additional data frequently serves only to bolster the arguments of Monkey Mind. And even if we move forward, we do so with reduced confidence and increased uncertainty about the course of action we have chosen.

Monkey Mind is the antithesis of the Authentic Self. Its roots are most likely in our earliest and most basic outer-centered training, which, like the ramblings of Monkey Mind, leverage our own fears against us by focusing on and magnifying only the negative possible outcomes. Once you are aware of it, however, the reasoning of Monkey Mind is easy to recognize since it is circular and frequently does not respect realities, such as when we *must* take action. Monkey Mind will argue against each and every choice equally effectively and with fear-based counsel.

By contrast, the Authentic Self has its roots in inner-centered reality in which we look to ourselves and our higher power to determine what course of action is right for us. The Authentic Self recognizes that fear can be conjured up at any turn and that it is in our best interest to proceed in spite of the fear— indeed, at times, *because* of it. Finally, the Authentic Self is not dependent solely on cognitive reasoning of any type because it synthesizes the physical, mental, emotional, and spiritual realities of our lives. That synthesis provides a foundation for creative and intuitive thinking in addition to data-driven cognitive reasoning.

When faced with an attack of Monkey Mind, our natural tendency is to argue with it, just as we might argue with a parent, authority figure, or a close friend who has just attacked us. We find ourselves protesting that we are not failures and offering all the reasons why a particular course of action will work. Arguing with Monkey Mind is actually the worse thing we can do, because it is impossible to win. Like a four-year-old child, Monkey Mind turns into a wellspring of "yes, buts" and "what ifs" that deflect every logical and rational answer we might offer in defense of our own reasoning. You cannot outlast Monkey Mind's ability to produce "yes, but" arguments.

Worse, arguing with Monkey Mind turns the Law of Mind Action against you. The more you argue, the more you actually focus on the negative result which Monkey Mind is advancing. By focusing on it, you direct your energies toward it. It is just like when young children learn to ride bicycles; they do fine until they spot something they are worried about running into—and then, sure enough, they steer right into it!

That seems to leave us with a considerable problem: We cannot eliminate Monkey Mind, and at the same time, it is useless to argue with it. But you will not be at the mercy of Monkey Mind if you learn to *manage* it.

A technique that has worked increasingly well for me over the years is to use what I call the "cancel command." When Monkey Mind starts presenting me with one disastrous scenario after another and I realize what is happening, I tell it sternly, "Cancel!" As simple as this sounds, you will be astonished by the seemingly overwhelming negative images you can disperse using this technique. Try it. The next time Monkey Mind starts presenting you with a series of calamitous images of the future, just say, "Cancel!" At first you may have to use it several times—one time right after another. Make the cancel command an automatic habit and you will discover that Monkey Mind will begin to respond to it instantly. Just as one would expect of a trained monkey, my Monkey Mind has gotten more responsive to the command over time, just as I have become more sensitive to the wiles of Monkey Mind itself. I am discovering that the need to use the cancel command is becoming less frequent with time.

Another technique that works well when dealing with decision paralysis is to leave the arena of your mind and refuse to engage in the internal debate with Monkey Mind. You do this by getting the pros and cons out in a graphic form in front of you—where you can see them all at once. They lose a lot of their mystery and power that way. And because Monkey Mind relies on sheer cunning to create confusion in your mind, you will vastly improve your ability to circumvent its arguments when you can see things more clearly.

Take a piece of paper and run a single vertical line down the center, forming two columns. Label the left column "Reasons to . . . ." Label the right column "Reasons not to . . . ." Then just receive all the arguments that enter your mind, with or without Monkey Mind's participation, for doing or not doing whatever the action is that you are considering. For example, let's say I am thinking about taking a two-month assignment in Panama. In the left column ("Reasons to . . .") I might write, "Good chance to travel and see a part of the world I've never seen before." Immediately, I think, "I would be away from my family for two months." I put this in the right column ("Reasons not to . . ."). It is important to place your "Reasons not to" directly opposite your "Reasons to."

The process is designed to empty your mind of everything that you have thought of around the pros and cons, and this includes all the things that Monkey Mind has suggested to you in the course of attempting to make a decision. This is not a process to determine which of the two alternatives has the largest number of reasons and then choose that one! It does not matter how many items end up in one column or the other. The sole purpose of this exercise is to get the decision—and all the little pieces of it floating around in your mind—*out* of your mind, which is where Monkey Mind plays its home games. After expressing the issues involved, as you have done in the exercise above, you are likely to experience a sense of relief, even a kind of emptiness, around the subject. In that void, you can make a choice rather than a decision, and actions based in choice are always best.

Learning to manage Monkey Mind liberates you from its tyranny so that you do not waste time attempting to counter its attacks. When you are starting new projects, you want your attention on doing your best, not on dealing with your inner demons and phantom inadequacies. You will be a better, more productive, and successful employee.

Also, learning to manage Monkey Mind can prevent you from marching into the swamp of indecision and getting mired in its quicksand. *Any* decision is better than no decision. One lesson from my training as an officer in the United States Army stands out in my mind more than any other. During a training exercise in which the team I was leading was moving through hostile territory, we came under attack. There were several possible responses, any one of which was acceptable in terms of getting a passing grade. The only *unacceptable* response was paralysis. It was hard to believe how many young officers stood completely paralyzed in the simulated heat of battle from the indecision caused by Monkey Mind.

The monkeys in your mind carefully guard the door to your Authentic Self. When you are doing battle with them, you are on the wrong side of the door. The more you engage Monkey Mind in an effort to defeat it, the harder it is to access your Authentic Self and the gifts it offers. Interestingly but not surprisingly, ignoring or otherwise managing Monkey Mind and going directly for your authenticity causes the monkeys in your mind to flee in terror.

9

Take a Break!

*It's important to be heroic, ambitious, productive, efficient, creative,
and progressive, but these qualities don't necessarily nurture soul.
The soul has different concerns, of equal value: downtime for
reflection, conversation, and reverie; beauty that is captivating
and pleasuring; relatedness to the environs and to people; and
any animal's rhythm of rest and activity.*

—Thomas Moore

During my years in corporate life, there were far too many days when I felt like
a steel ball in a pinball machine at the mercy of some wound-up teenager with a
roll of quarters. You probably know the feeling. You get in early, scrambling from
the moment you arrive, and you don't stop all day—that is, if you don't count a
few trips to the restroom and standing still long enough to wolf down a sandwich
from the vending machine or the cafeteria around lunchtime. On such days, you
may find yourself almost out of breath, your heart pounding in your chest, and
your body running purely by virtue of adrenaline, which is probably the case.

51

It is at times like these that we become vulnerable to what I call the "one-more-thing" mentality. It probably sounds familiar to you: "Just let me get this one-more-thing completed, and then I'll stop, slow down, or take a break!" This mentality is dishonest from the start, of course, because for me, I know that beyond *this* "one-more-thing" there looms yet another and another. And each one seems more critical than the last.

In addition to increasing friction in personal and business relationships and diminishing the quality of one's work, this seemingly minor act of dishonesty has several other seriously negative side effects. First, the demands of working at the one-more-thing pace are bad for the body, mind, emotions, and spirit. When we are in the throes of one-more-thing thinking, the first thing that disappears from our consciousness is any awareness that we need to take care of ourselves. With respect to the body, there is suddenly no time for exercise, no time to eat properly, and no time to get an appropriate amount of rest. Mentally, driving ourselves to complete one-more-thing usually results in overtaxed cognitive abilities without benefit of escape, and as a consequence we do not think as well as when we are in a more relaxed state. Emotionally, one-more-thing thinking causes us to get cranky and impatient with anything or anyone that seems to be inhibiting our ability to complete that task. Finally, faced with the downward spiral of body, mind, and emotions, the spirit doesn't have a chance. A results-driven—*crazed* is more properly the word!—version of the Corporate Self takes over while the Authentic Self goes into hiding until it is safe for it to come out again. The truth is that the one-more-thing mind-set plays right into the hands of our natural tendency to put ourselves last anyway.

The second negative impact of one-more-thing thinking is that it turns us into habitual breakers of our word. When we say we will do just one-more-thing before moving on to something else, we have made an agreement with ourselves. When we jump immediately into the next one-more-thing without taking that promised break, we breach that agreement. The agreements we make with ourselves are the easiest ones to break, and consistently breaking them invariably results in the loss of self-esteem and self-respect. Remember, a person who cannot be trusted to keep agreements with himself cannot be trusted to keep them with other people. In this light, completing that next one-more-thing becomes an expensive proposition.

Lastly and possibly worst of all, the more we permit ourselves to work in a one-more-thing state of mind, the more likely it is that we will become insensitive or even numb to it, and we can let it become the new baseline against which we gauge our productivity. We then believe that anything other than a one-more-thing attitude and approach to our work just isn't good enough. Indeed, many people become addicted to the way this mind-set energizes them and soon come to believe that they are unable to work productively without the kind of pressure it engenders. I would submit that these folks will be among those 40 percent experiencing Monday-morning heart attacks.

In today's work environment there is probably nothing you can do about the pace of your workday and the rate at which the challenges come at you, but most of us exacerbate the problem of overwork by adopting a one-more-thing approach to it. By doing so we signal that we can handle anything and any amount of it. *No limits* becomes our personal theme! The employment workload algorithm is very simple: The more you do, the more you get to do. Your employer will probably not notice the impact that getting work completed may be having on you as an individual, but he or she *will* notice that the work is being completed and that there's someone around who can apparently handle the load. It is your responsibility—not the company's—to pace yourself.

One way to accomplish this is through the simple act of scheduling and then taking frequent breaks. Breaks can be as simple as a short midday meditation or a walk outside. One good way to find relief from thoughts of work is to watch the show that nature puts on for us "everywhere at once," as philosopher Alan Watts once put it. Try stopping to focus for a few minutes on something as mundane as watching a bird searching for food on the lawn where you are sitting. Or you may wish to lose yourself in the meditative movement of your breath going in and out of your body. Losing yourself entirely in the moment is the important thing, not the manner by which you do it. It need not take long. I have felt rejuvenated after as little as a brisk, three-minute walk around the building, in which my senses were alert to the natural world around me.

Les Hewitt of Achievers International suggests that everyone take time for "TPM" several times every day. "TPM" stands for "twenty peaceful moments," which can be anything from the preceding suggestions to a nap on the floor of your office. There have recently been a number of articles published about companies that recognize the revitalizing effects of catnaps and are consequently providing places where their employees can go to take those short naps. Since none of the companies I ever worked for provided nap rooms, I took ten- or fifteen-minute naps in my car in the parking lot when I felt it necessary.

The most important component for taking a break is that it actually be a *break* from your work. Too many people take a break by simply moving the location of their work, either from their office to the cafeteria or from the computer on their desk to the computer in their mind. If you feel a walk would be helpful, make sure you do it *outside* the building. Walking around inside the building is an invitation to engage in additional work-related discussions—hardly a break! Forcibly preventing yourself from thinking about work and work issues for just a few minutes can be remarkably refreshing.

As with everything else in life, forewarned is forearmed. If you are aware that your work life leads you right into your one-more-thing habits, make certain that you set up reminders for yourself. I recommend a fifteen-minute break every two hours. If you live by your calendar, write down "break appointments," just as you would record an important meeting. And if your calendar says it's time for a break, take a break! Do not ignore them, or you do so at your peril. Set an alarm clock in your office or your cubicle to remind you. Have your computer, your administrative support person, or someone else tell you when it is time for a break. Set up a frequency that you know will work for you. And when you are reminded—and as soon as you are reminded—*take that break*. Do not put it off until you complete one-more-thing. You already know where that leads!

If you find that your break time arrives and you are concerned about your ability to recapture your momentum when you return, grab a Post-it pad and write yourself a quick note that tells you how to get back into the project when you return. After your break, read that note and you will get right back into your project without missing a beat. Always keep in mind that you will be more productive as a result of your break.

The truly wonderful thing about taking frequent breaks is that each one is an opportunity to get back in touch with the Authentic Self. Any break that takes you out of your mind is usually enough to put you back in touch with your physical, emotional, and spiritual being. That integration, no matter for how short a period, will usually open the door to your Authentic Self. You then have the ability to bring your Authentic Self and the creativity, innovation, and intuition that it contains back with you to the job that is still awaiting your best efforts.

10

Firmly Grasp Forgiveness

Forgiveness does not change the past, but it does enlarge the future.

—Paul Boese

For most of us, the idea of forgiveness is laden with misconceptions. One of the key misconceptions is that it is about letting someone else off the hook. It isn't. Forgiveness is about *you* and your relationship with yourself. That is why this chapter appears in the "Being Authentic with Yourself" part of this book. The truth is that acts of forgiveness have absolutely *nothing* to do with the *other guy*, except for the fact that our relationships with other people give us the opportunity to exercise our ability to forgive.

We often hesitate to forgive because of our mistaken belief that by ceasing to feel resentment toward someone, we are gifting that person. Perhaps this belief goes back to those times when our parents or teachers insisted that we accept the apology of a friend when we were still angry or hurt by something they had done. To accept would be to let the other person off the hook, even while we were still afire with anger and hurt. To move beyond that mind-set, we have to seek a deeper understanding of forgiveness.

Because the need for forgiveness has been such a major issue in my own life, I have participated in, and even facilitated, dozens of workshops, men's groups, retreats, and seminars on this theme. As I've listened to others tell about the difficulties they have with forgiving people in their lives, I am struck by the common underlying theme: It is the false belief that the person we feel we cannot forgive is somehow hurt by our holding on to our resentment and that to forgive them would be to release them from that bond.

Is that really the case? In workshops on forgiveness, we've often probed the reality of whether or not a person who lives a thousand miles away is hurt in any way by our resentment. Does the hold you have on this resentment accomplish anything at all, even if they happen to live in the town where you live? And what about clinging to resentment aimed at people who have died? In the clearer light of reason, we have to admit that the notion seems ridiculous. Think about it. Do you really believe that the person you have a grudge against is anxiously awaiting the day that you will release him or her from your wrath? You already know the answer to that question: Of course not! The greatest impact is felt by the person who is holding on to the resentment.

I have painfully watched this scene play itself out in the course of over forty years in my own family. My father believes that his older brother did something despicable to him in the late 1950s. They do not speak or have any contact with each other. The resentment that my father holds against my uncle is solid substance to him and lives in his heart and mind like a virus carrying the most deadly disease. If you mention either my uncle or the alleged incident to my father, his breathing becomes hard and labored, and he becomes visibly agitated and red in the face. Anger flows out of him like lava from an erupting volcano. Worse, I doubt that a day goes by that my father does not think of his brother in the context of this resentment.

And my uncle? When I talk with him—our relationship is good, despite my father's wishes—it is apparent that while he is certainly aware of my father's resentment, it has had absolutely no effect on him. His life is good, and the fact that my father despises him does not appear to play any part in his life. Why should it?

Take a minute to reflect on how holding on to resentment has affected you—in any way. Sit quietly and see who needs to be forgiven in your life. Determine what it is that is preventing you from forgiving any person who comes to mind. What are the positive effects on you, if any, of refusing to forgive and continuing to hold on to your resentment? What are the negative effects on you? At the very least, holding on to resentments sends your Authentic Self into hiding. Spirit *is* forgiveness, and to the extent that the Authentic Self is a reflection of Spirit, it too is steeped in the warm waters of forgiveness. Discard forgiveness as a living and healing element in your life, and your Authentic Self gets discarded along with it.

A Course in Miracles takes special note of a concept it calls "justified anger," that is, anger or resentment that you feel or can "prove" is "justified" because an offense actually occurred. The writers point out that it is our being convinced that it is justified which really hooks us. To forgive we first have to realize that "justified anger" is an illusion which we need to address in and of itself and that no matter how justified we may believe our resentment is, the act of another that led to it is still forgivable.

Some of our resistance to forgiveness may result from the mistaken belief that forgiveness means we must welcome the forgiven person back into our life with open arms. Do not confuse "forgiving" with "embracing." Forgiving is a one-way street—you forgive someone *within yourself* without any participation by the forgiven party. You are the one being released, not the other person. Embracing, on the other hand, is a two-way street, and traveling that street is independent of your own experience of forgiveness. Forgiveness is completed when you no longer feel that knot in your stomach at the thought of your offender and you can feel a sense of peace around the entire incident. Whether or not you want to welcome the person back into your life at that point is your choice—but it is *not* a requirement of forgiveness.

There are many people I have forgiven for past transgressions but whose company and companionship I no longer seek or expect. This is not inconsistent. Rather, it makes both common and spiritual sense. It makes common sense because there is a time to move from one stage of life to another, quite independent of any issues around forgiveness. At such times we may change our friends and associates anyway, but we cannot do so as long as we are tethered to them by the bonds of resentment. It makes spiritual sense because we cannot really move on until we have completed our business together, and very frequently, that business involves forgiveness.

My father doesn't want to have anything to do with his brother, and he thinks his unwillingness to forgive him is keeping his brother out of his life. Yet I am certain he spends some portion of just about every day with my uncle living rent-free in his head. My father will not be able to move on until he gets his brother out of his head, and that will not happen until he forgives him. Meanwhile, my uncle goes about the business of his own life free of any bond of resentment my father feels.

The dynamics of forgiveness and resentment in the workplace are no different than in families, except that the results of holding resentments and withholding forgiveness have the added ability to negatively affect your career and your finances.

It is easy to find reasons for feeling resentful in the workplace. No matter how large or small, the organization in which you work invites comparisons; indeed, it *relies* on comparisons to make many of the necessary decisions about its products, its markets, and more pertinently, its employees. Some of these comparisons are built into the structure of the organization, such as performance reviews, job titles, reporting relationships, and organizational charts. Other comparisons may be less formal but no less evident. These include such things as seeing peers you feel are less qualified than yourself getting promoted or receiving the choice assignments. Comparisons in the workplace are commonplace, and where there are comparisons there is likely to be envy and its jolly companion, resentment. Then, of course, there is the possibility that someone may do or say something which you view as being malevolent, something directed at you and jeopardizing your interests.

As a manager, it rarely escaped my notice when one of my employees was holding resentment against another person in the company. There is an energy around resentment that is unique and difficult to hide. Even the most casual observer will know something is amiss, even if he or she cannot identify precisely what it is. Resentment energy is not pleasant to be around, and you don't need people steering clear of you in the workplace because *your energy is bad*—even when they don't understand the underlying reasons for it.

Rare is the person who can hold resentment silently. Part of the payoff of withholding forgiveness and holding resentment is the opportunity to complain, to gather together a group of associates who agree how awful this offensive person is and how badly he or she has treated you. As a result, people holding resentments are not quiet about it, and soon they develop the reputation they deserve: complainer, whiner, grumbler, gossip, malcontent, and so forth. As you read this, I'll bet at least one person from your workplace has come to your mind because of his or her reputation as a malcontent, whiner, or gossip. You don't want that kind of reputation for yourself. It doesn't support your authenticity or your success.

On a metaphysical level, by holding resentment against others in the workplace, you are not placing obstacles and impediments in their way but in your own! Metaphysical writer Joseph Murphy says, "Actually, when you entertain these negative states of mind, you are hurting and injuring yourself, because you are thinking and feeling it."[1]

When people start to look at the need for forgiveness in their lives, they frequently discover that their inability to forgive others stems from their inability to forgive themselves. Again, it does not matter what the source of a resentment is—whether that resentment is directed against others or against one's self—it is the holding of the resentment, the unwillingness to forgive, that does the damage—and it does its damage to *you*! In your attempts to get a firm grasp on forgiveness, do not overlook forgiving yourself. The fact that it may seem an exercise in nonsense to you should be your first clue that there is more to the concept than immediately meets your eye. Do your work on forgiveness, but for heaven's sake—as well as your own—include yourself as one of the subjects of your forgiveness work. The payback can be monumental.

Naturally, a situation may arise in which you feel that you cannot find it in your heart to forgive that particular instance. Not that. Not them. Not this time.

When I am similarly experiencing difficulty in forgiving, I have found it immensely helpful to pray for the *willingness* to forgive. Believe it or not, this works. Try it sometime.

Another tool that helps me firmly grasp forgiveness is a forgiveness journal. As part of my mental and spiritual preparation for each day, I take the "Book of Forgiveness" off my desk and hold it quietly in my hands for a few moments. In this book I have a list of names that I started keeping several years ago. The process is simple: Each day I search my heart and mind for those people—including myself—who I feel the need to forgive. Some people show up in my consciousness day after day for weeks on end and then do not show up ever again. I do not question the reason why someone's name comes into my mind as a person I need to forgive, although sometimes the reason is very clear. I simply write the name of each person who comes to mind on one line in the journal without any notation about why I feel that forgiveness is necessary. Remember, forgiveness is not about the other person; it is about the need to forgive that resides in our own hearts. Then, while holding the closed book in my hands, I affirm my willingness to forgive. Then I get on with my day. This is one of the ways in which I ensure that I am taking a firm grasp of forgiveness.

Try starting your own "Book of Forgiveness." Make it a discipline every day to discover who you need to forgive—without spending any energy determining *why* you need to forgive them. List their names in your journal for as many days as they come into your consciousness during this process. Do this for a month and see what happens.

Interestingly, when I look back on the long list of names in my book, rarely can I remember what might have prompted me to put some of them there. Even when I do remember, the joy is that I discover I have absolutely no negative energy on the person or the "offense" which prompted me to include that person on my list in the first place. And *that* is a fine result.

There are hundreds of books and thousands of processes to help you push through your barriers of resistance so that you can learn to forgive under even the worst of circumstances. Read a book on forgiveness and do the exercises;

take a seminar that deals with forgiveness issues; go on a spiritual retreat; work with your spiritual counselor, minister, rabbi, sheikh, or priest. It doesn't matter what process you use in your own forgiveness program. What matters is that you take definite action to firmly grasp forgiveness as a practical tool for moving your life forward—and that includes your life in the workplace.

11

Build and Protect
Your Sanctuary

*The trouble in corporate America is that too many people with too
much power live in a box (their home), then travel the same road
every day to another box (their office).*

—Faith Popcorn

Have you ever noticed the shift that takes place within you when you return to
your home? It makes no difference if you have been away for only a few hours
at the mall or if you are returning from several weeks abroad. Although the inten-
sity can vary, the feeling of arriving home is always the same: a calming sense
of security and peace. Your home is a unique sanctuary that you have created.

Everyone needs a similar sanctuary in the workplace. Whether your workspace is a grand office, a cubicle, a desk among many others in a large open
space, a classroom, a checkout aisle, your car or truck, or even just your briefcase, it is important that it become a place of personal refuge for you. You must
learn to build a sanctuary for yourself and then protect it.

A personal sanctuary is a reminder to you of who you are, and as such, it
will allow you to get back in touch with the personal and communal significance of your work and the larger meaning of your life. I am not suggesting any

particular type of reminders. For your workspace to operate as a sanctuary, it must speak to you—and perhaps *only* to you.

When I worked at Intel, I had a few small but powerful reminders of the importance of certain aspects of my life that I kept in my gray, otherwise nondescript cubicle. These included a few photos of my wife and daughter, a small porcelain angel that my wife gave me many years ago, James Dillet Freeman's world-famous "Prayer for Protection" laser-engraved on a small wooden plaque, a reminder on my calendar that "God Means It for Good," a small colorful sign proclaiming "Metaphysics is not an option" next to my computer screen, and a small quartz crystal that sat silently but powerfully on my desk.

These reminders were for me alone. They acted as tethers to my center of calm and authenticity no matter how difficult that last meeting was or how much anxiety I was experiencing with whatever was coming up next. In the middle of a company that exists on the cutting edge of turmoil and change and that proclaims paranoia an admirable characteristic, my office sanctuary provided me with the opportunity to experience this all-important sense of peace whenever I returned to it. The reminders were there, and soon I subconsciously trained myself to seek and experience their power as soon as I reentered my workspace.

At this time in my life and career I do a lot of my writing in places other than my home or my home office. Most of my poetry has been written at various locations all around the world. During the summer I often work in a cabin in the midst of the "Big Trees" giant redwood country of the Sierra Nevada mountains. I convert the space into my own personal writing sanctuary by bringing items that give me a calming sense of security and peace. These include scented votive and pillar candles, a small Zuni fetish, a good supply of incense, and that same quartz crystal which sat on my desk at Intel for so many years. I also bring with me a feather wand, some dried sage bundles that I made while I was in the Navajo Country, and an abalone shell, all of which I use to ceremoniously "smudge" the cabin, inside and out, to commemorate my arrival and the work that will be done there. Over the course of many years, I have instilled these items with a compelling sense of ritual, with the result that each is so filled with personal meaning that merely casting my eye on any of them has a tremendous centering effect on me.

The personal reminders in your sanctuary need not be overt. There is no need for them to speak to anyone other than to you, although they might do so. I have discovered that when my workspace becomes a place of refuge and sanctuary for me, others sometimes experience a similar sense of safety merely from being in this space. Even in the largest corporate environment, it seemed that when someone whom I perceived as living almost totally in his or her Corporate Self came into my workspace, none of my personal sanctuary reminders registered on that person's consciousness. On the other hand, when those who were either being authentic or were open to being authentic came in, something about my sanctuary would resonate with them and the conversation could quickly move to a more authentic footing.

Frequently, these people would ask me what "Metaphysics is not an option" meant when the sign proclaiming these words caught their attention. The door was then open, and if it all felt right, I could walk through it. I could not possibly list all the significant friendships and relationships which developed from the deep and personal conversations prompted by that simple little sign, reminding us that the principles of metaphysics are not optional but are part of the human landscape—like it or not—and that we had best take into account those metaphysical principles as we travel through life.

Creating your sanctuary is an easy enough thing to do, but the rewards are incalculable. What you are striving for is a workspace that will center and ground you so that whenever you walk into it, no matter what disastrous or uncomfortable situation you've just experienced, you get that feeling of "coming home," and a calming wave of security and peace flows over you.

I know of salespeople who have created sanctuaries in their briefcases with a simple reminder—perhaps a small sign, a photo, or some other personal item that they see every time they open their briefcases. The same can be accomplished if your office is a car, a truck, or some other vehicle. Even a piece of special jewelry, such as a ring, a brooch, or a pendant around your neck, can create a sanctuary. Take a look around you and you will notice that many people these days wear thin gold or silver chains with perhaps a small crucifix, or a Buddha, or a silver or gold casting of an animal. Others wear lockets with a photo of a loved one.

Your sanctuary needs to be *consciously* created. Once you decide that you want to build a sanctuary, items to include will suddenly start coming into your life. (The Law of Mind Action will be at work here, because as you focus your attention and intention on building your sanctuary, the outer world will reflect that attention and you will find yourself with plenty of possibilities.) Your responsibility is to choose those things that will work best to remind you of who you really are—your Authentic Self—and that are likely to produce within you a sense of security and peace when you see them. What those things are and how you use them is unique to you.

Of course certain items in your workspace can *unconsciously* contribute to feelings of anxiety and distress, and those feelings make it more difficult for you to be authentic, because the Authentic Self and fear do not easily cohabit the same space. A good friend of mine, who is a shaman in the Native American tradition, told me a story that illustrates this point:

> *For many years I had a photo of an Indian in full cere-monial regalia that a client had given me as a gift. She had thought it colorful and interesting, but in looking at it I was reminded of how the Indians have been exploited and realized this photo had been posed for the tourist trade. It represented a lot of bigotry to me. I'd kept it on my wall to honor my friend's gift. But I finally had to admit that I was really offended every time I looked at it. So I discarded it.*

To minimize the influence of negative elements, take inventory of all the objects in your workspace. Focus on each one and allow yourself to experience the full range of thoughts, feelings, and emotions that each object evokes in you. If something is not contributing 100 percent to your sense of well-being, get rid of it. If you cannot do that, put it someplace where it is not a constant negative reminder.

Do this for your work papers, materials, and tools also. Keeping your work area organized and eliminating stacks of paper lying here and there will do much for your peace of mind. I find that unfinished or unpleasant work lying about tugs at my consciousness and makes it difficult to focus. My work practice is to only have one thing on my desk at a time, and that one thing is whatever I am working on. Everything else is organized into a set of "work in progress" files that I keep close at hand but out of sight. Develop the habit of keeping positive reminders in full view and the necessary negative ones accessible but out of the way.

Once having built your sanctuary, it will be necessary for you to continually and consciously protect it, both accumulating and eliminating reminder objects as your experiences change. Do you find that you are drawn to a common theme among your reminder items? If so, make a game of looking for more of the same kinds of items when you are shopping. Vacation shopping trips are particularly wonderful for finding sanctuary personal reminders because these items are already imbued with the positive energy of your vacation. At the same time, you may find there are some items in your workspace that you still like but that no longer *sing* to you. Consider passing those things onto someone who will find them new and exciting. Items that have held intense meaning at one time may not always. And reminders that once held positive energy for you may now affect you in just the opposite way, and then you need to have the willingness to let these items go. It is a continuous process of awareness, selection, and reselection.

A workplace sanctuary is *not* an expendable luxury—it is an absolute necessity.

12

Become Disciplined
in Meditation

*The fact that I practice meditation doesn't mean that I am always
calm or kind or gentle, or always present. There are many times
when I am not. It doesn't mean that I always know what to do
and never feel confused or at a loss. But even being a little more
mindful helps me see things I might not have seen and take small
but important, sometimes critical steps I might not otherwise
have taken.*

—Jon Kabat-Zinn

The summer after I graduated from college in 1970, I took a trip to New York
City and stayed with my friend Craig. I spent less than a week with Craig, but
that visit changed my life forever. Soon after my arrival, he told me that he had
been introduced to something called Transcendental Meditation (TM), which he
had just begun practicing on a regular basis. Maharishi Mahesh Yogi, an Indian
guru who had trained the Beatles in the discipline, had recently introduced this
particular form of meditation to the United States. Craig explained that the
practice required that he sit quietly and undisturbed for twenty minutes in the
morning and again for twenty minutes in the afternoon.

Craig was good to his word. Every day, morning and afternoon, no matter what else was going on, he would sit silently with his eyes closed and his hands resting comfortably in his lap. I would read or just quietly wait for him to finish. Sometimes I would pay some attention to Craig's state of repose; mostly, I would not.

What caught my full attention, however, was the change that was apparent in my friend. Until that time, I had seen Craig as a fairly anxious fellow. However, that no longer seemed to be the case. Craig's demeanor had taken on a tranquil, more confident aspect. I was intrigued. Craig attributed the change to his practice of TM.

When I returned to Washington to begin graduate school, at Craig's urging and following some surprising drive within my own mind and heart, I sought out the local TM office, paid a modest fee, sat through an evening orientation and training in the TM discipline, and received my personal mantra for use during my meditations.

That was over thirty years ago, and I have been meditating nearly every day since then in one form or another. Meditation is now a way of life for me, although I no longer observe the TM discipline exactly. Since my first exposure to meditation, I have made a study of its various techniques and traditions from around the world, and I have learned from a variety of teachers.

I believe that meditation has contributed more to the quality of my life than any other single practice I could have pursued. The daily practice of meditation in almost any form can also make significant differences in your life. If you have practiced meditation at some point, you will know the truth of these words: *Nothing can give you a higher return on your investment of time in terms of clarity of mind, a sense of well-being and peace, and access to your own brand of authenticity than can meditation.*

The discipline of meditation is an amazing gift. As little as fifteen minutes a day can help you to relax and focus on the things that really matter in your life—including the important aspects of your job. There is simply no better way to disengage from life's activities and from the chatter of Monkey Mind. As we practice the discipline of meditation day after day, we get better and better at it and the rewards expand geometrically.

Meditation is almost like a commercial for your soul in the midst of what could otherwise be a day where Spirit had no opportunity to give you guidance. It is an opportunity to break away from the mind and its cognitive constructs and to move into the limitless flow that life actually is. When we tap into that flow, for however short a period of time, we can obtain great insights. We momentarily eliminate the mental filters that in the course of a busy life can separate us from Spirit. We see our lives more clearly, and the grand patterns that course through our lives and through all of human history become apparent to us, striking us with the combined forces of intuition and inner knowing. In meditation, the alternative paths we can choose to follow are made clear; frequently, the future outcomes of those alternatives are also made clear.

The benefits of meditation extend far beyond mental clarity. Even Harvard Medical School now teaches meditation principles for fostering health. There are few, if any, alternatives that can provide the same benefits as meditation. While there are tranquilizers and other powerful medications that can relax us and reduce symptoms such as depression and anxiety, none of these produce their positive results without a tradeoff of uncomfortable or even dangerous side effects. Meditation, on the other hand, not only has no side effects, but its benefits cover a wide range from mental relaxation to normalizing heart rate.

Do you have to join an ashram and study Eastern religions with a guru to develop your meditation skills? Absolutely not. You can become your own meditation teacher. You need understand only that meditation is a technique for quieting the distractions of your mind. It is being "mindful" *without* your mind being full of thoughts.

The steps are simple and easily adapted to your own personal tastes: Find a quiet place where you can sit comfortably and erect. Close your eyes and relax. Begin by focusing on your breathing. Don't worry about any mind chatter that might come in—just acknowledge it when it shows up and immediately return your attention to your breathing. Some people count their breaths or inhale, hold, and exhale for slow counts of from ten to twenty. Do this for as long as you can, which initially may be as little as three minutes. Try to work up to fifteen or twenty minutes. If you like, you can silently repeat a single-syllable mantra such as "Peace," "Om," or "Still." You don't need a guru to develop a blossoming meditation practice. *You* are all you need.

I was raised in the Roman Catholic Church. As an altar boy, I was introduced to the Novena, a prayer devotion lasting nine days that a person would undertake for a religious intention. Our parish held a Novena service every Monday evening, and I became the regular altar boy for those services. I loved them, but it was only later, after I began a discipline of meditative practice, that I understood why.

The Novena service basically consists of audible prayer in the form of an initiation by the priest and a response by the congregation. The Catholic Rosary is used for structure, with the result that the same prayers are repeated over and over again—a few of them dozens of times in a single service. Before long, the repeating prayer becomes a rhythmic beat. Indeed, after a short while it is often hard to understand the words being spoken, but the rhythm of Spirit is both unmistakable and compelling. In actuality, these spoken prayers become a mantra resulting in a transcendental meditative experience for everyone involved. There is a tangible sense of peace and connection to the community of worshippers that is both mesmerizing and addictive, just as I now find in meditation.

And meditation does not even have to look like, well, meditation. Many activities can give us the opportunity to transcend our minds and ourselves and put us in direct contact with the Spirit that resides within each of us. Many people have transcendental experiences while engaged in activities such as gardening or repetitive aerobic exercises such as cycling, swimming, or running. The transcendental quality of these activities is created and then deepened by the focus and mindfulness with which each activity is approached. The Zen Master says, "When you wash the dishes, wash the dishes."

Assess your present meditative practices, whether formal or informal. Is there an activity you are already doing (e.g., gardening, walking, or even cleaning the house) that could serve as a meditative practice if done with the appro-

priate mindfulness? Determine what you can do to expand your overall meditative practice to get maximum benefit from it. If you presently have no meditative practice, begin one—possibly by taking a class, reading a book, or listening
to an audiotape to learn the basics. If you do meditate now, try an alternative
discipline either instead of or in addition to your present discipline. Gauge the
effects of the alternative discipline on your sense of well-being and peace.

At any time that we quiet the chatter of our minds and become mindful of
whatever is at hand—whether it is the silent, barely noticeable movement of our
breath coming in and going out or the turning of soil with a trowel—we are
practicing the discipline of meditation, and its benefits are immediate and deep.
For one thing, it gives us the opportunity to get in touch with and actually
become our inner selves. We move from the world of doing into the realm of
simply *being*, and nurturing being is what the Authentic Self is all about. For
another, it gives us perspective on the events that make up our individual life
stories, and this includes the events that occupy us in the workplace.

13

Use a Personal
Discovery System

To know how to wonder is the first step of the mind toward discovery.

—Louis Pasteur

People are always surprised when I tell them that I have been a tarot card reader for nearly twenty-five years. I suppose the surprise comes because most people associate tarot cards with fortune-tellers. Certainly it's not something they ordinarily associate with a corporate executive. "You're kidding, right?" is the most common response I receive when I bring up the subject during a talk or a workshop.

No, I am not kidding. Tarot offers a powerful method of personal discovery, one that assists me in making choices and learning the truth about my feelings in both business and personal situations. It is not that the tarot cards contain any answers. On the contrary, the cards contain something more important: *questions*. As James Wanless says in his book on the use of tarot in business, *Strategic Intuition in the 21st Century*, "Tarot is a spark, not the fire. Tarot is a map, not the traveler."

Most of us operate on the level at which much of our experience is created by our subconscious minds working in conjunction with the Law of

Mind Action. We think we are consciously creating everything in our lives—choosing this path, selecting that course of action—but all too frequently the actual creation mechanism is invisible to us. Indeed, we may even be misled by what is apparent in our conscious mind versus what is invisible but working in our subconscious mind. For example, we may consciously think or affirm, "I am going to close this sale!" Or we may tell ourselves, "I really deserve this promotion!" And then we are surprised when we lose the sale or the promotion falls through. At this point, many people jump to the conclusion that the Law of Mind Action does not work or that it had no impact this time around.

Not true. Where the Law of Mind Action is concerned, the mind cannot distinguish between conscious thoughts and subconscious or unconscious ones. If you are *consciously* telling yourself that you deserve that promotion while *subconsciously* holding on to reasons why you do not deserve the promotion, then, at best, the negative subconscious thoughts will cancel out the positive conscious ones. At this point, it is easy to draw the conclusion that the Law of Mind Action failed to operate. And whenever your negative subconscious thoughts overwhelm your positive conscious ones, the Law of Mind Action will appear to have worked in reverse, creating a reality just the opposite of what you believe you intended.

And that is precisely where a personal discovery system—like tarot—can be of immense value to you. It draws out the full range of your thoughts and feelings, both conscious and unconscious. When I lay out the cards for a reading, I always have a specific situation in mind. As I shuffle the cards, I ask that I be given the gift of seeing the whole truth about a situation—*my* truth, which means the totality of what I think and feel about it, including the subconscious and unconscious parts of my mind.

Tarot, with every symbolic card and layout, presents a rich tapestry of possibilities that can stimulate our thinking about a particular situation and provide information on what is going on in the deep recesses of our subconscious. The real value of the tarot is that it contains *evocative questions*, that is, it motivates us and suggests new questions and new possibilities to probe. It is the very process of encountering those questions that provides me with valuable insight. The tarot acts as a mirror, using symbols that can potentially reflect back to me my own thoughts and feelings—some of which may lie buried in my unconscious—about a given situation.

There are many personal discovery systems besides tarot. Some people like runes, which is a system that originally came from the ancient Vikings and is thought to have first been used in ocean navigation. There's also the Chinese *I Ching*, which consists of sixty-four hexagrams, or possible readings. Thousands of people have made a regular practice of studying *A Course in Miracles*; others use the Bible or other scriptural writings. Still others partici- pate in stichomancy, which is simply the practice of seeking insight by opening a book to a random page while holding a question in your mind, reading a random passage, and then reflecting on what associations come up that are relevant to the issue you are trying to understand. Many people use traditional psychotherapy as their personal discovery system. In that particular discipline, a therapist acts as the mirror, bringing the client's innermost thoughts and feel- ings into the light of self-examination so he can learn from the subconscious and progress along the path of personal and spiritual growth.

What is your attitude toward adopting a personal discovery system such as tarot, runes, the *I Ching*, or perhaps even *A Course in Miracles* or the Bible? Do you have some beliefs or preconceptions about these approaches? If so, what are they? Are you willing to set aside those beliefs and preconceptions if they are standing in the way of you obtaining valuable new insights into your moti- vations and subconscious thought processes?

If you do desire to find your personal discovery system, start by doing some reading to explore what might appeal to you. Go to a local metaphysical bookstore and look at the various options. Hold the tarot cards, the rune stones, the *I Ching* coins, or *I Ching* yarrow sticks in your hand, and peruse *A Course in Miracles*, and then see what speaks to you. Something will. Open yourself to the possibility of synchronicity—i.e., that the right personal discovery system will find *you* when you are ready to receive it. Whatever this turns out to be, give it an honest trial.

A friend of mine—a psychiatrist, as a matter of fact—carries around a single ordinary six-sided die. He has assigned sayings to each number, which he has memorized. As I remember, they are well-chosen, thought-provoking sayings like "Perception is projection." Whenever he needs to, he asks a question, holds intent, rolls the die, reads what comes up, and applies it like a tarot reading!

Your personal discovery system will give you surprising insight into your inner feelings and thoughts. It will provide you with the opportunity to understand your concerns and fears about situations that arise in your life. Most importantly, the seeds for the answers to your concerns and fears will be contained in the questions your personal discovery system will require you to answer. It is not the cards, it is not the stones, it is not the tiles, and it is not the books you use that will make the difference—it is *you* and your willingness to dig deeper for answers and insights.

Besides providing the kind of assistance we have been discussing, looking deeply has at least one additional benefit. When you use a personal discovery system to access your subconscious thoughts and feelings, you learn more about what motivates you and what holds you back. In short, you get to know yourself better, and knowing yourself better is an expressway to your Authentic Self.

It does not matter what personal discovery system you choose, but you must enjoy working with it. Recognize that using one regularly can catapult you along your path toward greater success and authenticity. For this to happen, however, you will need to embrace your personal discovery system as a discipline. By *discipline*, I mean something you do regularly and take on as part of the process of growth in your life. Work with your chosen system often, and study it seriously. Over time that study will pay off a thousandfold.

Whatever you select to use as a personal discovery system, you will also want to make sure that it is fun! You simply won't practice it or use it on a regular basis if you find the system tedious. My love affair with tarot is well into its third decade, and I have literally enjoyed every minute of it. While I have a large and interesting collection of books on the subject, I have always held it lightly, which I believe has helped to keep it a fun and yet very valuable pastime.

14

Harness the Power
of Your Dreams

✦ ✦ ✦ ✦ ✦ ✦ ✦ ✦

*Dreams are a reservoir of knowledge and experience, yet they are
often overlooked as a vehicle for exploring reality.*

—Tarthang Tulku

There is an important source of wisdom that many of us tend to disregard more
than any other: our dreams. Dreams contain valuable information that we can
apply in our daily lives. They often reflect what has happened, is happening, and
perhaps will happen to us during our waking hours. At the barest minimum,
dreams contain intelligence from the deepest parts of our souls. They are direct
links to the Authentic Self and the wisdom it possesses.

The Swiss psychiatrist Carl Gustav Jung wrote, "The dream describes
the inner situation of the dreamer, but the conscious mind denies its truth and
reality, or admits it only grudgingly.... It shows the inner truth and reality of
the patient as it really is: not as I conjecture it to be, and not as he would like it
to be, but *as it is*."[1] A dream reveals; it does not conceal.

History is filled with the stories of the power that dreams have had over
the lives of men and women. The book of Genesis in the Bible describes how
Joseph, sold into slavery in Egypt by his envious brothers, rose to incredible

power and wealth because of his ability to understand and act in response to his own dreams. He even advised others, such as high-ranking prisoners and Pharaoh, on the wisdom their dreams contained. The Prophet Mohammed reportedly had a high regard for dreams. Each morning he asked his disciples to tell him their dreams, and then he gave them dream interpretations and shared his own dreams with them.

Dreams have also been a constant source of inspiration to artists and philosophers. Robert Louis Stevenson, the author of such works as *Treasure Island* and *Dr. Jekyll and Mr. Hyde,* wrote that he received many of his best stories from his dreams. Edgar Allan Poe, whose poems and short stories include "The Raven," "The Telltale Heart," and "The Murders in the Rue Morgue," is reported to have relied on his dreams to inspire the moods and themes of many of his tales. Giuseppe Tartini wrote his masterpiece sonata for the violin, "The Devil's Trill," after hearing it performed in a dream. The French philosopher Voltaire composed a canto of "La Henriade" in a dream, and Samuel Taylor Coleridge's poetic masterpieces, "Kubla Khan" and *The Rime of the Ancient Mariner*, were inspired by dreams.

Nor has application of the power of dreams been restricted to religion and the arts. In 1865, German chemist Friedrich August Kekulé dozed in his chair while trying to solve the forty-year-long mystery of the structure of benzene. He dreamt of serpents whirling around each other and catching each other's tails to form a circle—an arrangement that provided the perfect model. Nineteenth-century chemist Dmitri Mendeleyev understood in a dream that the basic chemical elements are all related to each other in a manner similar to the themes and phrases in music. When he awakened, he was able to write out for the first time the entire periodic table, which forms the basis of modern chemistry. Niels Bohr, dreaming of how horses run at the racetrack, had an insight into how electrons remain in their orbits. Based on this vivid image from a dream, Bohr was able to formulate his quantum theory, a scientific breakthrough for which he was eventually awarded a Nobel Prize. And young Albert Einstein dreamed that he was sledding down a steep mountainside, going faster and faster, approaching the speed of light, which caused the stars in his dream to change their appearance. Meditating upon that dream, Einstein eventually worked out his extraordinary theory of relativity.

There is a great variance in how much of their dreams people remember. It is likely that most people forget their dreams because they simply do not care to remember them and take no action to preserve the memory of their dreams. Traditional Western culture does not regard dreams as important, and the pressures of modern life—particularly for the employed—generally require that we get ourselves out of bed immediately, often to the blare of an alarm clock. Since most dreams occur at the *end* of the sleep cycle, they are often interrupted. Even if dreams are not interrupted, the need to get up fast to deal with the coming day and to focus on our hectic schedules prevents us from thinking about our dreams in the morning.

Despite what you may believe, everyone dreams nightly. If you do not think that you do, what is most likely true is that you simply do not remember your dreams. But there is something you can do to expand and reinforce your experience of your dreams: Train yourself for maximum dream recall, bid yourself to dream by sowing the seeds of your dreams, and harness their power to your use. By doing this, you can turn your dreams into yet another personal discovery system that will provide you with clues and information to your subconscious and unconscious thoughts and feelings about any situation in life.

This is important because the more you know about what motivates and inspires you and the more you know about the inner workings of your heart, your soul, and your unconscious mind, the more you become your Authentic Self. This is so because the Authentic Self is the sum total of all of these aspects that make up who you are.

The process of seeding your dreams is much easier than you might think. Just before you go to sleep, "seed" your subconscious by asking for guidance in the form of a dream to assist you with whatever issue you're facing. *Don't* focus on the issue; focus on the request to dream about it. Try saying something as simple and nonspecific as "You know what? I need some answers," and then let the dream come that will provide you with those answers.

But what about remembering your dreams? Dreaming the answers to challenging issues in your life will be of no benefit if you cannot remember the dream. The solution comes as a two-step process. First, before going to sleep, suggest to yourself that you will remember your dreams when you awake in the morning. It may not happen the first night or even the second, but repeating the reminder just before sleeping will eventually give you results. As with any new skill, time and practice bring results.

And second, as soon as you open your eyes in the morning, and before getting up, try to remember your dreams. I cannot stress this strongly enough. If you do *anything*—get a cup of coffee or even use the bathroom—before making some effort to capture the content of your dream, it will be lost to you for all time.

One good way to capture your dreams is to keep a journal next to your bed and then write down your dream impressions *before* you get up. Admittedly, this is a difficult habit to start and then to develop as regular practice, but once you do, it becomes easy. I find it particularly useful to record dreams in first-person narrative as though I am still in the dream and describing what I am seeing there. You need not write down every scene or symbol in your dream. My experience is that so long as I capture the essence on paper immediately upon waking, my mind retains the details that I can later bring up and review. Many times, in the wake of a particularly powerful dream, I have captured the essence in a few short sentences, and then much later, when there was more time, I have written out a complete and detailed accounting of the dream, which I can then review at my leisure. Frequently, when I happen upon notes of dreams written years ago, the dream itself returns to my consciousness with an astonishing clarity that seems more than just a recollection of a long-past dream.

Whatever you do to learn what your dreams mean, recognize that your dreams are a source of incredibly powerful information about your subconscious mind and your hidden emotions. Accessing that information gives you a greater chance of understanding more about yourself—and that means bringing more of your Authentic Self to the fore.

Once you have begun seeding and remembering your dreams, start looking at them for the answers they might contain. Look for obvious and not-so-obvious symbolism. You might consider obtaining a dream dictionary that will give you clues as to what some of the symbols in your dreams might mean. The key is to mine your dreams for their gems in the same questioning approach you would use with any other personal discovery discipline. Ask yourself what the symbols mean to *you*, notwithstanding what any dream dictionary might say about them. Ask yourself what the story in a dream means to you in the context of the issues and events you are experiencing in your life. Look for common connections between different dreams, because sometimes the subconscious will give us answers in pieces, and we must consciously fit those puzzle pieces together to get the picture.

15

. . . . Practice Imaging

Perhaps the truth depends on a walk around the lake.

—Wallace Stevens

Faced with the many complexities of today's work world, there are times when not only do we not have solutions to the problems confronting us, but we have even run out of ideas for how to *get* help or find the solutions we need. This conundrum can quickly develop into a descending spiral of your energy as well as your confidence.

When I arrive at this stage, whether in my personal or professional life, I feel so at odds with myself that I am unable to access even the tiniest shreds of creativity, innovation, or intuition. All these valuable elements of my Authentic Self seem to have gone into hiding. And, indeed, it is my now elusive Authentic Self that I most need for reversing the course of my downward spiral.

Over the years, I have turned to "imaging" to help me with those times when I am out of ideas and out of ways to get them. Imaging is not the same thing as "visioning," although people frequently confuse the two. Visioning is useful for those times when you *can* voluntarily visualize a result that you want. For example, suppose you are working with a team of five people and you visualize them all working together smoothly and cooperatively, completing a particular job by a certain date and with absolute perfection. In this case, you are able to bring a goal into reality by focusing your attention on all the emotions, feelings, thoughts, and visuals associated with the successful completion of the project. This application of the Law of Mind Action will ultimately re-create your vision in reality because whatever you hold in your consciousness will manifest.

However, that's impossible to do when you have no idea what the vision should be and you seem hopelessly stuck. It is in such times that imaging can help. The underlying principle of this practice is simple: Just hold the issue or a question in your mind and ask for an image to help jog your creativity into action. As you sit with the issue in your mind, an image will flow into your mind's eye that at first may seem irrelevant. Stay with the image, even though you might not at first understand what it has to do with the issue you are facing.

A friend of mine—call him Allen—once told me about using imaging to help a friend who telephoned him because his brand-new car wouldn't start. Allen was a pretty fair mechanic, but he didn't have any experience with his friend's car and didn't even know what it looked like under the hood. So he simply sat, centered himself, closed his eyes, and waited for an image to come to him. What came to mind was something that looked like a rubber ball with an open collar on opposite sides. He had no idea what this could possibly mean, but he related the picture to his friend and they hung up. Later, when Allen asked his friend if he'd gotten his car started that day, his friend said, "Sure. It was exactly like you said. One of the collars of that rubber thing had come loose and I had to reattach it. After that, it worked fine."

Not all images that come to mind will be this accurate or directly related to the problem. Some will seem to have nothing to do with the actual physical reality you are attempting to resolve. When you finally recognize the image for what it is, however, you will find that it will hold keys to the answer you are seeking.

The crucial requirements for successful imaging are openness to the possibility that the image really does have something to offer and the willingness and ability to extrapolate from seemingly unrelated imagery.

In a way, my experience with imaging is that it is not so very different from using the tarot or any other personal discovery system. The power of the practice is in the questions it raises for you, not necessarily in its ability to provide ready, easily understood answers. This is particularly the case when dealing with the more complex issues of life or work.

You may remember in the last chapter how the chemist Kekulé fell asleep while pondering the problem of the benzene ring. What came into his mind in the form of a dream was a snake with its tail in its mouth. He could have easily come to the conclusion that snakes have nothing to do with chemistry. But he trusted that the image was meaningful. By asking himself what the snakes had to do with his chemistry problem, he saw his solution. Whereas Kekulé utilized a dream to get his answer, similar dynamics work with imaging.

The next time you are dealing with a knotty issue, do an internal imaging process—*internal* meaning that you expect the image to present itself to you from your own consciousness. Sit quietly where you will be undisturbed and begin by paying attention to your breathing—breathe deeply, exhale fully, and perhaps count your breaths. You may notice that this is also the way you begin a meditation session. Close your eyes if it feels right to you. When centered, begin focusing your attention on the issue at hand—*feel* it rather than just thinking about it—and ask for an image to guide you toward a solution. Even the asking is more of an emotional and intuitional "reaching out," a felt rather than verbalized process. For example, rather than articulating a specific question (e.g., "Should I . . . ?"), you might allow impressions of your feelings about the situation, the people involved, or even your own frustration or confusion to come into your consciousness and see where those lead.

If you find yourself distracted during this process—whether by the problem itself or by extraneous thoughts or interruptions—bring your attention back to your breathing. When you again feel centered and calm, gently focus on the issue to be resolved.

When an image presents itself to you, do not discard it, no matter how unrelated to your issue it may seem. Instead, allow your mind to freely associate with and extrapolate from the image presented. Allow yourself to engage in a miniature flight of fancy—perhaps a word, image, or concept association. For example, if the image you saw were a kite, you could allow your imagination to move into one of a number of intriguing directions: flight, wind, string, tether, sky, clouds, child, diamond-shape, and so on. Sometimes the image will be another person or even an animal with thinking and speaking abilities. For example, you may find yourself face-to-face with a talking bear or a bird whose thoughts you can read and who will respond to yours—and you can engage in a direct conversation, asking questions and seeking guidance. The key thing is to hold these images lightly and to play with and expound upon them.

Another way to access hidden solutions is through external imaging processes. In external imaging we seek "guidance" from the outside world. It is somewhat similar to games you might have played—or still play—in which you tell yourself, "If the next car coming down the street is red, it means I'm supposed to do so-and-so, and if it's not red, I don't have to do it." External imaging is much the same except that it isn't a game of "yes-or-no" or "this-or-that."

Instead, external imaging acknowledges a connection between all things and the one mind that is the source of all. It is based on the knowledge that each of us creates our own experience of reality and that the forces of the universe are at our disposal—including forces that are ready and willing to give us the answers to life's most perplexing issues. We need only quiet ourselves long enough to see and hear.

Because external imaging depends on images in the world around you, it is best to seek those images in an environment that *seems* unrelated to the area where you are struggling with the problem. I say "seems" because it is clear to me—as I suspect it is now clear to you—that there are no accidents and that everything in life is connected in some wonderful way to everything else. Nevertheless, removing yourself from the scene where the difficulty is taking place clears your mind and makes you better able to engage successfully in external imaging. If the issue is work-related, leave your office building and take a short walk or sit quietly on a park bench. If the problem is at home, consider a drive to a quiet woods, a scenic lake, or the seashore. I find that getting out into a more natural environment helps the process.

As with internal imaging, start by focusing on your breathing, calming your body, and placing your full attention on the issue at hand. Then, instead of seeking an internal image, look for an external sign that will indicate a better way in which you might deal with the situation. While observing the world around you, pay attention to even the smallest detail, because the answers are everywhere.

David Whyte tells a wonderful story about his experiences with external imaging in his classic book, *The Heart Aroused: Poetry and the Preservation of the Soul in Corporate America*:

> *I remember being completely overwhelmed as the director of a residential education program in the Pacific Northwest. Finally, pushed over the edge one day by a small incident, I walked out into the woods surrounding the center and told myself to look for a sign or image that would indicate a better way of dealing with the whole stressful state of affairs. Though the immediate image before my mind was that of a branch from which to hang myself, I did quiet my mind enough to recognize the teaching image when it appeared—a small bird, working its way up a decaying cedar stump, pushing its beak without fail into every minute hole in the stump, looking for a supper of insects. The bird did not overlook any part of that log as it slowly, over twenty minutes, worked its way to the top. It wasn't what I wanted to see, but it was pure gold as far as what was needed. One step at a time, and don't miss any of the steps, not even the smallest! One step at a time! My sanity for the year that followed hinged*

on the physical presence of that image, conjured not only
as a reminder but as a way of being.[1]

It is important to understand that imaging—whether internal or external—is not miraculous but simply the uncovering of something your inner self, or your subconscious, already knows. In reality, it is merely the expression of yet more of your Authentic Self.

16

Map Your Future

The future is not a result of choices among alternative paths
offered by the present, but a place that is created—created first in
the mind and will, created next in activity. The future is not some
place we are going to, but one we are creating. The paths are not to
be found, but made, and the activity of making them changes both
the maker and the destination.

—John Schaar

I am a strong believer in what I have come to call "management by graphics," which is akin to the nearly ubiquitous saying that *a picture is worth a thousand words*. It seems that the human mind can capture and retain concepts contained in images much better than it can capture and retain those same concepts when they are presented only verbally. Recognizing this, it is only a small jump to understanding how graphics can help us achieve and maintain our own dreams and desires. Over the years this graphics process has taken several forms such as "mind mapping" or "treasure mapping."

Mapping could not be easier. Basically, you look for and collect images, such as photos, clippings from magazines and sales brochures, or even pictures that you have drawn, of the things you want to create in your life. Then you place these where they will act as constant reminders to you—and, most particularly, constant reminders to your subconscious.

Collect graphic representations that most accurately reflect the fulfillment of your desires. For example, if you are dreaming of buying a new car of a particular make, model, and color, make sure that the image you select for your map is of the exact make, model, and the color that you desire. (Why manifest a blue Toyota sedan when you want to drive a red Mercedes convertible?)

How you actually create your map is up to you. Some people choose to create a photo album with their selected images. Others simply take one image and place it in a location where it will be seen each and every day, such as on their bathroom mirror, on the dashboard of their car, or on their desk at work. I have discovered that the best mapping approach for me is a small cork bulletin board that I keep on the wall near my desk in a somewhat private corner of my office. The board is covered with paper to create a colorful rainbow background, and my mapping images are clustered in groups on the corkboard. These groups represent several areas of my life for which I am seeking new or different results. I cannot help but see this collection of images every day, and they act as reminders to my subconscious to keep working on those things that I want to create in my life, even while I am pursuing them with my conscious mind and through my daily activities.

Try mapping for yourself. Begin by going on an image search. Several times each week sit down with some magazines and a pair of scissors and begin cutting out images that appeal to you and that may represent items you would like to manifest in your own life. Let your imagination run wild. If you really want a cabin in the woods, don't settle for an image of anything less. See yourself possessing and using each item as if it is yours and as if it is the most natural thing in the world for you to have it.

Once you have collected a significant number of images, create a map for yourself. Use any method that you think will work best for you. Remember to make your map with colors and textures you find attractive and appealing. Either place your map in a location where you will see it every day or make arrangements to ensure that you will take it out each day and look at it. When you are working with your map on a daily basis, be sure to imagine yourself possessing each item and using it as though it is yours. The most important part of this process is that you feel good about your map and that when you look at it, which should be often, it creates in you some sense of the pleasures and joys to come as your desires manifest.

I believe that the extraordinary results which many people experience with these techniques derive from the map's ability to give a graphic representation in a form the mind can understand at all levels. Too frequently our conscious statements about what we want to manifest in our lives are tinged with limitation or lack. Just thinking about *wanting* something is a clear acknowledgment that the item is lacking from our life. And focusing on lack does not get us any closer to obtaining what we desire. In fact, the negative energy associated with lack only pushes what we would manifest away from us. This is yet another demonstration of the Law of Mind Action: When we verbally pose a desire, the absence of that object or situation is what we are holding in our minds—and so that absence will continue to be manifested. When we are focused on the lack instead of the attainment or fulfillment, it can be an insidious, self-defeating, and frustrating situation because what we end up manifesting is only more desire for something—and not its attainment.

Mapping, on the other hand, works for several reasons: First, surrounding yourself with the images of your desires creates an environment in which the desired objects begin to feel appropriate to your situation and circumstances. When you have pictures of something you want around you as constant reminders, your unconscious mind gets quite accustomed to that object or situation being there. We know that the human consciousness does not discriminate between a real and an imagined object or situation. To the unconscious mind, a picture of a new car is no different from a real car. And so, as far as your unconscious mind is concerned, it no longer seems out of the question for you to have possession of the actual thing. Perhaps some level of comfort is developed between you and your possession of the desired item that replaces the comfort of the feelings of desire.

Second, mapping works because the graphic images override any negative self-talk from the subconscious mind that might interfere with the manifestation process. When your subconscious mind is frequently and consistently presented with the same image—one which supports a belief that you can and will have what you desire—it ultimately begins to accept that image as the truth about your future. Once the conscious and subconscious elements of your mind have become converts to a revised future, as represented by your map, the Law of Mind Action takes over, and manifestation of your desires is assured.

And mapping is also a declaration to the universe—albeit a *graphic* declaration—of your desire to manifest something different from what you have. While there is immense power in our words, this power is magnified and expanded exponentially when we consciously move that intention into the deepest levels of our subconscious. Because of the simplicity of the graphic interface, mapping accomplishes that task remarkably well.

I have never known anyone to have failed to manifest their desires when they have used mapping with high intention and commitment. Why it isn't more prevalent as a conscious tool for building the lives we want continues to amaze me. I do know, though, that many people have significant resistance to manifesting the things they *say* they want in their lives. My own experience tells me that the fear of success—of having what we truly want from life—can be as much an obstacle as our fear of failure.

Werner Erhard once observed that with respect to the condition of our lives there were only two things possible: People either have results in their lives or they have the reasons why they have had no results. "Too many people," he said, "are satisfied with the reasons for not having results."

Do not be satisfied with the reasons for not having results in your own life. Do not let anything get in the way of your manifesting all the good you can in your life. Don't let concerns about what others may say or think prevent you from collecting your own symbols of prosperity, if this is what you want. To paraphrase Jesus, it is Spirit's good pleasure to give you everything you desire. There is only one person who can prevent you from manifesting everything you want in your life, and that person is *you*.

Because life frequently seems filled with travail, it can be hard to believe the truth, which is that your Authentic Self, through its direct connection with Spirit, wants you to have the most spectacular life possible. The more of that life you successfully manifest, the more you are expressing your Authentic Self. Mapping is an excellent tool you can use to create a life consistent with your Authentic Self—and to do it both effectively and efficiently.

17

Keep Your Perspective

If you're proactive, you don't have to wait for circumstances or other people to create perspective expanding experiences. You can consciously create your own.

—Stephen R. Covey

Most of us take life way too seriously, and this includes life in our workplaces. So much of our lives seems to be centered on work that many of us have lost all perspective about it. We believe that we are working so that we can have the things which we want in life, but the demands and related fears of today's workplace conspire to form a reality in which many of us no longer work to live, but rather live to work—and only to work! We think we are doing our jobs so we can have real lives, but our job situations don't let us have even a small portion of the lives we envision.

There is a story from the ancient world that I believe is relevant in today's work situation, and to the degree that it has become the accepted norm, it is also relevant to the new work ethic. Diogenes the Cynic was one of the most interesting philosophers of the ancient world, and he was greatly admired by one of his most famous contemporaries, Alexander the Great. Alexander visited Diogenes at one point early in his life, and Diogenes had the audacity to ask him what his plans were. Alexander answered that he planned to conquer and subjugate all of Greece. "And what after that?" asked Diogenes. Alexander said he then planned to conquer and subjugate all of Asia Minor. In response to the obvious next question, Alexander said that he then intended to conquer and subjugate the entire known world. Not easily dissuaded from a line of inquiry, Diogenes asked the same question again. Alexander answered that after conquering the world, he intended to relax and enjoy himself. Diogenes responded by inquiring whether Alexander could not save himself a great deal of difficulty by simply undertaking to relax and enjoy himself *now* and skip all the intermediary steps.

History would suggest that Alexander did not take Diogenes' advice, leading me to ask how many of us have followed in Alexander's footsteps in our approach to our jobs and our lives? How do you see the role of work in your life? Are you living to work at the expense of your life, or do you have things in perspective? For one week, monitor your activities. How much of your life do you spend preparing for work, commuting to work, being at work, commuting from work, thinking about work, and recovering from being at work? What, if anything, are you willing to change to keep your perspective?

To keep your perspective about the role of work in your life, you will need something to take your attention *off* work and put it on something else for a period of time—something that engages your entire being and invites your Authentic Self out to play. It could be something as simple as gardening or as complex as learning a difficult language or a highly technical art form such as sculpture, painting, tai chi, or playing a musical instrument. Such opportunities are chances to practice a discipline of pure presence in the moment, to be *mindful*. These times can be personally and spiritually rewarding, helping us to learn to live not by clocks and the requirements of the world around us—standards set in an outer-centered reality—but in accordance with our own inner clocks, our inner wisdom, and our intuition.

Living in the moment also hones our ability to perceive inner guidance, giving us a clearer experience of the blessings that surround us at all times. While living at Walden Pond in the 1850s, Thoreau wrote, "God himself culminates in the present moment." Mindfulness is one of the keys certain to open that inner door to God and to the Authentic Self.

One of the methods I developed late in my corporate career was to bookend the workday. What I mean by "bookend the workday" is to arrange your day so that there are things unrelated to your work that you do *every* day before you go to work and also after you return home from work. This technique creates a subtle but significant shift in your perspective about the role of work in your life. These additional activities, when adopted in a regular and disciplined manner, convert your day from being about getting to, being at, and returning from your job to your day being about your own life's activities which are then punctuated by your job. Thus, your job becomes just one of the things that you do during a day which you consider otherwise yours. In the final analysis, this is a far more productive and appropriate perspective.

To bookend my day, I began by getting out of bed at four o'clock in the morning—having gone to bed at a reasonable hour the night before. I would meditate, write in my gratitude and forgiveness journals, and see what presented itself to do at that time. I might, for example, sit in the living room and quietly read. I might write a personal letter or card at my desk. I might exercise by running, skating, or biking. I might go for a walk in the pre-dawn air, write poetry or an article, listen to music, or watch a movie video that was of keen interest to me but that I knew was of little interest to my wife and daughter. Regardless of what activity I chose to do, I would have several hours to myself before it was necessary for me even to begin to get ready for the office. Even today as one of the self-employed, bookending continues to help me keep my perspective about the role of work in my life.

When traveling, which I did frequently during my years as a corporate person, I might do other things unique to a particular place that I could not do at home. For example, when I stayed in a hotel in Hong Kong, I met the night manager at the door of the hotel's music salon at 4:15 each morning. A waiter carrying a silver tray with a large pot of English tea accompanied him. During what others considered a business trip, I would spend an hour or two each morning sitting at a nine-foot concert grand piano in that beautiful music room filled with English and Chinese antiques enjoying my morning tea and practicing my piano lessons. In the end, those practice sessions at that fine piano in that elegant room are what I remember of my trips to Hong Kong and not the meetings, not the completed contracts, and not the business successes and failures. I had created a significant shift in perspective.

There are a lot of exciting and memorable things you can do in a few hours before it is time to get ready to face the workday, whether you are at home or in some exotic location. Come up with a list of things you might enjoy doing before going to work and a second list of things you might enjoy doing after you return home from work. Develop a plan to implement some bookending elements for yourself. Commit and follow through on that commitment for thirty days. At the end of that thirty-day trial period, see how you feel about your efforts to bookend the workday. Make adjustments and continue the practice.

Besides helping me keep my perspective, my practice of rising early and learning to bookend the workday offered another interesting side benefit. When I got to the office, I was already in full stride rather than still in the process of shaking off sleep. While others were stumbling back from the cafeteria with the morning's first cup of coffee, I was well into or completely through with my e-mail. By the time my co-workers were just beginning to get some traction, I had already made major inroads into what projects the day held for me—not a bad perquisite for my employer, derived from a practice I was undertaking to make *my* life better.

By the time the traditional lunch break rolled around, I had invested about half of the day's hours in activities for myself and about half of the day's hours in activities for my employer—and, I believe, both at a higher level of efficiency and effectiveness than I otherwise would have had.

The period after lunch would frequently be a mirror image of the morning hours—working diligently at the office and getting home to participate, again, in activities that had nothing whatsoever to do with work but which were of special interest to me. People always expressed surprise when they learned that, although I held a more-than-full-time position, I did most of the shopping and cooking, while my wife, Betsy, who was not employed outside our home, took on most of the home care and gardening. From my perspective, rather than yet another chore, preparing the family dinner was a break from my standard corporate fare and gave me the opportunity to practice being present and mindful in a very deliberate way.

Sometimes the whole family would shake things up a little, which also helped to keep things in perspective. (Kids tend to develop the same sense of "droning" around school that many of us have developed around our jobs—in other words, they, too, lose their perspective.) On occasion we would declare a family "Adventure Day." These were days without plans. Whenever we were ready, we would pile into the car and head off in whatever direction took our fancy. Sometimes there were days when we just shamelessly played hooky—me from work, Annalisa from school, Betsy from the house and the laundry. We'd go wherever there was to go, see whatever there was to see, experience whatever there was to experience—with no expectations about the outcome. The lack of plans and schedule always made Adventure Days special. We never knew what was in store, and such times together were always spectacular. I believe that one of the significant factors which made those days special was that we approached them with a simple mindfulness, and that changed everything. Indeed, it changed our perspective so much that when we returned to our jobs—whether at work or at school or at home—we were always refreshed and ready for whatever was to come next.

Try declaring an Adventure Day for yourself. Keep yourself and your spouse or significant partner home from work, keep the kids home from school, pile into the car, and just let the first impulse take you in some direction. Make your Adventure Day mindful by being fully present to everything that comes into your path. Be sure to gauge your perspective about your work the next day when you return to the workplace. If your Adventure Day contributes to you keeping your perspective, be sure to have another. Repeat as needed.

It really doesn't matter what you do to regain and then keep your perspective about the role of work in your life. What is important is that you do take control of the situation and develop a program that will make it easier for you to keep things in their proper perspective.

PART II

Being Authentic with Others

18

Create Name Recognition

Who hath not owned, with rapture-smitten frame,
The power of grace, the magic of a name?

—Thomas Campbell

Our names hold immense power. They represent who we are, and as such, using someone's name connects both of you at a deeper level.

Consider your own experience. When you run into someone you've met once or twice and that person begins the conversation by saying, "Steve, it's good to see you again!" you feel recognized and acknowledged. All of that comes simply from another person remembering and using your name.

What other word of any substance do you hear more frequently than your own name? What sound *could* you hear that calls your entire body and being into the present more than this? You're walking down the street and suddenly you hear your name. Immediately, you are at full attention. You turn to see who it is that has summoned you. If perchance you discover it is only someone being called who has the same name, you move on, frequently feeling a bit embarrassed. That embarrassment arises from the sense of openness and vulnerability that the sound of your name has triggered in you. Such incidents hint at the power of our names.

The power of names is a tradition with ancient roots. For example, names were very important to the ancient Hebrews and were used with great care and respect. To name someone was to have power over that person, and to use the name of God was believed the same as using God's power. Hence, there were sacred laws against speaking the name of God.

The earliest references in the Bible show us the importance and power of names as understood by the ancient Hebrews. In the first chapter of Genesis, we read that "God called the light Day, and the darkness he called Night." In other words, having named it, God created it and then had power over light itself. Similarly, we learn that "God called the dome Sky" and "God called the dry land Earth, and the waters that were gathered together he called Seas" (New English Bible). Ultimately the naming is the source of everything over which God has dominion.

Not just in the Judeo-Christian tradition but also throughout history and all over the world, names and naming have held unique and often spectacular power. In some languages, the words for "name," "breath," and "soul" are synonymous. In North American Zuni theology, there is no name for God because for humans to have one would be presumptuous—it represents exercising power too great for humans.

To some primitive societies, that which had no name simply did not exist. In many tribal traditions, only after a person was named was he or she deemed to have acquired a soul. Even modern Jews have special naming ceremonies, preferably held in the child's first year. And in the christening ceremony, the name of the child is committed to Jesus.

In general, the American Indians consider their names to be distinct and separate parts of their physical selves. Coupled with this is the belief that injury can result just as surely from the malicious handling of one's name as from a wound inflicted on any part of the body.

Australian aborigines believe that an enemy's life may be taken by the use of his name in incantation. In Java the indigenous people believe that a person will die if his name is written on a piece of bone and buried in a damp place; as the name gradually fades away, so will the person to whom it belongs.[1]

Human history teaches us that names are important, and the spiritual traditions of many, if not all, religions teach us that names contain power. But for the most part in our workplaces, we have discarded these historical and spiritual traditions and make no use of the power of each other's names. (One of my colleagues has suggested that this may be deliberate, much as is the case in the military and in prisons.) Notwithstanding intent, the result is an almost anonymous approach to dealing with others in the workplace. This approach creates a sense of nonexistence, and where individuals are not recognized in their uniqueness, there is no sense of individual identity and no sense of community, and individual effort and responsibility are diminished.

As powerful as using names can be, it is an amazingly simple thing to learn. I am not talking about remembering and using the names of your organization's executives, your managers, your peers, and your staff members. You probably already know these. I mean learning and using the names of absolutely *everyone* with whom you come into contact during the workday: the security guards in the lobby, the facilities personnel who clean the restrooms, the mailroom clerks, the cafeteria employees, the UPS driver, your regular customers and suppliers. Learn the names of your customers' assistants. Ask the names of the receptionists at your vendors' establishments and write them on your primary contacts' business cards. Then, when you call you can say hello to the receptionist by name. Even if it is a different receptionist next time, you stand out as someone special—after all, you know the *other* receptionist! Learn the names of everyone you can and use those names at every opportunity. It's a simple gift you can give to everyone you encounter in your work no matter how casual the interaction might be. Remembering names makes you memorable and special in another's experience. And while you're at it, create an organizational culture that makes it easy for other people to learn your employees' names. If you manage a company or department, have your employees answer the telephone with a format that includes their personal names. For example, "Good morning! XYZ Corporation. This is Gerald. How may I help you?" This kind of greeting opens the door to a deeper interaction for both the caller and your employee.

Start noticing how many people there are in your workplace whose names you do not know and with whom you have some contact—no matter how tenuous that contact might be. Every day for one week, learn the names of three people you see at work on occasion but whose names you do not know. Then, use those names regularly. Gauge the results on the relationships with the people whose names you begin using regularly.

If you're saying to yourself, "Well, I'm just not very good at remembering names," realize that every time you affirm that you are not good at remembering names, you make it more real and you make it more your truth. You can change all that by starting a regular program of affirming your ability to remember names. A few tips may help. For one thing, don't be embarrassed when you have forgotten someone's name. You know the situation well—you're at a meeting or party, you introduce yourself to someone who then gives you his or her name, and not three minutes later, even as you are still standing there talking to this person, you haven't a clue what his or her name is! The standard approach is to attempt to hide it. You hope that someone will come over and say something to the person like, "Oh, hi, Jill. How's the family?" or "Jack! What a surprise to see you here," but that never seems to happen.

I've developed a different approach that has had surprising results. When I've forgotten the name of someone I've just met, I tell the truth about it immediately. I look the other person in the eyes and say something like, "Please excuse me, but I've already lost your name. Would you tell me it again?"

Rather than being disturbed, their faces light up. They seem to be thinking, "Here's someone who actually cares about my name, wants to know it, and is even willing to risk the embarrassment of admitting that he has forgotten what I told him three minutes ago." After all, they've been there, too. I've even had someone admit that he had already forgotten *my* name, and we had a good laugh about it. I believe there are two reasons for this remarkable response. First, this situation is so much a part of the human condition that I cannot imagine anyone who is immune to it. Something about admitting our common human foibles manages to connect us at some deeper level. Second, when you ask a second time, it cannot be lost upon the person that you are truly interested in him or her. Only the value you place on knowing and being able to use his or her name would drive you to ask again in those circumstances.

In asking for people's names, we honor them in their uniqueness. Check it out for yourself: When you meet a person who indicates that your name is important to them, how does it make you feel? Chances are pretty good that it makes you feel that this person is genuinely interested in you.

We all want to be around others who are interested, not necessarily those who are interesting. When you take the time to admit you've forgotten someone's name and ask for it again, you've suddenly shifted from being potentially interesting to *definitely interested.*

A participant in one of my workshops suggested that it is a good idea to use the person's name several times in the first few sentences you exchange. It assists you in remembering the name, and she says, "It makes cocktail chatter less like cocktail chatter." It's a good suggestion that works well.

Learning and using people's names in the workplace is a wonderful gift you can give to others every day that costs you nothing to give but is valued beyond measure by the receiver. In a short time, you will begin reaping the benefits as others in your life begin to treat you with the same special care with which you treat them. Through our names we create a sense that each one of us really matters, and with that a powerful sense of authentic community is born.

19

Assume Responsibility

In dreams begins responsibility.

—William Butler Yeats

There are many definitions of responsibility. Most of them, however, are restrictive in the sense that the boundaries of responsibility are outlined for us either by ourselves or by others. It is almost as if we learn about responsibility by clarifying what it is for which we have *no* responsibility. It is no wonder that most people view responsibility as a restriction rather than as an expansive opportunity.

I call this the "that's-not-my-table" mentality, T.N.M.T. for short. It's a familiar situation: You ask a server at a restaurant for a clean fork and instead of getting what you asked for, you hear, "Sorry, sir, that's not my table." But this mentality extends to our homes and workplaces as well.

You will change your experience of work, and probably your entire life, if you take a careful look at where you might be taking the T.N.M.T. approach in your own life and, instead, make your definition of responsibility as expansive as you can.

Expanding your definition of responsibility may not be an easy thing for you to do, particularly, if like most of us, you were raised in an environment in which responsibility was the equivalent of fault or blame.

In their best-selling book, *The Corporate Mystic*, Kate Ludemann and Gay Hendricks explore the sources of our ideas about responsibility to show how we can arrive at "Breakthrough Responsibility."[1] The sources generally fall into three categories:

The first category can be summarized as "Who did this?" We learned this one during early childhood when a parent entered a room where we had just completed some mischief. The second category occurs frequently in our schooling. You may remember when the teacher leaves the room for a moment and in her absence pandemonium breaks loose. Upon her return to the room, the teacher scowls and demands, "Who started this?" as though the ones who participated have less responsibility than the culprit who started it. The third category involves the efforts to deny participation in a chain of events that led to an undesirable situation. We often see this posturing during investigations of government snafus and political scandals where people accused of contributing to the problem do everything in their power to sidestep responsibility. Examples include Watergate, Iran Contra, and any one of a number of notorious scandals involving members of the Clinton administration.

With these experiences in our background, it is easy to understand why the vast majority of us respond to *responsibility* and *fault* as if they are synonyms. How do we separate the two? *Webster's Third New International Dictionary* (unabridged) defines *responsibility* as "the quality or state of being responsible; moral, legal, or mental accountability; reliability; trustworthiness." It defines the word *fault* as "a defect in quality or constitution, an imperfection in character or disposition; failing, weakness; a blameworthy moral weakness less serious than a vice; a blemish, a damaged part."

Making a conscious distinction between responsibility and fault is important because you cannot make any changes in the circumstances of your life unless you feel responsible for having created those circumstances in the first place. And feeling blamed instead of responsible impedes the process. An understanding of blameless responsibility is necessary for you to take charge of those situations you might normally sidestep if you associated them with "fault."

Blameless responsibility can be learned and even mastered, with practice. This begins with paying attention to what you actually hear internally in your heart, mind, body, and spirit when you use the word or think about responsibility. Do concepts such as blame and fault come up? If so, make a conscious effort to move your thoughts, feelings, and emotions back onto the positive side of the scale. How do you do that?

Change comes about quickly when we say to ourselves that it's time to put blame and fault aside and move forward. Responsibility now takes on a new meaning—"the ability to respond to the present." We now take on the cause of letting the past go to create a new future.

I think Ludemann and Hendricks hit the target dead center when they defined Breakthrough Responsibility as "taking responsibility for something regardless of who did it, regardless of who started it, or regardless of who participated in the chain of events leading up to it."

What this means in the context of your relationship with your workplace peers, managers, employees, vendors, and customers depends entirely on how you choose to implement your own brand of expanded responsibility. A good rule of thumb is that every time you participate in solving a problem you neither created nor took part in, you are expanding your personal definition of responsibility. In other words, it is as far from the T.N.M.T. mentality as one can get. You'd be like the restaurant server who responds to a request for a fork by immediately getting one, apologizing for the oversight, and asking if there is anything else the customer needs—even though the customer is not sitting at the server's table. The bonus is that operating from blameless responsibility with others will allow you to operate from blameless responsibility with yourself. That opens doors!

I was lucky enough to spend a significant portion of my business career at Intel Corporation, where a similar concept called "Assumed Responsibility" is an integral part of the corporate culture. Assumed Responsibility means that if you find something critical that needs attention and no one else is doing anything about it, *assume* that it is your responsibility to do it. Things tend not to slip through the cracks that way.

Because of Assumed Responsibility, I experienced one of the most exciting and rewarding jobs of my career. In 1990, I was asked to help design the
now ubiquitous Intel Inside cooperative marketing program. Initially, I was
working on the project as an attorney overseeing marketing and antitrust issues,
but it became clear that with our limited time and resources, our tiny team of
five people would have to contribute more personal effort than any of us had
anticipated. Like everyone on the team, I found myself assuming personal
responsibility for things I had never done before: writing video scripts for the
CEO to explain the program to Intel's customers, developing trademark usage
and advertising guidelines for customers, creating sales presentations for the
sales department, participating in the design of the logo, becoming the company expert on the intricacies of trademark law and licensing, negotiating
variations of the program for international customers—the list was endless.
Assuming responsibility for the things that needed to get done to make the program a success—even though any of us could have argued that none of it was
"my table"—forced us to stretch beyond any self-imposed limits we may have
had in any of a number of directions. Remember, my *official* role on this project was as the company lawyer.

Instead, through Assumed Responsibility, by the time my stint with the
Intel Inside program was completed a few years later, many doors had opened to
me. I delivered product demonstrations at the Intel booth at various trade shows,
participated in focal-group market research, worked with creative advertising
folks to develop advertising campaigns for both print and broadcast media,
became part of a television-commercial production crew, built a worldwide
trademark-enforcement organization, and participated in the creation of an Intel
IMAX film and frequently commuted to Hollywood to deal with filming
issues—all things I could never have experienced if I had stuck only to those
tasks that belonged to my assigned role of "company lawyer." Assumed
Responsibility is a good deal for you *and* for your organization.

Take a look at your own life and try to remember a time when you might
have knowingly or unknowingly expanded your definition of responsibility or
assumed responsibility. What were the results of that risk? How did you feel

about it beforehand? Afterward? Next, try expanding your definition of responsibility. The next time you identify something that is not being done but that needs to be, tell your supervisor or manager that you are assuming responsibility for it unless she or he has another idea. How does that feel to you? What is your manager's reaction?

Assumed Responsibility is a valuable technique for managing your career and your various duties at home and at work. As you gradually take on more of the things you personally choose through this approach, there will be opportunities to let go of some of the areas of which you are less fond. By this process you can keep refining your job duties to include the things you like to do—and at which you will naturally excel—while releasing those duties you consider burdensome. Interestingly, it seems that just when I am eager to release something that I find tedious, invariably someone comes along who is drawn to that particular task for the excitement and advancement it represents. The result is that things get better for me, for the person excited to pick up my released "burden," and for the organization.

Expanding your definition of responsibility and then following through by acting on appropriate opportunities not only can change your experience of your work and your workplace, it can change your entire life. When you place no artificial limitations on how you can make a contribution, your innate gifts of creativity, innovation, and intuition blossom forth. Giving yourself maximum access to these three internal gifts is one sure way of accessing your Authentic Self.

20

Mend Relationships

There is no hope of joy except in human relations.

—Antoine de Saint-Exupéry

Many of us do not realize that our workplaces are communities because too frequently they are places of discomfort, and the word *community* doesn't seem consistent with any level of discomfort. But community is not a word of value or judgment. There are communities that contribute to an individual member's sense of well-being and peace, and there are communities that not only do not do that but actually tear at the fabric of the individual's well-being. Nonetheless, both ends of this spectrum and all the points in between are communities.

There is a certain danger in not recognizing our workplaces as communities. In almost any other community in which we participate—families, circles of friends, neighborhoods, and churches—when we find ourselves in a relationship where there is rancor or mistrust, most of us will make at least some effort to rectify the situation. Sometimes we succeed; sometimes we fail. But the point is that we are sufficiently uncomfortable with being on the outs with a person in our community that we will make an effort to resolve the source of conflict. This just does not seem to be the case in the workplace. If we do not see the workplace as a community, we simply avoid those people with whom we are having trouble. Consciously or unconsciously we operate under a set of rules that causes us to limit our interactions with that person. We may even cut off all interactions with them. I've actually heard myself think, "Oh, I can't go into the coffee room now; *she's* in there!"

Let's face it. We seem to follow an unspoken law that we will interact with the people we like and who we believe like us. If we have a difficult relationship with someone, it is natural to avoid that person. We all do it.

However, this tactic sets us up for a self-fulfilling prophecy wherein we remain alienated from other people because we have no interactions with them. There's no opportunity for getting to know who they really are; rather, they remain exactly the people that we have created in our mind. We see only what we already believe to be true. Mary Baker Eddy, the founder of Christian Science, said, "The mind sees what it believes and then believes what it sees."

What often happens in the workplace is that we have a negative interaction with someone, and that interaction causes us to begin confusing this person's behavior with who they are; thus, we forget that a single action does not define the whole person. For example, early in a new relationship with a co-worker, I might have an exchange in which my co-worker shows herself to be impatient or even unkind—and my perception of her behavior may be inaccurate, or even accurate, for any of a variety of reasons. From then on, however, this person wears the labels of "impatient" or "unkind" in my mind. As I keep this person at a distance, I witness her behavior through the filter of whatever opinion I have already made about her. When I continue to avoid her, I am robbed of any opportunities to learn new facts about her behavior, personality, and motives.

The most challenging thing I have had to learn about being around people I do not like is the realization that, on both psychological and metaphysical levels, what I find objectionable or even repulsive in other people is usually just some aspect of myself that I do not wish to acknowledge or accept. When I am faced with some unlovable part of myself being mirrored back to me by another person, the natural tendency is to push such revelations away. See if this might be true in your case, too. Make a list of all the qualities and traits you find objectionable in someone with whom you may be having difficulty. When completed, review each item on the list to see if perhaps it mirrors some part of yourself that you dislike or would rather not own. As difficult as it may be, recognizing that my own undesirable traits are the source of my discord with the other person has proved invaluable in giving me the impetus to move beyond impasses of noncommunication.

If we are going to be comfortable at work, we need to treat the workplace as if it already *is* the community we want it to be. If you are having trouble with someone, do them and yourself the honor of handling the discord with them *directly*. Do so gently and truthfully, without attacking and without defending. You will likely be amazed at the reception you'll receive if you speak from your heart and if your intention is to put harmony and balance back into the workplace community.

If you find that you simply cannot bring yourself to address relationship issues directly with this person, at least commit yourself to increasing your interactions with him or her and reevaluating your preconceived notions. By doing so, you can short-circuit the cycle that causes you to attribute negative motives to this person, and you can then make a clearer distinction between the whole person and the individual's behavior.

Over the years I have counseled many people who have had a genuine desire to be part of a healthy and supportive workplace community. Most of them have complained of politics, cliques, and petty behaviors among co-workers that throw the entire community out of balance.

These folks are quite right in their observations. If any member of a community is not getting along with any other member, the entire community *is* out of balance. The discord will spread beyond the two squabbling members. Such a community is not unlike a circle that has 340 degrees of perfect roundness but 20 degrees of flatness. The wheel can no longer turn efficiently, even though only a small portion of the circle is dysfunctional. Communities are like that— the 20 degrees of flatness disrupts the circle, in some cases causing the whole system to screech to a halt.

In traditional cultures that live in a *conscious* awareness of community, when the balance is disrupted for any reason, it is the responsibility of *each* member individually, and of *all* members collectively, to fix it. There is no such thing as not wanting to get involved. Members of the community are already involved by virtue of their membership. They instinctively know that their total well-being, and their greatest potential individually and collectively, is dependent on everyone acknowledging the contribution that each part makes to the whole.

As often as not, the people who have spoken to me about wanting a greater sense of community in the workplace also feel powerless to effect any changes that might bring this about. Most of them feel that the problem is bigger than any single person and that surely they are not the right person to be attempting to fix it. At this point, you may be thinking exactly the same thing about your own workplace.

In your workplace community you may need to be the one to start mending the relationship for others who are unwilling to pursue that challenge themselves. If some part of your workplace circle is "out of round"—that is, if two co-workers are not getting along—make a conscious effort to see what you can do to help them mend their relationship. Such a course of action may have its risks, but the potential benefits to the community and to you may well be limitless. Indeed, expanding your sense of responsibility to the entire community is a soul-stretching activity of the highest magnitude.

To understand how we might effect positive change in a community, let's take a look at what I call the "Three Levels of Human Consciousness" and how they would be applied.

The first level of consciousness is being responsible for *what we do to other people*. Most of the time the world is operating at this level, but on occasion I see behavior suggesting that someone has not even reached this level yet. For example, a couple of years ago I was sitting in a restaurant when a young mother slapped her young child and then declared, "Look what you made me do!" as though the child's behavior had directly caused an involuntary muscle reaction in the mother's body. Clearly, the young mother's level of consciousness did not include being responsible for what she, herself, did to others. Moments later, an older woman who had been sitting at the next table approached the young mother, apologized for intruding, and then helped to wipe the child's tears. I could not understand the conversation that ensued, but it was clearly a helpful gesture on the older woman's part that was appreciated by the younger woman. The older woman was not only evolved to this first level of consciousness but took the initiative to perhaps extend a helping hand to someone who wasn't. Such interventions are rare and even risky, particularly with strangers, but when they do occur they can provide models that the rest of us might follow.

The second level of consciousness occurs when we take responsibility for *what others do to us*. At this level, we begin to understand the causal relationships between our own actions and thoughts and the actions and thoughts of others toward us. This is not unlike the concept of *karma* as taught in Hinduism. It embodies an understanding that your own thoughts and actions have triggered the kind of treatment you are receiving from others.

The third and highest level of consciousness is the ability to feel responsibility for *what other people do to other people*. This is a level of universal consciousness in which you are consciously aware of your connection to all things. The older woman who interceded at the restaurant would be an example of this.

This third level of consciousness has as many names as there are disciplines to assist us in getting there: Krishna consciousness, Christ consciousness, cosmic consciousness, global or universal consciousness, and so on. Operating at this level means that you comprehend your responsibility for the deaths in a war halfway around the world, for the starvation of humans on every continent, and for the destruction of the biosphere. It is a lofty level from whose heights you can actually see what can be done about these things at an individual level *because* you have taken responsibility in the broader scheme of things.

Taking responsibility for your workplace community, and working to keep it in balance, is a way of practicing this third level of consciousness. Surprisingly, it takes little more than your willingness to be responsible at that level for things to begin improving. You will find, in most cases, that you will have no need to even seek solutions to the problems you are seeing in your workplace community. Those solutions will come part and parcel with your recognition that there is a problem to be resolved. This may sound like a contradiction until we realize that every problem—even a technical one—embodies its own solution. A simple willingness to see the solution is frequently all it takes to unveil what, until that moment, was the hidden answer.

Remember that your workplace community will only be as good as you're willing to have it be—and that will undoubtedly include taking some risks.

21

Manage Your
Communications

* * * * * * * *

*Most conversations are simply monologues delivered in the presence
of witnesses.*

—Margaret Millar

You do not have a choice about whether to communicate. You do have a choice
about whether you *manage* what you communicate.

When we are listening to other people, most of us put great emphasis on
their choice of words, their tone of voice, and their body language. But it's
uncanny how negligent we are about those things when we are the ones talking.

Some of us, particularly in the work environment, have the mistaken belief
that there are times when we *are* communicating and then there are times when
we are *not* communicating. We seem to think we are analogous to television news
reporters who have a "backstage" life and an "on camera" life. In your workplace,
there is no such thing as being backstage. Everything you do or say—as well as
everything you don't do or don't say—communicates something to somebody.

There is nothing that can be done about that. Indeed, it is impossible to
plan communications to target and ensure an exact result because communication is ultimately in the mind of the recipient. But the point is that without a

good dose of consciousness and intention in our communications, we never know exactly how the other person is interpreting what we have communicated. Then, like characters in some comic opera, we act surprised when others haven't received the communication we believe we've transmitted.

Put humans together in any environment and communication takes place with or without any words being spoken. You may think you are not communicating with those neighbors with whom you haven't spoken in years. Think again. They are being affected by your silence. We'd all like to believe that others pay attention to us only when we are consciously making an effort to communicate, for example, when we are speaking in front of a group of employees or sitting down with a staff member to discuss his performance review.

Say it's time for you to make an announcement to your staff. You get into your manager's state of mind, put on your manager's face, pull out your manager's lexicon, and tell them what you need them to hear. And *are* they listening? Probably not. They know that what you're saying is prepared, packaged, practiced, not real, and, well, not *authentic*. Instead, your co-workers may be paying close attention only in your seemingly more authentic moments—unprepared, unpackaged, and unpracticed—such as when you are upset and not paying attention to what you're saying, how you're saying it, and to whom and where you're saying it. The simple act of being mindful of your communications can help you make significant improvements in your work environment and your work experience—not to mention your credibility.

Communications management involves more than only focusing on the words we choose to say. Of course, the words themselves are important, but what's said *between the lines*—in vocal tone and body language—might just mean even more. Results of decades of research at the University of California, Los Angeles, have shown that words themselves contribute only 7 percent to a listener's understanding. A full 38 percent of a listener's understanding comes from the vocal tone being used by the speaker, and body language accounts for 55 percent of total understanding! If you are honing only your vocabulary or your use of words in an effort to better your communication skills, you might just be wasting your time.

If you are skeptical about the results of this research, just think for a minute how much trouble and misunderstanding you have encountered using e-mail to communicate. E-mail-based communication is difficult because it consists almost exclusively of the 7 percent of communication based on words and none of the vocal tone or body language elements, with the possible exception of the occasional smiley face or other emoticon.[1] Our grandparents didn't have this difficulty with handwritten communications, because an individual's handwriting also contains significant elements of "tone" and "body language." Have you ever noticed how different your handwriting looks when you have written something in anger?

If it sounds hopeless, don't despair. All that is required to become an excellent communicator is a conscious effort on your part to manage your communications. Start by slowing down. Choose your words consciously and make an effort to determine what the result of those words is likely to be on your listener. Are you using a misleading vocal tone to soften a statement you think will be difficult for your listener to hear? Notice your body posture; is it consistent with the message you are attempting to deliver? Are you making eye contact when you're talking to the other person? Are you telling the truth as you see it? Are you fully present or are you thinking about other things? In short, are you fully engaged in that moment of communication?

Begin consciously monitoring your communications in the workplace and make adjustments as you deem necessary. If you notice you are having particular difficulty communicating with another employee—whether boss, peer, or one of your staff members—pay special attention to what you say and how you say it when you are communicating with him or her. Consider having a meeting with that individual to obtain feedback on how you can communicate with him or her better.

The hardest thing to accept is that you are *always* communicating and that you have no choice in the matter. You, your actions, and your words *are* the message. Only with this full awareness can you make choices about what you're communicating. You can and will get better at it in time. It's simply a game of self-awareness.

Pay attention, also, to what and to whom you listen. Michele, a participant in one of my workshops, complained that her department was filled with negative and unproductive gossip about nearly everything and everyone—management, corporate decisions, workloads, deadlines, and so forth. Everyone gossiped and complained. As a result, morale was down and she found that her stress level at work had increased significantly.

After some discussion among all the workshop participants, Michele decided that she was going to change what she had been unwittingly communicating. She determined that by being polite and listening to all the negativity without objection, she had been communicating that she agreed and that it was fine to talk about it with her, even though she had never gone into explicit agreement with anything that had been said. When she returned to work, she began to politely but firmly tell those who started down that same road to negativity that she was not interested in listening. She then simply removed herself from the conversation.

About six months after the workshop, I received an e-mail from Michele in which she was delighted to report that everything had changed—at least for her. She said that it was a bit difficult at first to communicate her position without judgment and refuse to participate in the negativity, even if that meant physically walking away from the conversation. Her concerns were the same as yours would be; generally, that the others would think her snobbish or haughty and that her actions might negatively impact some of her working relationships. This turned out not to be the case. Instead, the result was that no one brought any negativity of this kind to her! The gossip was probably still going on, but it was completely invisible to Michele. Additionally, she reported that there were no unfavorable consequences as a result of her having told her truth. Indeed, she said that several other department members came to her privately to tell her that they felt the same way. By managing her communications in this one area, Michele single-handedly transformed her experience of her workplace.

Now it's your turn. What have you been listening to in the workplace that you would rather not hear? What have you been communicating by your apparent willingness to listen? Do something about it! Gauge your results.

Managing *everything* you communicate in the workplace will ensure that every communication is an accurate representation of your Authentic Self.

22

Always Tell Your Truth

The moment we begin to fear the opinions of others and hesitate to tell the truth that is in us, and from motives of policy are silent when we should speak, the divine floods of light and life no longer flow into our souls.

—Elizabeth Cady Stanton

One of the casualties of living an outer-centered reality is that we can easily lose our ability to tell our truth honestly, openly, and freely. Sadly, this doesn't just mean being unable to tell your truth to others, it also means not being able to tell your truth to yourself. This state of affairs is part of the learned response that motivates us to give others what they want or at least what we *think* they want, even if it means sacrificing what *we* want. In the worst scenario, it means putting ourselves last.

Some of the difficulty we all have in this area comes from three possible sources besides our training in outer-centered reality: First, we believe that truth-telling will cause us to appear dictatorial and unyielding. We must each realize that there is no truth with a capital *T* in the human condition; there is only "my" truth and "your" truth and "her" truth and "his" truth and "their" truth. Even if we assume that there exists such a thing as "The Truth," it is impossible for any of us to determine either for others or ourselves what elements of what we feel, believe, and say might constitute "The Truth" and what represent individualized personal truths. And therein lies the solution to this widely held belief—i.e., the understanding that each of us is capable of telling the truth *only as we see it*. It has been my experience that when I make it clear that I am telling *my* truth, which necessarily includes speaking from my feelings, I am not viewed as being either authoritarian or immovable in my position.

Second, we confuse "tell your truth" with "tell your *whole* truth." I am not suggesting that all of the truth be told all of the time. Such an approach would lead to needlessly telling your co-worker that her new hairdo, of which she is so proud, actually looks awful to you or that you believe your father-in-law's taste in neckties is atrocious. A "tell your whole truth" requirement is one with which few of us could live comfortably and would give people license to be unnecessarily cruel. What I am suggesting, however, is that whatever you choose to say, make sure it is the truth for you. But at the same time, make sure that it is not misleading because you have omitted some important part.

Third, there is a general belief that we genuinely serve others by putting their desires before our own. I have come to understand, though, mostly through trial and error, that I best serve others in any given situation by being clear about what I want. Even if no one agrees with me or is willing to let me have what I want, my clarity and clear communication about what I want provide us all with valuable information to determine a course of action that will work for everyone. Too frequently we attempt to steer others toward accepting our own hidden agendas without making a plain statement about what we want.

Sometimes, too, we withdraw from the truth because we know it is not something an authority figure wants to hear. And this is the case most particularly in the workplace. For example, most of us have been in a situation where our boss has come to us excited about some intended plan of action. We instantly spot the flaw in the logic or we intuitively know that this is not the right approach, but we also know that the boss does not take kindly to being told that his ideas are not good ones, so we say nothing because it's dangerous to tell the truth.

More generally in the workplace, we fear we'll lose our jobs if we say something out of the ordinary or something that voices our personal truth. We fear we'll make enemies that will cause difficulties for us either immediately or in the future. We fear that by asking the "wrong" question or making the "wrong" comment, we will reveal how little we know or others will judge us as ignorant or as not conforming to the accepted norms of the organization. These same fears of reprisal come into play when we are faced with acknowledging a mistake we've made. Admittedly, these are not easy hurdles to overcome, but it is essential to negotiate them if we are to live an authentic life in the workplace.

Take a minute to reflect on your ability or inability to tell your truth, particularly in the workplace. Notice how frequently you say things that are safe or politically correct and don't say the things that are true for you but are not necessarily as safe. Don't do anything about this; just notice how frequently or infrequently you are willing to tell your truth in the work environment.

It is important to recognize the cost of withholding our truth, both for ourselves and for the organizations in which we work. For ourselves, each time we do not say what we think, another moment of authenticity is lost. Worse, we deny the value of our own contribution and the intellect, creativity, and intuition that are its foundation. As we habitually reject those inner stirrings to say what is on our minds, our connection to our inner self in the context of the workplace drifts farther and farther away, until like an unrequited lover, it stops calling for our attention. In short, another tiny piece of us dies in the process.

The organization loses even more. Information and knowledge are among the most important resources available to organizations in these times of global competition. Holding back the truth—*your* truth—hampers the organization from recognizing and making the best use of your knowledge, your experience, and your intuition. Multiply this loss by the hundreds, the thousands, or the tens of thousands of employees all operating the same way, and the loss to the organization is incalculable.

In companies where mistakes are hidden because employees fear reprisal, or where the proverbial buck is passed from one employee to another, with everyone avoiding blame for a mistake, nothing is learned. In a climate such as this, half-truths, strategic omissions, and doctored information contribute to spiraling organizational losses that have a negative impact on everyone.

The only solution is to create a working environment where open communication becomes second nature and where owning up to our mistakes is not only tolerated but also celebrated. In such an environment, better ways of doing things are discovered, the atmosphere becomes creative rather than defensive, productivity increases, and people find real pleasure in going to work.

I once worked in a very enlightened company where the approach to mistakes was exemplary. Not only was it refreshing and fun to work there, but the environment gave the organization the best possible chance to recover as fully as possible from errors. Our corporate procedure for dealing with mistakes was this: When you found you had made some significant error, you would go to your manager and announce, "I screwed up, and here's how I am going to fix it." Then, without making any excuses—which are nearly always irrelevant anyway—you would explain what had happened and proceed to outline your plan for getting the matter rectified. What invariably followed was a dialogue, sometimes with others called in to assist, that focused on the corrective action without in any way berating the person who had caused the problem. The result was always in the best interest of the individual *and* the organization. As I said, this was a very enlightened company.

It is just as critical to tell your truth in interpersonal relationships in the work environment, even though they pose a unique risk because of the emotions involved. I've certainly had my share of experiences where I failed to tell my truth because I feared reprisal. And I also know that for every time I failed to tell my truth, I gave away another piece of my authenticity. Interestingly though, it is not the times that I failed to be authentic and speak my truth which stick in my mind; it's the times that I took the risk and declared my truth, no matter how horrible it seemed at the time. Sometimes, we just have to be big enough to acknowledge to another human being how small we can be and bravely tell the truth about how we are seeing things and feeling about them.

Fairly early in my career in high technology, I worked for a software company that had fallen on hard times. The investors brought in a Harvard MBA type to manage the reorganization and downsizing, which was dramatic by any standards. The company laid off half of its employees within two months of Mitchell's arrival and half of the remaining employees within two months after that. It was a difficult and frightening time for everyone involved. Things looked particularly bad for me, as it was apparent to me from the start that Mitchell intended that I be laid off as well. For reasons I still do not completely fathom, that never happened.

A year passed. Mitchell was no longer an outside consultant but had become part of the executive management team, of which I remained a member. I was forced to work shoulder to shoulder with him, even traveling with him, all the while loathing him for his serious but failed attempt to cause me to lose my job. For that and many other reasons I had accumulated, to me he represented everything bad that had happened to the company.

One day Mitchell and I arrived in Boston only to learn that our business meeting had been cancelled before our flight had even left San Francisco. We were grounded in Boston together for about thirty-six hours. Mitchell, who was from Boston, suggested that he show me around during our free day together. It is a testament to my level of unwillingness to face the truth—*my* truth—that I agreed. In retrospect, I think I was still in survival mode about my job and found it necessary to keep Mitchell happy. In other words, I was being run by my fear and using my outer-centered reality skills to provide Mitchell with whatever he wanted—including my personal company—that would make him happy and keep me safe.

Then it happened. I had spent the better part of two hours or so glumly accompanying Mitchell while he showed me the sights in downtown Boston. I was no longer willing to put up with this charade—whatever the cost. I decided to tell Mitchell right then and there what I was thinking and feeling.

"Mitchell," I said, stopping and turning to look at him, "there are a couple of things I need to tell you before we do anything else."

"OK. What is it?"

And so I told him—everything. To this day, I'm still not sure what it was that prompted me to do that, but my sense is that my Authentic Self had just had enough of me being something and someone I wasn't, even in the name of self-preservation. As I told him everything I thought about him—that I believed he had tried to get me fired when he first arrived and that I felt that his approach to dealing with the company's problems caused many people a great deal of grief—Mitchell just calmly stood there listening to me with what I can only describe as honest interest in his face. He wasn't offended. He didn't get upset. He didn't defend and he didn't attack. He just listened.

When I was done, he told me that in looking over our interactions since his arrival at the company, he could certainly see how I felt that way. And, yes, he had wanted to get rid of me when he first arrived. But what I didn't know—and he took responsibility for me not knowing it—was that he no longer saw me as part of the company's problems, but rather, for many months he had viewed me as one of the people who held the keys for solving those problems. He then went on to justify his revised view by underscoring some of the things he had seen me doing over the past twelve months.

I was flabbergasted with the results of telling my truth to Mitchell in the most brutal and uncompromising way. Mitchell had listened. I've discovered many times since then that people will listen when you are telling your truth. People *want* to hear your truth, even if that truth is "I hate you." We humans seem to have an innate understanding that we cannot move through a space such as "I hate you" to whatever is next—frequently, it is just the opposite of hate—unless there has been an acknowledgment of where we truly are—i.e., our truth. Without speaking our truth, we are doomed to stay stuck right where we are.

The ending of the story with Mitchell is that, nearly nineteen years after that conversation in Boston, we are still in each other's lives, and we have supported each other emotionally and professionally on several occasions. This will not always be the result for everyone, in every situation, but telling the truth lays the groundwork to make outcomes like this possible.

I am not suggesting that you show up for work on Monday and line up all the people with whom you are having trouble to tell them honestly what you think of them. You may need to wait until your own special kind of lightning strikes you. Be aware, though, that your lightning can be as simple as that voice in your head saying, "You can't say *that!*" when something suggests itself for you to say. Why not? Just remember that when you are coming from your truth—and nothing but your truth—people will often listen with an open heart. The next time you think of something to say that you know is true for you and your mind offers something like, "You can't say that!" ignore your mind and say it anyway. Be sure you are telling your truth and be sure to include a statement of your feelings. Stay aware of and gauge the reaction of your co-worker or co-workers.

My friend Kathy Kirkpatrick once shared with me a five-step process for dealing with particularly gnarly interpersonal issues. She calls it the "Five Steps to Assertive Communication," and I have used it with great success as an alternative method for approaching someone with whom I have an issue.

Assertive Communication allows you to tell your truth in a nonthreatening and respectful way. The Five Steps to Assertive Communication are as follows:

1. *When you . . .* Start out by describing the specific activity that you are upset about, focusing everything you say on the *actions* of the person you are addressing. For example, you might say, "When you come into my office and interrupt me when I'm on the telephone . . ."

2. *I feel . . .* Then describe what it is you feel under those circumstances. For example, you might say, "I feel angry . . ." Here you name the feeling that the objectionable incident or activity raises in you. Careful! It is *not* a feeling when you say something like, "I feel that you don't respect me." That's a judgment, and there is no room for judgments in successful Assertive Communication. Remember, too, that people do not get upset when you come from your genuine feelings.

3. *What I'd like . . .* After describing the situation that upsets you and the feelings it evokes, state what you'd like to do about it. Say, "What I'd like us to do in the future is . . ." and generally

describe the relationship or situation that you'd like to replace the objectionable incident or activity. Again, it's important to avoid inserting judgments. The best plan is to speak in broad terms; describe the situation in a way that you think will work best for both of you.

4. *What I'd like you to do* . . . Now offer a course of action for the other person that will alleviate the problem you've just defined. Say, "So, what I'd like you to do is check to see if I'm on the phone before you enter my office." Describe as specifically as possible what new behavior you would like the other person to exhibit when similar situations come in up in the future.

5. *What do you think?* Lastly, and most importantly, say, "I'd like to know what you think about this." This gives the other person the chance to respond and the chance for the both of you to work together to negotiate a win-win solution.

I have used the Five Steps to Assertive Communication on many occasions, often in those situations that are highly charged with emotion (mine) and where I require something of a script to assist me in getting through the process. These five simple steps have never failed me. Try them yourself. Make a list of at least five people with whom you are having difficulty telling your truth. Rank them in order of difficulty—most difficult at the top to least difficult at the bottom. Write out an assertive-communication script to deal with the most difficult person. Practice it and then perform it, staying present during the entire session. Keep working down your list.

It's important to realize that you don't tell your truth for the other person's sake. You tell your truth for *you*. That's not to say that it won't have some effect on the other people, even if they give you no indications whatsoever that your truth-telling has affected them. I've had people tell me I'm wrong. I've had people respond by telling me, "Oh, you can't *possibly* feel that way!" and then going on to explain why this is so. I've had people shut down because I've struck too close to something they were hiding in themselves, and they steered clear of me after that. On more than one occasion, I have even had people get angry because I'd told the truth as I saw it. I've had people deny that what I had said to them had any element of truth in it, only to have them reveal years later that what I'd said had forced them to face a difficult truth in their own lives. In a few cases, my willingness to tell the truth became a turning point not only in my own life but also in the lives of others. The important thing to remember in every situation is that you aren't telling your truth for the other person; you're telling it for you!

I once interviewed a young man right out of graduate school for a position at a high-technology company that was known for its no-nonsense attitude, late hours, and overachieving culture. During the interview, he asked a series of questions I would never have had the courage to ask when I was his age: "I understand that employees receive three weeks of vacation during their first year. Do we really get those three weeks or is that just on paper?" Later he wanted to know if he could be successful if he worked just forty or fifty hours a week in the face of the company's reputation for having employees who worked an average of sixty to eighty hours each week. At first I was a bit taken aback, but then I realized that his commitment to a balanced lifestyle was something I wanted to encourage in all the company's employees. Consequently, I was impressed with his candor and by the presence of his Authentic Self during the interview process as evidenced by his willingness to ask those questions. He got the job and went on to do extremely well.

Consider for a moment what might have occurred if he had not been willing to risk "offending" the interviewer—me—by telling the truth and asking questions about what he could expect his life to look like if he were employed by my company. He might have gotten the job nonetheless—indeed, conventional wisdom would dictate that he would have been *more* likely to get the job—and both of us could have been in for some very unpleasant surprises. So stay completely conscious during your interviews, tell your truth, and present your Authentic Self in its full glory. Quite simply, if your potential employer does not "take to" your Authentic Self, *you do not want that job*. The right job for your Authentic Self will present itself to you if you pass up the ones that do not support its presence.

I cannot tell you the number of people who get into trouble in the workplace because they are not willing to tell the truth as they see it. They'd rather not hurt somebody's feelings. They'd rather not be in touch with what's really going on with them. They'd rather do or say anything but their truth. But what *always* works is to tell your truth!

23

Practice Genuine Trust

The chief lesson I have learned in a long life is that the only way to make a man trustworthy is to trust him; and the surest way to make him untrustworthy is to distrust him and show your distrust.

—Henry L. Stimson

Trust or the lack of it takes many forms in the workplace. There is the opportunity for trust in the relationships with staff, peers, and managers. There is the opportunity for trust in the organization and its goals, its general direction, its courses of action, and the individual steps it takes to achieve its end results. There can be trust that the administration of processes and procedures are fair to all employees. There are opportunities for trust with vendors and with clients and customers. On a personal level, each of us has the opportunity to trust ourselves and our choices as well as in the bigger picture, the opportunity to trust the career path we have chosen.

I have entitled this chapter "Practice Genuine Trust" because, in my experience, we often give a great deal of lip service to trust, and many believe they actually do practice it, but the reality is that where the rubber meets the road, *genuine* trust—in others and in ourselves—is missing. We all seem to have developed the ability to apply "qualified" or "conditional" trust. We trust people until their words or actions begin to raise doubts or fears in our minds. At that point, we jerk back those strings we've always had attached to our trust in a last-ditch effort to save the situation from what are, in all actuality, our own fears and doubts.

In the workplace, we see this most frequently when a manager delegates a specific task to an employee. First of all, it is rare for such delegations to include the necessary two legs—responsibility *and* authority—on which to stand. Too often, employees will be given responsibility without authority. Even if sufficient authority is initially given, it can be taken away the instant the person making the delegation disagrees with the course of action steered by the employee. At this point, the employee may find his authority, and often his responsibility, sharply and instantly curtailed.

I am not suggesting that managers in such situations have anything but their company's best interests at heart. Even granting this, most of us have known managers who cannot see beyond their own methods for doing things. Their rigidity about how things should be done is imposed on every single task they delegate. And if things are not done *exactly* the way they would have done them personally, they are quick to withdraw an employee's authority.

Employees who experience this level of highly conditional trust in the workplace often feel disenfranchised and correctly diagnose that they have no real voice in the organization's decision-making and policy direction. If you are working in conditions like this, you know exactly what I mean.

Other than removing yourself from the situation, there may not be much you can do about gaining the trust of your superiors if they are not able or willing to give it to you. But there is plenty you can do about giving your own *genuine* trust to others in the workplace, including your employees, your peers, your managers, and the administration. And let's not forget the people outside your organization, such as vendors, clients, and customers.

The number of people I meet who say, directly or indirectly, that they do not trust their employers always surprises me. I have always wondered how and why these people continue to work for people or organizations they do not trust.

The giving of trust in our work relationships has its own set of conditions and practices. For one thing, I think many of us have it backward. On one level or another, most of us withhold trust from another person until that person proves to be trustworthy in our estimation. That may have been an appropriate methodology one hundred years ago when employment meant being one of three or four clerks in a general store, or even fifty years ago when a dozen or so people worked together in a small group in a manufacturing plant and interacted with each other all day long. But in today's complex and highly matrixed working environments there is neither time nor opportunity to scope out the other employees to assure yourself that each one is trustworthy.

Just as with learning to lead with gratitude, where giving gratitude *up front* provides the energy and impetus for miracles to take place, the giving of trust up front—unearned, as it were—creates an environment in which trustworthiness will be the most likely response. Giving trust is the fuel that makes others trustworthy. If you do not trust me initially, there is *nothing* I can say or do that will make you trust me—precisely because if you do not trust what I say and do, how can anything I say or do earn your trust? Trust is a gift you give to others unconditionally, not a reward or compensation that must be earned.

How do you hold trust? Do you begin by trusting someone absolutely, or do you wait, expecting that your trust must be earned first by specific deeds? Realize that your approach and expectations have enormous power over the outcome.

Yes, there is risk involved, and I am not saying that, like a fool, you should continue to trust those who have consistently proven themselves untrustworthy. (One plausible definition of mental illness is doing the same thing over and over and expecting to get a different result.) But if you hold people as being less than fully trustworthy until they prove themselves, they will probably never prove themselves. Remember the Law of Mind Action? This is another place where consciously applying this principle can cause a dramatic shift in how you relate to people—and in how they relate to you. If you are focused on someone being trustworthy, then that is likely what you will get from them. If you are focused on finding out why they might not be worthy of your trust, you're likely to find that, too. Ask yourself, if someone were scrutinizing you to determine your trustworthiness, would you pass with a rating of 100 percent absolutely trust-worthy? Probably not.

I have found that even when a person has done something which I perceive as having violated my trust, there are often other factors at work. I'm a firm believer in what Edward de Bono calls "logic bubbles," those things in a person's environment that cause him or her to act in a certain way. A logic bubble is a set of perceptions—including circumstance, structure, context, and relationships—within which a person is acting at any given moment.[1] To those of us outside someone's logic bubble, that individual's actions may appear to make no sense at all. But inside the bubble, things can look very different, such that the person's actions and choices appear reasonable given what he or she knew and had to deal with at the time. So it's good to keep in mind that at times a person's apparent untrustworthiness is merely the result of their operating in a different logic bubble than you are—and one that's frequently invisible to you.

I once held a position with a large corporation where one of my responsibilities was to determine when a specific customer-service issue was to be "escalated" to another department. If it was, I would discuss it with the person who managed the department that handled escalated customer-service issues. If we both agreed that escalation was necessary, as was generally the case, he would take it. When a new person moved into that position, I suddenly found I was having extreme difficulty getting this new manager's agreement to accept escalations, despite what I thought were very persuasive arguments that it was in the best interests of the company that he do so. I simply could not understand his position, and I began to think of him as being untrustworthy—at least, as far as his ability to determine what was good for the company.

Then I discovered that he was operating in a completely different logic bubble than I was. When he was hired into the position, *his* manager, who was under increasing pressure to cut costs in the department, set up this new manager's bonus compensation so that it was based, in large part, on his ability to limit the number of escalations he permitted into the department. No wonder he was obstreperous! He saw every escalation as money coming out of his pocket! It wasn't that he was untrustworthy; he was just operating in a different logic bubble than I was. Once I realized what the true situation was, the door was open for communication regarding the best interests of the company, and appropriate changes were made.

The next time you find yourself moving into distrust because of someone's actions, make a serious effort to determine what in that person's logic bubble is causing the response you are witnessing. You will probably find an explanation that will convert the apparently illogical act into something quite logical and trustworthy.

Sometimes someone's apparent untrustworthiness is caused by the very nature of our communication to that person. A few years ago, I was having difficulty with a friend and I found myself unwilling to discuss the situation with her directly until I could determine an approach that I felt would work. A mutual friend told me she could see that something was going on and offered to help. After she agreed to keep things confidential, I told her what I was dealing with and that I was working on a plan to get things cleaned up.

The next day the phone rang, and it was the friend with whom I was having the issues. She was upset—alternately confused, angry, betrayed, and hurt. Our mutual friend had told her everything I had discussed with her! After some initial heated discussion about who had said and done what to whom, we started talking. By the time the call ended, things were nearly cleared up. And what about the mutual friend who had promised to keep things confidential? What I realized is that when she had offered to help and to keep things confidential, she had no idea what I was about to dump on her. My mental image is that she willingly held out a tiny teacup, but I, unaware of the limits of her offer, poured forth bucket after bucket of accusations about and issues with our mutual friend that completely overwhelmed her. Neither her teacup nor she could hold it. *Who*, I had to ask myself, was responsible for *that*? Right. Me! It is extremely important to understand the extent of someone's abilities. If we overwhelm them and they crack, it's easy to label them as untrustworthy, but where does the real responsibility lie?

Many of us have the greatest difficulty in genuinely trusting ourselves and our choices. We second-guess the process we are in or the path we are on. We look at some small thing that we believe has not worked out for us, and we use it to make a case against our ability to make *any* right choices. How many times during some "dark cloud" moment in your job have you told yourself—or perhaps even someone else—that you made a mistake coming to work there? It is vital to trust your choices, your path, and the processes that lie along your path. Your ability to trust others can be no greater than the limits you have placed on trusting yourself.

Your Authentic Self is both a trusting and a trustworthy being. It is hard for your Authentic Self to make an appearance in an environment where trust is lacking. Recognize that sometimes it is necessary to disarm yourself first, because when you do, you disarm others as well.

If you find yourself having difficulty extending complete and genuine trust to anyone, don't be disheartened. Extend what you can. Go as far as you can see, and when you get there you will be able to see farther. The important thing is to not make a limiting decision about someone's trustworthiness and then operate from that perspective for all time.

Learn to grant genuine trust to your employer, your manager, your peers, your employees, and most importantly, to yourself. If you find that you cannot do that, make some changes, because your Authentic Self will continue to hide if you don't.

24

Be Curious

I believe that the first test of a truly great man is his humility.
I don't mean by humility, doubt of his power. But really great
men have a curious feeling that the greatness is not of them,
but through them. And they see something divine in every other
man and are endlessly, foolishly, incredibly merciful.

—John Ruskin

When I say "Be curious," I am not talking about being nosy or prying into other people's affairs. Rather, I am referring to an approach to dealing with other people that builds on the concept of practicing genuine trust. Ordinarily, we don't think of trust and curiosity going hand in hand, but in fact they do, as you'll soon come to understand.

We have all had the experience of working ourselves into a frenzy over what someone else has said or done, only to find out later that there was some motive for those words or actions that had absolutely nothing to do with us. Just as with the "logic bubble" approach that we discussed in the previous chapter, curiosity can take us beyond the limits of our own perceptions. Indeed, like the logic-bubble concept, being curious allows you to check out the world from inside another person's mind and prevents that person from feeling in any way threatened or attacked.

Sometimes we discover the mitigating circumstances that caused someone to behave in a way that hurt or angered us only *after* we have confronted the presumed offender in a showdown. In the worst cases, bad feelings between the two people can go on for years because the offended person fails to find out why the other person did or said the things he or she did. Being curious as soon as a potential problem arises can prevent the situation from snowballing. Let me explain:

When we have an experience we don't fully understand, our minds naturally "build a case" involving the other person. Instead of assuming that you are absolutely right, as we all often do in these situations, you can carry your case to the alleged offender and ask him or her about it, in the true spirit of curiosity. The asking makes all the difference.

When you bring your case to this person, you do so not in an accusatory way but in the context of benign curiosity. You do so with the spirit of genuinely seeking an explanation, because the best explanation you have been able to come up with leads you to some uncomfortable conclusions about the relationship. The "Be curious" approach signals that, rather than accepting those conclusions unquestioningly, you are checking your data and observations.

Think about it this way: When you approach people with this kind of curious communication, they are being honored. First, you honor them in your stated hesitancy to think that they would do anything consciously to anger or hurt you. There is genuine trust implicit in that hesitancy. Second, you honor them because you obviously value the relationship enough that you do not want to adhere to those uncomfortable conclusions without first checking them out. Third, you honor them because you are evidently willing to take a risk before traveling down the path to cementing the conclusions you have drawn thus far.

The most important aspect about coming from the "Be curious" space is adopting what is called "inner silence" in many Eastern traditions. Inner silence is basically "not knowing." It is not a matter of feigning ignorance so much as it is a letting go of all your decisions and conclusions. You are suspending belief in what you think you know about the situation, so that you can approach the other person from the pure and innocent place of *not knowing*.

Practice being in inner silence. During your quiet time see if you can fully release all of your preconceived knowledge about a situation you find unsettling. Do this with the spirit of fully expecting to get complete and satisfying answers to your questions about the situation.

Our own prejudices and preconceptions can block us from hearing or accepting the truth. Remember that the mind sees what it believes and then believes what it sees. In truth, questioning that comes from a place of pre-conception or prejudice, rather than coming from a place of inner silence and being curious, quickly becomes the preamble for expressing your anger or upset. In the worst-case scenario, it is your prelude to an attack—one that you will defend with your belief that your attack is "justified."

On the other hand, it's amazing what you can learn when you enter into the space of asking questions without being convinced that you know the answers beforehand. When you practice inner silence, you empty yourself of your preconceptions. This process is made more challenging, of course, when you attempt to apply it in situations where past experience with a particular person tells you that the case you've built is probably right. But even here the "Be curious" approach often produces real breakthroughs in relationships that you might have once believed were impossible.

The "Be curious" approach has three basic steps:

1. You outline your understanding and expectations in a very simple and unemotional way. It's a good idea to write these points down before meeting in any situation where you have strong feelings or judgments about what occurred.
2. You make it clear to the other person that the result you got, or *think* you got, was not the result you expected, and this has raised your curiosity.

3. You ask about it, because, after all, it appears to you that the person you are addressing is at the center of the issue and you believe that coming to them would be productive.

Let's say, for example, that you are the head of a team that has been assigned to work on a project with a team headed by Jack. Both of you came to realize, at some point, that your teams were having trouble working together. You and Jack have met to discuss this, but while you have not come up with any solutions yet, you have agreed to not discuss the matter with other people until you have the teams working more smoothly. Meanwhile, it appears that Jack did not honor the agreement but has spoken to his manager, and you are angry with him. Your "Be curious" approach might look something like this:

1. "Jack, my understanding was that you and I agreed that we would not discuss the difficulties our staffs are having working together with anyone else until we had made a sincere effort to work out the issues." (*Your statement of what your understanding and expectations were.*)
2. "Yesterday, I heard that you had discussed the situation with your manager, which may or may not be true." (*Your statement of the facts you have learned that appear inconsistent with your understanding and expectations.*)
3. "I'm curious about this. Can you enlighten me?" (*Your expression of curiosity and request for an explanation.*)

At this point, Jack might tell you any number of things. Perhaps the purported conversation with his manager never took place. Or maybe it took place because one of the employees had complained to Jack's boss, who in turn snagged Jack and demanded an explanation. Or it could be that Jack has a different understanding of the agreement he made with you. Or perhaps Jack's understanding of the agreement was the same as yours but he broke the agreement inadvertently and now realizes his error. Just keep in mind that the potential range of explanations is nearly infinite and that you can't know for certain anything about Jack's perceptions of the matter until you ask—in a benignly curious way.

When Jack does explain in response to your calm and curious request for information about his actions—even if your worst suspicions are confirmed—you can *then* decide what your most appropriate response will be. Recognize that your response, whatever it is, is now based on far more accurate and complete information than you could have had prior to this latest interaction with Jack.

If you are coming from the place of inner silence and the space of truly being curious, you will not know what the answer is going to be. If you even *think* you know the answer you're going to get, you're not there!

My father and I have had a difficult past. Off and on, for a period of nearly twenty years, we were estranged. Shortly after my mother died, Dad remarried and his outlook on life changed significantly. As a result of that, and personal growth on both our parts, we reestablished contact about four years ago and have had few problems since.

At the time that we reconciled, my daughter was ten years old, and my father had seen her but once, when she was about two months old. In fact, when my daughter was born, my parents never acknowledged her birth, not even with a card or gift. The Father's Day following our reconciliation, I called Dad to wish him well and to talk a bit about what was going on in our lives but also to hear him acknowledge the fact that since I had a child it was Father's Day for me as well. While I recognized that Father's Day was a time to honor our fathers, not for them to honor their children's fatherhood, past hurts made it important to me to hear Dad say something about my status as a father. He never did.

When I got off the telephone, I was livid. "Is it possible that he doesn't understand that *I'm* a father?" I asked my wife. "Apparently, he doesn't care! He hasn't changed. He'll *never* change. Why do I bother?" I admit, I was really hurt.

It took me a week, but I finally moved to the place of true curiosity in which I just could not understand how the result that I got was so far off the mark from the result that I expected. After much meditation and prayer, I was able to calm myself sufficiently to realize that, with our joint history adding fuel to the fire, I could come up with hundreds of reasons how that interaction could have happened, but in truth I really didn't *know*. So, I decided to ask. Worried that my emotions would run away with me if I tried to deal with this on the phone, I sent him this note:

> *Dear Dad,*
>
> *I'm really curious. There's something I cannot put together in my mind. Maybe you can help. When I called you on Father's Day this was also the tenth year since I became a father myself. I realized that I had wanted you to acknowledge that fact. I understand that you and I were estranged when my daughter was born, but thankfully we no longer are. After talking with you on Father's Day, I began to wonder why you never acknowledged my fatherhood. I don't know how to put that together in my mind. Can you help me with this?*

Within four days I got a letter back from Dad. In it he explained to me what was going on in his life. His new wife of less than six months had discovered a lump in her breast that turned out to be malignant. When he had talked with me on the phone, they had just received the news and were bracing for an upcoming radical mastectomy, with months of chemotherapy and radiation beyond that. He said that when he got off the telephone with me, he realized something had been missing from the conversation, but he couldn't put his finger on it. And then he apologized for having neglected to give me the respect he clearly felt I deserved. That letter was filled with love as well as with the pain of his own circumstances, something else he had never shared with me.

I am convinced that had I been anything other than curious in my communications with my father, the result would likely have been very different. Had I simply stuffed my hurt feelings and decided to simply forget that

Father's Day phone call, it would have plagued our relationship for years. I might have convinced myself, on the surface, that things were OK between the two of us, but there would have been quite another message festering in the recesses of my mind.

Being curious is easy to implement, though admittedly it can be difficult to remember this tool when you are in the heat of anger or upset. For that reason, you want to begin rehearsing this approach in your mind *now* so that when you need it as a tool it will be accessible. If you understand the concept and focus on using it at every possible opportunity, it will become a comfortable habit. When it is a habit, it will be the automatic response you have to any situation in which you feel confused, upset, or angered by someone else's behavior.

The next time you find yourself angry or upset about something another person has done, work yourself through the steps of inner silence and move into the space where you can simply be curious. If you think it will help, write out a simple three-step script so that you can approach the person you are having difficulty with from the space of being curious. Gauge the response to this approach by checking out what you are experiencing within yourself and how the other person is responding to what you've said.

When someone does something that doesn't match your expectations of what should have happened in the circumstances—whether at work or any-where else in your life—before you are angry, before you are hurt, before you counterattack, "Be curious." When you address the situation from that perspec-tive, you will always be coming from a place of authenticity.

25

Honor Silence

Under all speech that is good for anything there lies a silence that is better. Silence is deep as Eternity; speech is shallow as Time.

—Thomas Carlyle

Most of us find silence uncomfortable. This may be a product of our Western society where the air always seems to be filled with sound. Whatever the cause, few of us tolerate silence for long. Even with a conscious effort, it has taken me decades to appreciate the power of silence and to draw it willingly into my life as an important source of creativity, inspiration, and most importantly, peace.

Because my father had a keen interest in the television industry, a television set was already a fixture in my parents' home by the time I was born. Television had a powerful influence on my childhood and our family dynamics. It *totally* replaced silence. The first one up in the morning turned the television on, and it stayed on all day long, until the last person to go to bed would turn it off. What I find amazing, in retrospect, is that the television would be on in our house even when nobody was watching it. It provided background noise while we did other things—homework, preparing and eating meals, doing the dishes, performing other chores, and even talking. The sound of the television was ever present, filling what otherwise, and in other times, would have been spaces of silence. In our home today, where silence is revered and honored, it is almost impossible to believe that I once lived that way.

I do not know why the television became so ubiquitous in my parents' house, but I believe to some extent it served to keep us from experiencing the "sound of silence," as Simon and Garfunkel would so eloquently put it a short time later. There was something in the silence that frightened us, and so we used the television to keep it at bay.

There is some of that same fear, I believe, in all of us. Most of us look upon silence as something to avoid. In our lives outside work, it takes the comparative safety of being with someone we love and trust, and who we know loves and trusts us, before we can simply be together in silence for any period of time. How many times have you been haunted by the specter of unexpected silence in your own life and immediately done something to break that silence, such as turning on the radio or television, playing some music, or calling someone?

Life at work provides ample opportunities to see how we all tend to react to silence. You have undoubtedly noticed how uncomfortable it can get in a meeting when suddenly there is complete silence—even if only for a few seconds. As though responding to some interpersonal variation of the law of physics that "nature abhors a vacuum," someone, perhaps you, will fill the empty space by saying something—indeed, almost anything.

I firmly believe that we are all engaged in an unacknowledged conspiracy against silence. That conspiracy robs us of much. First, without silence it is virtually impossible for us to be authentic. Silence allows us to focus and get in touch with what we are thinking and feeling. Second, silence itself has a beauty all its own, helping to provide clarity and understanding. When we fill the silence just for the sake of filling it, we are robbed of its benefits. As my author friend James Dillet Freeman writes, "Is not music more beautiful because there are rests? Is not eloquence more passionate when it has pauses?" Third, we lose the gifts that silence can bring us, if we would only listen.

The Navajo people have several traditions that honor the gifts of silence. For one thing, a Navajo will never interrupt another person who is speaking.

Indeed, they wait for a respectful period of time to pass before offering any response. This period of silence serves two purposes: First, it gives the speaker an opportunity to reflect and possibly to elaborate on what he or she has already said. The listener shows his respect for that by remaining silent, knowing that it is in silence that we often complete our thoughts. Second, it allows the words of the speaker to wash over the listener so that he fully comprehends both the words and their meaning. By waiting, the listener's response is more likely to be in tune with both the spoken and the unspoken messages of what the speaker has conveyed.

Contrast this ancient practice with how we, in modern life, tend to operate in a conversation. When we are "listening," we are usually preoccupied with what we are going to say in response to the listener. We are usually framing our own response at the same time the other person is talking, and we interrupt the speaker with our response: "No, no, it's not like what you're saying at all . . ." or "I know, I had the same thing happen to me except . . ." or "I totally agree with what you are saying, but let me add that . . ." We seem to have forgotten that silence is an integral part of the rhythm of a conversation. We've forgotten that it sets the rhythm of our lives in the same way that rests are an integral and necessary part of a piece of music, or for that matter, that the rest between heartbeats and breaths is literally what nurtures life.

My own love affair with silence began in 1970 when, as I have previously mentioned, I began practicing Transcendental Meditation. For the first few weeks of sitting in a quiet room for twenty minutes in the morning and afternoon, the silence was maddening—deafening! Then something clicked for me. Silence had suddenly become my friend, and now I spend time every day in silence, sometimes for an hour or more.

I have picked up other silence-generating habits as well. For example, a few years ago a friend told me about the ancient practice of the vision quest, where a person goes alone into the wilderness to fast for several days and be alone. I tried it myself, and since that time I have disappeared for several days each year, traveling to the desert of the Four Corners area of the Southwest where I go on my own quest. I go there for the beauty. I go there for the natural wonder.

But mostly I go there for the days of silence. In that silence I am renewed and refreshed. Poetry pours itself through me, and I am once again filled with the wonder of life, simply by being alone in the silence.

Many people find silence in certain types of athletic activities: long-distance running, bicycling, wilderness hiking, cross-country skiing, lap swimming, and in-line skating—all activities that provide opportunities for solitude and, if we choose, silence.

It is as a result of practicing silent meditation that many people discover the feeling that we are never really alone. Some describe it as the experience of "communing with nature" or of feeling "at one" with God or Spirit. Others may talk about silence opening a window to their inner self or of it helping them to get in touch with what spiritual teachers for thousands of years have called the "soul." However you happen to describe such experiences, prolonged periods of silence seem to put us in touch with the highest parts of ourselves, parts that reside within each one of us but which are too easily drowned out in the busyness of our lives.

Silence is the only route to that place of peace within you. Stillness itself fills that place. Look at the examples of the masters. Jesus often drew apart from crowds and activities and was renewed by the experience. Again and again he went into the mountains, completely apart from all others, to be alone and to be in silence. Gautama Siddhartha became Buddha while sitting in silence under the bodhi tree during what the Buddhists now call the "Sacred Night." Confucius tells us, "Silence is a friend who will never betray." Mohammed's vision in which he was commanded by God to preach, resulting in the founding of Islam, occurred while he was alone during a silent retreat in a cave at Mount Hira, north of Mecca.

In the introduction and throughout this book, I have talked about various practices for honoring your truth and manifesting your Authentic Self throughout your life—not just at your place of employment but *everywhere*. Certainly we move closer to this Authentic Self through the practices we have discussed so far in these pages. But perhaps the biggest changes and the greatest benefits of working from your integrity are born when you ally yourself with silence. Silence is the key that unlocks doors to your own inner strengths and gifts, gifts that make your interactions with those around you easier, more productive, and certainly more personally satisfying.

Creating silent time for yourself could not be easier. It requires only two things: you and your willingness. You can use some of the other tools and techniques you will find in this book such as meditation, visioning, imaging, and building your sanctuary to create times when you can be silent even in the middle of the most hectic day. You can spend some silent time alone after work or even just before entering the workplace. Sitting silently in your parked car for ten to twenty minutes before going into your office can give you the opportunity to touch the silence, remember the source of your authenticity, and remind yourself of the higher intents you wish to bring to the workplace.

Bringing the concept of honoring silence into the everyday interactions of the workplace itself need not be difficult. While people can be uncomfortable with silence at first, it is amazing how quickly they can get used to it—or even require it. In particularly difficult or stressful situations, such as when there is an apparent logjam on a decision, I suggest that you announce to everyone present at that moment to take a few minutes just to be silent and to see what emerges in that silence. I have never had anyone object to this suggestion, even when I wasn't in charge of the meeting. People seem to inherently know that periods of silence are beneficial. More often than not, after silently assimilating what has happened to that point, we have come out of silence with several new ideas and approaches which carried us that much closer to a solution.

When you are engaged in conversations, begin practicing the Navajo discipline of taking a rest before responding. Wait some ten or twenty seconds before responding to what someone has said to you. See what gifts that short period of silence gives you. You will also discover that people will catch on to your rhythm and adopt it in conversations with you as you set the pace. If you feel uncomfortable doing this with other people or if you sense some discomfort, announce what you are doing. For example, you might say, "I want to just take a few moments to be silent and take in what you just said. I find I am better able to process things that way." Then take half a minute or so to be with the thoughts and feelings the conversation has brought up for you thus far.

Begin honoring silence for the gift that it is, even if you don't yet understand what these gifts will be for you. Honor it in your life in general, and in your workplace in particular. You will soon be reaping sources of personal power that will champion you in all things, not the least of which will be your authenticity. The creative and inspired ideas that your time in silence will give you will repay you in both spiritual and practical terms at work, at play, and in all your relationships.

26

Mentor Someone

A teacher affects eternity; he can never tell where his influence stops.

—Henry Brooks Adams

At some point in your career, your work and the workplace may become stale and unsatisfying—the commute is too long, the work duties are too routine, the responsibilities are burdensome, the personalities are challenging, the politics are frustrating, and you are sure that you are not being paid the salary you deserve. The same work that once excited you now seems to drag down your spirits.

When this happens, *you* start going missing from your work. And you are not going to be the only one who notices this. Oh, you still show up on time, make all the right moves, and perhaps your results are as good as always. But something is missing, and that something is the energy of your heart, that spirit within you which used to bring excitement to your work and made every day an adventure. Your Authentic Self has retired and is no longer showing up for work, even though your body still is.

For many of us, this state of affairs constitutes a mid-career crisis of tremendous proportions, one that we don't always fully acknowledge even to ourselves. But if we are truthful with ourselves, we have to admit that we have invested a large part of our lives in our jobs. By the time such disillusionment sets in, we may have spent years, possibly decades, gaining valuable on-the-job experience and honing our knowledge and skills. This may have included specialized vocational schools, staying updated on skills and technologies, and obtaining the required certification. Some people have spent years in college and graduate school. Given all that, when we get to the point of feeling uninspired or even disillusioned with our work, it is no wonder that we begin to get a little panicked.

If you have been or are now at this crossroads in your own life, the questions running through your mind may go something like this: "Well, what *else* am I going to do? Isn't this what I have trained to do? Indeed, isn't this the *only* thing I am trained to do? Isn't this where my experience is and, hence, where the money is for me? Can I possibly stand feeling like this until I reach retirement age?"

These circumstances and thoughts can conspire to make us feel trapped, and most people don't know that anything can be done about it. The first choice for some people is to chuck the education, leave their experience by the roadside, and go out into the world to search for something new that will feed their souls. They abandon their dreams, their financial goals, and even their lifestyle preferences attempting to regain the excitement they once associated with the workplace. Although this is a perfectly viable option, it is not the only one. You can stay at your present job and marshal back the forces of your enthusiasm, inspiration, creativity, excitement, and joy by finding something *more* within the context of your present job to give you back that sense of satisfaction and fulfillment. The best way to bring vibrant life back to your work is to "give it away," and the best way to give it away is to mentor someone.

By mentoring someone, I mean teaching what you have learned. I am not just talking about office skills, although these are important, too, and frequently deep mentoring relationships begin on that note. I am talking about mentoring everything that you have learned—all of your life lessons, including business skills, personal insights about life, what you know about dealing with other people, and most importantly, whatever you have gained about the importance of learning about yourself. Take risks, get personal, and go deep.

Teaching another person stretches *you* and gives you a way to give back some of what has been given to you. This is an excellent way to exercise your gratitude muscles. This is also a powerful way to fire up the engine of change in your life. Additionally, it is an incredible opportunity to learn. As sages have told us from the beginning of time, we learn best when we are teaching someone else.

Become a teacher, a mentor. Mentoring can be like having a new career within the successful career you already have. It gives you new eyes with which to see your work, your workplace, and the activities and interactions that go on there. Suddenly everything about your job becomes fresh and new. You are looking at it more clearly and, along the way, learning a new appreciation for your own accomplishments and your own experience. All of these serve to help you rediscover the interest and excitement that has been missing from your work, as you see things through the eyes of the person you have chosen to mentor.

One of the great rewards of mentoring is watching the people you are working with gaining skills and confidence through your teaching. There is something that responds within us, something that we find deeply satisfying, when a person in whom we have invested our time and energy becomes more effective or develops their own strengths.

There are plenty of opportunities to enter into mentoring relationships. Indeed, if you start using any of the tools and techniques in this book, people will be drawn to you, particularly young people who are just starting out. This is not to say that you must be older than the person you mentor but only that you have the willingness to extend yourself to the people around you who could benefit from your help.

Mentoring need not be a long-term relationship, but it can be. Sometimes the most valuable mentoring takes place in the blink of an eye with a seemingly casual comment. You'll find that opportunities will open to you; people will ask you questions or say things that, if you are really listening, are invitations to engage with them at a deeper level. You need only be alert to those opportunities and act on them. Ask the individual how you can be of assistance to him or her, and look for opportunities where you could step in and assist this person by sharing your own knowledge or experience. Formalize the relationship if the other person is willing. Set up a series of regular meetings with that person—perhaps once or twice per month. After a few meetings, schedule a special session where both of you give the other feedback about how the mentoring relationship is going and how it can possibly be made better. Make adjustments accordingly.

Read a book or take a course on how to mentor other people. Begin immediately to implement the skills you learn when dealing with other people in your workplace, even in the absence of a "formal" mentoring relationship. You will probably discover that you have already had some experience as a mentor in one form or another. Think back on those times when you assisted someone in a mentoring capacity and it turned out great. Draw from those memories to develop your mentoring skills in the present.

Mentoring means making yourself—actually, your Authentic Self—available to people. In order for that to happen, your Authentic Self must be available to *you*. It is an excellent way to practice and commit to being authentic. You cannot mentor another person and not be authentic. They'll see through you, and *you'll* see through you. The good news is that, if you find that you are not being authentic in any mentoring activity, you have the opportunity to choose again and discover new ways to express yourself in this way.

The best thing about mentoring is also the most frightening: It will give you insights into those areas in your own life where you are having your own issues and are stuck. There is no stronger magnifying mirror than mentoring someone. When you are mentoring someone and you find that the person is stuck and unable to move forward because of something in his consciousness that you can see and he cannot, it always means that it is time to take a close look at yourself. When I am mentoring someone who is stuck, I am usually able—with very little self-examination—to see where there is a parallel between what he's going through and what is at issue for me. While I always have the choice to *not* move through my own resistance, knowing that the person I am mentoring will not move through his resistance until I move through mine is a powerful motivator. This alone is a valuable gift, both for the person you are mentoring and for you.

In his best-selling book, *The Celestine Prophecy*, James Redfield tells us that the first of the key insights occurs when we take seriously the coincidences that seem to just happen in our lives. These coincidences make us feel there is something more, something spiritual, operating underneath everything we do. What this means is that everyone you meet in life has a message for you and there is a higher purpose to every meeting. And if everyone you meet in life has a message for you, then it must follow that *you* have messages for everyone whose paths cross yours. What is your message for that new intern fresh out of college? What is your message for the middle-aged middle manager who hasn't been able to get ahead in the organization and has lost his ambition and enthusiasm? What is your message for the employee who wants to grow and succeed tremendously in his job but who also wants a family and a *real* life outside the office? You *do* have messages for each and every one of the people who come into your life, both in the workplace and elsewhere. Mentoring is the best discipline I know to discover what those messages are and to deliver them. These are the kinds of messages that change people's lives. Most importantly, discovering and delivering those messages will change *your* life.

While being a mentor involves great responsibility, there is a mistaken belief that we need to be perfect role models to do it. But I sometimes think that some of the greatest precepts we have to teach are the lessons we have learned about dealing with our own imperfections. It may just be that the thing the person you are mentoring really needs to hear is your biggest failure—the disappointment and pain of the breakup of your marriage, your experience of having once been fired, or your battle to overcome some addiction. One of my own mentors has a sign over his desk that reads, "When we give ourselves permission to fail and perhaps play the fool, we also give ourselves permission to succeed and so be a hero." It is often our fear of failure that stops us from excelling, and any mentor worth her or his salt will by example pass along this truth to a student.

At one point in my career at Intel, I worked as a "Technical Assistant" (TA) to a vice president who ran one of the corporate divisions. Despite the title, there was nothing particularly "technical" about my job responsibilities. For the most part, TAs shadow their vice president in everything so that they can learn Intel's business at the executive level. These positions are highly regarded and much prized because there are so few of them and they are stepping stones to becoming a vice president. I thought that accepting a position as a TA would be a good opportunity to rise to the highest levels in the organization.

One day I received a phone call from a young Intel employee named Winston. He told me that he'd heard I was approachable, and he asked me if I would be willing to meet with him for an hour or so to talk about his career path. He believed that part of his own career path was to someday move into a TA position, and he wanted to "pick my brain" about it.

A few days later, Winston and I met. He was in his mid-twenties and had been out of college about three years. He told me that he came to Intel with his engineering degree immediately after school. As I listened to him tell me his plans, it was clear to me that he had thought everything out both logically and thoroughly. Nevertheless, I sensed some undercurrent or subtext to what he was telling me. That undercurrent was making me uncomfortable. It was almost as if he were talking about someone *else's* life; there was no animation, no "fire in the belly," as poet David Whyte would describe it. The more Winston talked, the stronger my gut feeling about this undercurrent grew.

Following that gut feeling, I asked him about it. "There's something that's just not right about what you are telling me," I said. "On a purely practical level, everything looks great. You've done all the right things; made all the right plans. But there's no fire, no excitement in what you are telling me. What is it that I am hearing here? Why am I feeling so uncomfortable with your story?"

Winston stared at me for a few moments. I was sure he had heard my question, but I was not sure he would be willing to answer me, at least not truthfully.

After just that moment of hesitation, he told me his story. He had come from an Asian family in which the work ethic was a powerful driving force. That, coupled with the cultural tradition of respecting the plans his parents had for his life, mandated that he follow the career path *they* had chosen for him, which was engineering. What he really wanted to do was to go to business school and get an MBA, but his father was dead set against him going into business and had insisted that he take the job at Intel. Winston's voice had an emotional edge for the first time as he talked about what he wanted versus what he was actually doing. When he talked about his dreams for a career in business, the fire was definitely there.

Winston's story stunned me! Here was this young man, easily twenty years younger than I, and he was telling me *my* own story! There were differences, of course: his parents were Chinese, mine Italian; my parents dreamed that I would go into medicine instead of law, and his parents wanted him to become a successful—and presumably wealthy—Silicon Valley engineer. Winston and I had this one thing in common: we had both succumbed to living other people's dreams and not our own.

I told Winston my similar story without giving him any advice or making any suggestions. I simply pointed out to him that the parallels surprised me. We met a few more times after that and continued our dialogue. Mostly I'd listen to him and answer any questions he had about my past, my process, and my decisions. On occasion, I'd ask him a question when it seemed appropriate to do so. Then, I suppose, we both got busy, and our meetings and contacts ceased abruptly.

Some six or eight months later, I received an e-mail from Winston in which he thanked me for all the time I had spent with him. He also wanted me to know that he was leaving Intel. He had been accepted into the MBA program at a major university in the Midwest and was starting the program the following Saturday.

I've never heard from Winston since then, but he is no less a part of my life and my path as, surely, I am a part of his. The time I spent with Winston had also worked its magic on me. I saw that the work I was doing at Intel at the time was not what I really wanted, and talking with Winston about doing something other than his dream in hopes of reaching a goal that wasn't even his own had operated as a powerful catalyst on me.

In truth, I had little interest in becoming another vice president running one of the line divisions. Within a matter of months, I had secured one of the other vice presidents as a patron, and he set me up as Intel's first Director of Business Relationships, where my talent in generating and maintaining healthy relationships could be best put to use. That position ultimately led me to my present passion, which is inspiring and encouraging people to be authentic in the workplace and giving them the tools to accomplish that goal. Those mentoring sessions with Winston were a great step forward for me, too. But notice that our real breakthroughs—for both of us—came when we got in touch with our Authentic Selves and spoke our truths.

There is someone out there who is in need of the knowledge of your life experiences. Find that person, give this very special gift to him or to her, and most importantly, give it to yourself. Go mentor someone. It will change *your* life!

27

Keep Your Agreements

*Never esteem anything as of advantage to you that will make you
break your word or lose your self-respect.*

—Marcus Aurelius Antoninus

We all make agreements of two kinds: First, we make agreements with ourselves, such as when we resolve, "I'm going to exercise three times a week
beginning tomorrow." Second, we make agreements with others, such as when
we say we will meet someone at a certain restaurant at 6:30 P.M. on Saturday.
While the latter kind may appear to be agreements solely with others, they are
also agreements with ourselves.

Failing to keep our agreements can certainly disrupt other people's lives
and leave them with unfulfilled expectations, but the greatest harm may be to
ourselves. This is the case whether the agreement is with another or with ourselves. For most of us, those agreements with ourselves are the easiest to
break and, at the same time, do the most damage when we don't honor them.
How many times can you promise yourself that you will start exercising
tomorrow and then *not* do it before you lose all trust and faith in yourself?
This kind of damage to ourselves undermines our self-trust and self-esteem

in ways that are not so easy to see or repair. Then, of course, not keeping our agreements with others has the additional complication of eroding our credibility in other people's eyes. Do it too frequently and you'll soon develop a reputation for failing to honor agreements. That only further decreases your faith and trust in yourself.

There is a commonly held belief that there is a sort of hierarchy of agreements, from those we truly must keep to those we need only keep if it is convenient to do so. Written, legally binding contractual agreements tend to fall into the first category. Agreements in our personal relationships too frequently get relegated to the latter category. My experience, both in law and in my personal life, is that people who believe that certain agreements must be kept while others need not be will place them into whichever category fits their particular needs at the moment, and this can lead to trouble.

If you wish to enhance your authenticity, it is important to look at how you handle agreements. From the viewpoint of your Authentic Self, there is no such thing as *not keeping* an agreement because it is not significant. Your Authentic Self would have you keep *all* agreements or renegotiate any you cannot or perhaps *should not* keep. When you simply dismiss your obligations under an agreement because you somehow decide it is insignificant, your Authentic Self goes into hiding.

There is no such thing as an insignificant agreement, because every time you fail to keep an agreement, your self-esteem and self-respect are involved. It makes no difference whether you think the agreement is small or large. The Authentic Self treats all agreements the same, and failing to keep a small agreement is as dangerous to your self-esteem and your self-respect as is failing to keep a big one. The ramifications easily spread to all aspects of your life.

Take the example of my acquaintance Gary. He rarely, if ever, keeps his agreements with me, and I assume from this that he also fails to keep his agreements with others. We are both part of a men's group that meets on occasion to view a film, have dinner together, and generally enjoy each other's company. About a month in advance, I send out e-mail notices to everyone in the group to tell them the date of the next get-together. Then, the day before the event, I send out the specifics of the evening. The rule is that no one need RSVP, and whoever wants to attend just shows up. For reasons I do not understand, Gary always writes back after each of my two separate notices to tell me that he will be there this time *for sure*! But he never shows up! Gary actually goes out of his way to make agreements he does not even have to make, and then he breaks them.

His entire life mirrors his difficulty with keeping agreements. Since I met him about eighteen months ago, he has lost his business, has had to sell almost everything he owns, and has a remaining personal debt of nearly a half million dollars. He has taken a low-level job to make ends meet at a company that used to be one of his competitors, and his marriage is in trouble. Now, I would grant you that it might be *possible* that Gary's problems have absolutely nothing to do with the fact that he doesn't keep his agreements, but I would bet you that they do. My own experiences in life tell me that those people who keep their agreements have lives which work and that those who do not keep their agreements have lives generously salted with difficulty.

How about you? Are you keeping *all* your agreements, with yourself and with others? Are you keeping even those agreements that you do not believe are particularly significant in the overall context of your life? Make a list of every agreement you made and kept or that you made and did not keep over the previous week. If need be, go back farther than a week. Get a sense of your completion rate. From your findings, see if you can find a pattern with the kinds of agreements you tend to let slide and the kinds you tend to complete. Begin to think of ways to get your agreement completion rate to 100 percent.

Remember that every agreement is an opportunity to prove that you value your word, your self, and the other parties involved in the agreement. If we are to fully grasp the power of agreements, we also need to understand how every agreement holds the potential for showing your disregard for your self, your word, and those around you. Once this fact is recognized, the way we deal with agreements must become a *conscious* choice.

Too frequently, we enter into agreements either unconsciously or because we simply have not thought them through. We tell someone that we will do something, but we feel no real commitment in our hearts to carry through. We need to understand that when people hear us say that we will do something, they interpret this to mean we have committed in the most binding sense of the word, irrespective of what we may have meant or how casually we have given our agreement.

There are many reasons why we make agreements without making internal commitments that will ensure we follow through. Sometimes we agree without understanding what's required of us. Sometimes we agree in order to get someone off our backs, such as when the kids are begging us to take them to the park or to play with them, and we're busy, so we promise to do it tomorrow. Sometimes we truly want to be of assistance, and so we sign on to do more than we are actually able or willing to do. Sometimes we agree because we think we have to or because we are afraid to say no, as when the boss asks us to take on yet another responsibility. Sometimes, agreeing without commitment is simply a reflex resulting from years of outer-centered reality training—or, to put it more simply, we've just never learned to say no.

Making agreements with commitment starts by simply developing some consciousness involving your agreements. Begin by making a firm commitment to yourself that you will make no agreements, either with yourself or with others, until you fully understand what the agreement will require of you. Take the time you need, whether it's a few seconds or a few days. The point is to make it a *mandatory* step in your personal process of making agreements to stop and think through what the obligation means and whether you are going to be able and willing to perform it. Check in with your feelings. Do you feel positive and excited? Do you feel ambivalent, burdened, or afraid to say no? Examine your motives. Is this something that you will enjoy doing or that will benefit you? Are you doing it only because you feel guilty or because you want people to think well of you? Look at all the different possibilities.

Take the time to project an image of yourself doing whatever you will need to do to fulfill the agreement. If the agreement requires you to do something in the future, take into account what other things you will be doing during that time. Of course, you cannot anticipate everything, but you can anticipate some things, and the self-examination suggested here will prevent you from entering into a lot of agreements for which you truly have no commitment. It is the agreement behind which there is no commitment that is the one most often broken.

By using this technique you avoid making agreements without feeling a real commitment to doing so. But does this mean that you must always keep every agreement which you ever make? No, of course not, although there are metaphysical teachings which would suggest that this could be the case. Certainly there are situations that make an agreement we've entered into suddenly less profitable, more inconvenient, less attractive, requiring resources that we don't have available, or even impossible. The question then becomes, what do you do about it?

One thing is certain: Don't ignore agreements you've made, not even the ones that you can no longer complete. What you need to do is to communicate with the people who will be affected by your new decision and renegotiate. As soon as you realize that you are unwilling or unable to keep an agreement, contact the party or parties who are relying on you to keep your agreement and tell them the circumstances. (It is important here, as elsewhere, to tell your truth. Making up excuses will do nothing for your self-esteem or authenticity, even though you might be the only one who will ever discover the truth.)

The next step is renegotiation, the results of which can range from being freely and completely released from your obligation to shifting the time or the very nature of your obligation. The renegotiated results will depend entirely on the situation, including the nature of the original agreement, the impact of your actions on the other parties, the extent to which they were relying on you to keep the original agreement, and your relationship with them.

As with making any agreements, take the time to carefully apply the methodology of consciously looking at the renegotiated agreement and any resulting new commitments *before* you agree. It's all too easy to agree to something while feeling pressured because of your unwillingness or inability to keep an old agreement. Remember, going back *again* to renegotiate will not do much for your sense of self-esteem and self-respect, and it won't contribute to your positive reputation with the other parties either.

The bottom line is quite simple and straightforward: If you want to be more authentic, enter into agreements *only* if you know that you will and can fulfill them—and then keep your agreements. If you find that you cannot keep an agreement, do the responsible thing—communicate and renegotiate.

28

Create and Honor Ritual

*To most of us on most occasions things are not symbols
and actions are not sacramental; and we have to teach
ourselves, consciously and deliberately, to remember
that they are.*

—Aldous Huxley

Even in our early childhood, rituals are important to us. When my daughter was
very young there were certain things that simply *had* to happen before bedtime
or she would not go to sleep. These items included reading a story together, the
"tucking in" of her favorite stuffed animals, and a series of three questions her
mother or I would ask her: "Do you feel warm? Do you feel cozy? Do you feel
loved?" This nighttime ritual completed her day and signaled her mind that the
time for sleep had arrived.

It is important to realize that the significance of any ritual does not come
from the ritual itself. Rituals do not spring forth already filled with meaning.
Ceremonial acts are meaningless unless and until we give them meaning. It is
we who bring meaning to the events and activities of our lives and instill them
with importance or treat them as unimportant.

As an example, a young co-worker in a small office where I worked many years ago came to work one Monday wearing a wedding ring. Everyone was surprised since he had never mentioned that he was even engaged. When asked about the wedding, he shrugged, indicating that the event seemed to have no more significance to him than going to see a movie over the weekend. At the opposite extreme, a single mother I knew went to great lengths to create a ceremonial ritual for the simple act of signing her will in favor of her young daughter. She invited friends, family, and co-workers to participate in what she consciously created as a joyous event. Who had the right approach? Neither is right or wrong, but each serves to illustrate that rituals are meaningful or meaningless according to what we assign to them.

Rituals are important because they create a sense of community and have the ability to draw members of a community into a sense of unity wherein we are reminded that common threads intertwine all our lives. Theologian and author Matthew Fox says that ritual is an opportunity for the community to gather to praise. That praise can be of some Higher Power, an individual, or the community in general. Indeed, says Fox, there is no community without ritual.

Our modern world has been stripped of conscious and meaningful rituals. We have streamlined our lives, removing whatever appeared to be superfluous. As recently as one hundred years ago, society was rich with ritual: community barn raisings, rites of passage for boys becoming men and for girls becoming women, an agrarian society's proximity to the cycles of the seasons, and so on. Additionally, most people participated as members of church communities, which were heavily laden with spiritual rituals of their own. Generations of the same family living within the same community created a sense of ritual that provided a continuity of tradition that people could point to and use to measure the passage of their own lives: "Oh, that was about the time the Smiths opened the hardware store" or "That was about the time Charlie Smith donated the bell to the church." For many of us, today's more mobile lifestyle and decreased participation in traditional church communities have diminished the sense of community that provided a context for our life rituals.

Notwithstanding the paucity of rituals in our lives, ceremony and ritual remain important to us as adults. They are so important, in fact, that we will subconsciously create rituals to fill the holes we consciously or unconsciously feel. Many people have the ritual of stopping at a coffee bar every morning before work to pick up their favorite coffee drink, and the day doesn't seem to go right when they fail to do that. People have unconscious rituals about things as mundane as the manner in which they get dressed in the morning and the route they take to work. We may have rituals about what must be done first when we arrive at work and what must happen before we feel the day is complete.

Look carefully at your own habits and you may find several activities that, when you fail to perform them, leave you feeling somewhat unsettled. These could be activities as simple as making the rounds to make sure all the doors are locked at night or as ritualized as saying a prayer or performing a time-honored religious ceremony. These are your personal life rituals. There are at least as many different rituals as there are people, and who is to say without significant individual analysis why one set of rituals is important to one person and another set important to someone else? Remember, it is what each of us assigns to our rituals—either by personal preference or a formally learned tradition—that gives them their meaning.

Look around your workplace. Is it not a virtual hotbed of ritual? This may not be obvious at first since the development of these rituals, and the performance of the rituals themselves, frequently tends to be unconscious in nature. Again, the ritual may be as mundane as going to the kitchen to rinse out a cup, make a cup of tea, and bring it back to one's office space before turning on the computer. Or it can be as formalized as placing a freshly cut flower in a bud vase next to the picture of one's religious or spiritual leader. While we may not immediately see such actions in the workplace as rituals, this does not change the fact that they are.

Workplace rituals are too often unconscious, both in planning and execution. When this is the case they can leave in their wakes exactly the opposite of what we might have consciously intended. A more conscious approach to these rituals can help to create a sense of community and maintain a consistent level of productivity in the workplace.

For example, examine what I call the "Ritual of the New Employee." This is one that happens daily in thousands of workplaces, so you probably know it well. A new employee arrives at work after some sort of orientation. He reports to his manager, who then takes him on a tour of the department to meet everyone. The introductions, consisting of five to ten minutes of meaningless chitchat, interrupt all the employees, who are probably already deep into their work. This ritual is repeated *seriatim* with each employee who happens to be in the office on the day of the new employee's arrival. As practiced in most organizations, the Ritual of the New Employee adds nothing to the sense of community and may, in fact, detract from it. Busy workers will accept this interruption, but they may resent it and, in the process, subconsciously resent the new employee. For at least a period of time, newcomers tend to disrupt the sense of order that any community of people has established, whether by design or by default.

Change the Ritual of the New Employee only slightly and the outcome for the workplace community will be entirely different. An employer usually knows several weeks in advance when a new employee will be starting. That's plenty of notice to get a first-thing-in-the-morning, thirty-minute meeting on everyone's calendar for the day the new employee reports to work. Arrange to have bagels, coffee, or other refreshments. Introduce the new employee to the entire department *at once*. This may be followed by the same kind of chitchat interchanges that would have occurred in the desk-to-desk ritual, but there are significant differences. First, no one is interrupted at the point in the morning when they just might be getting traction on their work. Second, the introduction is *to* the department community and *by* the department community rather than to a long string of individual employees. Third, this ritual takes significantly less time than the desk-to-desk ritual.

Another noteworthy benefit of a modified Ritual of the New Employee is that meeting the community as a whole eliminates some of the boss's stereotyping and prejudices about other people in the department. In my own experience as the new employee, I could not help but notice that my escorting manager would punctuate each visit with some commentary about the employee we had just met. "Joe is a great guy," the boss might say, "but he works a little slower than the rest of us, so I have to keep after him." Or he might comment, "It takes a while to get to know Frank, but once you do, you'll find working with him quite easy." Before the tour was over, I had pigeonholed nearly everyone, all based on the stream of consciousness offered by my host and new boss. Being introduced to one's co-workers in a group setting gives the new employee the best chance of drawing his or her own conclusions about the individuals he will be working with. Additionally, there is the opportunity of seeing members of the group interact with each other, which can provide valuable data to a newcomer.

Creating meaningful and constructive rituals in the workplace, ones that contribute to a sense of community and of belonging, is easy to accomplish when we understand the purpose of ritual and what makes it work.

A ritual has three requisite phases:

1. There must be a *disengagement*, which means that some event or action happens which takes the participants out of their normal habits and into a separate space and time. A moment is set aside, which says this is a special event; pay careful attention.
2. The participants must experience a shift in their *awareness* so that they recognize that they are part of something greater than themselves. This shift of awareness causes them to reach deeper or stretch higher than they otherwise would if this special space in time was not set aside.
3. *Assimilation* occurs when the group returns to its everyday world with a new sense of self-knowledge based on the recognition that the group is no longer the same as it was but that it has evolved as a result of the first two phases.

I am a strong believer in using ritual at work to mark times when shifts are occurring. These can be shifts involving events, status, membership, consciousness, and so on. Creating and honoring ritual in the workplace is so much a part of being human that in the process of our taking part in it our authenticity is naturally drawn to the fore. It is hard not to be authentic in an environment in which conscious and meaningful ritual plays an important role.

Look closely at your workplace. See if you can identify unconscious rituals that contribute to a sense of community or that may even be counter-productive in that regard. Ask yourself if the rituals help to create an environment conducive to authenticity, and eliminate those rituals that don't. At the same time, be on the lookout for opportunities to convert a regularly scheduled event into a ritual that builds community. Brainstorm with your co-workers to design meaningful rituals of your own. Remember that it is not the ritual itself but the meaning that you bring to the event which is important.

29

* * * * Learn to Manage Energy

For hatred does not cease by hatred at any time; hatred ceases by love—this is the eternal law.

—The Pali Canon

I once found myself working for a person who many described as one of the nastiest and rudest men on Wall Street. It wasn't by conscious choice. An extremely wealthy lawyer, Milt had purchased a significant interest in a company of which I was a vice president and the corporate secretary. He soon became chairman of the board, and my interaction with him increased dramatically.

Milt was not a likeable man. That would have made it difficult enough to be around him, but the situation was exacerbated by the fact that he seemed to dislike anyone else with whom he came in contact and made no secret about it. At the monthly board meetings, he would curse at people and call them the worst names you can imagine. On at least two occasions, in a fit of rage, he picked up an object from the head of the table where he sat and hurled it directly at the person speaking in the front of the room.

Shortly after his investment in the company and his joining the board, I scheduled a trip to New York for business unrelated to the board of directors.

Since I would be within blocks of Milt's office, I extended an offer to meet for lunch. Just before summarily hanging up the phone, he grumbled into the mouthpiece, "I don't eat lunch." As I said, Milt was not a likeable man.

As a young attorney and executive in a brand-new industry, I believed I had two options: learn to deal with Milt or leave the company. The second option didn't feel like such a good one at the time, so I made some effort to determine what, if anything, I could do about the way Milt treated people—or at the very least, how he treated me.

When I looked at my own feelings about the situation, I discovered that beyond my fear of him, I was feeling sadness. It seemed to me that Milt lacked any kind of friendship or love in his life and actually dissuaded anyone from extending friendship to him. What was I, a minor player in a minor company, among one of the many dozens in which Milt held significant stock, going to do to change his behavior and possibly his life? I was smart enough to realize that there really wasn't anything I could do to change Milt or how he dealt with people. It would have been useless, even counterproductive, for me to try.

At the same time, however, I was beginning to learn about energy and how it affects those around us. For the first time, I understood that energy could be managed in a way that could produce desirable results, as opposed to simply "letting things happen." I was also aware that the heart radiates its energy as far as twelve feet around us and can affect those its energy touches in ways that the mind doesn't consciously notice. I decided then that instead of sending negative energy to Milt when I was with him, which is certainly what every other person in the room was doing, I would work hard at sending only positive energy in his direction.

My "energy management" project was simple enough. At the monthly board meetings, I would quietly and unobtrusively send Milt positive energy. I would move my consciousness to my heart, feel myself present there, and then begin sending positive energy flowing through me to him. I didn't make eye contact with him. I didn't even look at him. I didn't make any gestures in his direction. This was simply a matter of focusing my own positive energy in one direction—aiming it, if you will.

I am not going to tell you that my relationship with Milt was suddenly better or that Milt now invited me for lunch in New York, because none of that would be true. On the surface, nothing changed. Milt continued to rant and rave, scream and curse, call people names, and work hard to make them feel bad.

Not too long after I began my personal "energy management" program with Milt, he fired every executive at the company except for the president, who still held a majority of the shares of stock, and me. I suppose this could have been coincidence, or it could have been because Milt was a lawyer and so was I, he felt some level of professional courtesy. I don't know, but for whatever reason, Milt was calling the shots, and I kept my job while nearly every one of my peers lost his.

Two years later, the same thing happened. Milt decided it was time for a change because the company had not done as well as his expectations, so he again fired every executive with a vice presidential title—every one but me. At the time, the only difference I could determine between me and the other vice presidents—besides my being a lawyer—was that I was using the time I spent in the same room with Milt during the monthly board meetings to consciously send him positive energy, and the others were consciously or unconsciously broadcasting intermittent fear, anger, and hatred.

Two more years passed. There was no significant improvement in the company's performance and no improvement in Milt's mood or manner of interacting with people. If you have guessed that there was another executive bloodbath, you've guessed correctly. Again, all the heads rolled, except for mine.

Now, by this time, I knew that my skills were significant, and I was no longer afraid of losing my job. Indeed, I had actively begun to look for a position outside the company, which I found shortly after the third in this series of every-other-year executive dismissals. Within a few months, I left the company on my own terms.

Before I left, I wrote to Milt informing him of my resignation and thanking him for everything that I had learned from him in the six years he had been involved in the company. I *had* learned quite a bit from him about business, although the only way I learned from his manner of dealing with people was by watching him and then making sure I did something other than what he did! Interestingly, I got a very nice letter back from this man. It surprised me to no end. I didn't expect to get any kind of response, much less a kind one. In it he thanked me for all my efforts over the years. He even went on to explain why he was always so frustrated with the company and its management. This letter came from a man with whom I had never, not even once, had a civil conversation. I am convinced that there was a connection which took place at some level too deep for him to understand and to which he responded positively.

Since that first time, I have used this technique dozens of times. It works. Period. You can transform your relationships with difficult people without even exchanging a single word with them. I have found this tool particularly useful when trying to clean up conflicts with people with whom every effort to talk simply makes matters worse. When words alone only seem to get the two of you deeper into trouble with each other, try managing the energy between you from a distance for a while.

I have even used this technique for quick, short-term fixes, such as when I am waiting in line and I become aware of a service clerk's negative approach to everyone. I start sending positive energy in the direction of the clerk. When my heart is open, it never fails to bring about a rapid change in the clerk's demeanor when it comes to be my turn.

And that is precisely what it takes—an open heart. Anything less and your efforts will be no more successful than a fake smile and condescending words of encouragement. This is not manipulation. Rather, it is the sharing of a gift, and that gift is your own Authentic Self. There is nothing contrived about an expression of the Authentic Self, although it may at first feel unnatural because most of us are not used to putting the Authentic Self forward.

If you are not quite sure what I am talking about when I say "an open heart," don't despair. You can practice. At first, sit upright in a comfortable chair in a dimly lighted room. Perhaps play some appropriate soft music. Close your eyes and take several deep but natural breaths. Move your consciousness down to your heart. Experience your heart beating. Imagine your heart expanding to encompass your entire body. *Become* your heart. Let yourself feel the comfort and peace that your heart projects at all times but which we are generally too busy of mind to notice. Bathe in this sense of peace while you sit quietly. What you will begin to experience is an open heart.

Practice sitting with an open heart at least three times a week for ten minutes each sitting. Then, work to expand the circumference of your heart's reach by imagining an increasing sphere around you. Finally, practice in your mind's eye focusing the energy of your heart and directing it at another person. Try this for several weeks, and when you feel ready, try it in public and see what happens. Use this technique when you find yourself with people who are frustrated by waiting and with service personnel who seem frazzled from dealing with frustrated people. Focus on your heart energy and expand it to include everyone around you. Even if it has no impact on the people around you, it will have a tremendous impact on you.

It is amazing what changes you can make by simply managing the energy between you and other people. You will not know how successful you can be at it until you make a conscious effort to open your heart and let your own unique form of positive energy flow to others.

30

◦ ◦ ◦ ◦ ◦ ◦ ◦ ◦ Learn to Let Go

*There is nothing that wastes the body like worry, and one who
has any faith in God should be ashamed to worry about anything
whatsoever.*

—Mahatma Gandhi

In organizations, the desire for control takes many forms: the desire to control
the flow of goods or services, the desire to control the balance of income and
expenses, the desire to control the actions of suppliers and employees, the
desire to control the responses of customers or clients to product marketing
and public-relations efforts, the desire to control the overall operation of the
organization so that there are no unpleasant surprises or, in any event, as few
as possible.

Given this reality, it is not surprising that so many of us develop a controlling facet of our personalities as part of the Corporate Self. The Corporate
Self believes that it must control other people and events in order to orchestrate
the precise results it wants. And that kind of demand filters down to everyone
in the workplace. Those whose lives are completely dominated by the priorities,
needs, and procedures of the Corporate Self find themselves in the unfortunate

position of demanding the same level of precise compliance from themselves as they do from others. This, as you might guess, can have disastrous effects on that person's self-esteem—as well as on the self-esteem of everyone around him or her. My old boss Milt, in the previous chapter, is a prime example of this.

The Authentic Self seems to have no difficulty understanding that we control absolutely nothing. In Jesus' Sermon on the Mount, he asked, "Is there a man among you who by anxious thought can add a foot to his height? If, then, you cannot do even a very little thing, why are you anxious about the rest?" (Luke 12:25–26, NEB.) And the Buddha, in his great sermon, "Setting in Motion the Wheel of the Law," told us that the end of human suffering is found in letting go of attachment. Keeping our attachment is simply another way of saying that we have not "let go."

We live on two planes: the physical and the spiritual. The Corporate Self is a creature of the purely physical plane, whereas the Authentic Self, while still very much part of the physical plane, also has access to the spiritual.

Deep within ourselves we know that our lives on the physical plane are subject to forces beyond our direct control. Is there anyone reading this book who knows, without even a shred of doubt, that life will proceed tomorrow exactly as he or she has planned it? No, of course not. But even though we lack the omnipotence to ensure that future events will fully match our expectations, we should continue to seek ways to make things work well. It is important to "Pay Caesar what is due to Caesar, and pay God what is due to God." (Mark 12:17.) In other words, it is important to understand that in any effort there are things that must be done on the material plane ("what is due to Caesar") but that there are *also* things to be done on the spiritual plane ("what is due to God"). In our efforts to cause certain desirable results in our workplace—and in our lives, for that matter—we make great haste to do all that's required on the material plane. We have gotten very good at paying what is due to Caesar. It is in dealing with the other side of the equation—the spiritual side—that we could greatly improve. And nowhere is this lack more apparent than in our inability to simply "let go" of something once we have done everything that we feel we can do on the material plane.

The Corporate Self is unable to fully trust our own efforts, the efforts of others, and the process by which results are obtained. As a result, the Corporate Self frequently judges the present from its experiences of the past and has a hard time trusting the process without continuing to think of ways to intervene. By contrast, the Authentic Self knows when to let go and thus allow the best possible results to be achieved. If there remains something to be done, the inner guidance present in the Authentic Self will make the additional requirement abundantly clear. Through these dynamics, those who are operating in authenticity simply are not plagued by the worry and fretting that drive the Corporate Self.

The inability to let go occurs most often around issues of delegation. As a management consultant, I am frequently brought in to assist in resolving conflicts between two or more levels of management. Invariably, lower levels of management want to address senior management's policies around delegation. The four most common delegation problems identified are these: (1) there is no delegation whatsoever and, instead, everything is tightly controlled from the top; (2) responsibility for a result is assigned, but the person to whom it is assigned is not given the authority to accomplish it; (3) responsibility and requisite authority are seemingly granted, but the delegating manager nevertheless continues to "micromanage" the project; and (4) responsibilities and appropriate authority are delegated to an employee, but then the delegating manager's stress and anxiety levels rise, and the delegated work and authority are suddenly and inexplicably withdrawn.

Each one of these four delegation issues is simply a variation on the same inability to let go. For the most part, the Corporate Self is mind-centered and materially based, whereas the Authentic Self is heart-centered and spiritually based. When you are focused on a solely mind-centered approach, your mind will play endless "what if" scenarios and no action will seem adequate, even after that action has been initiated. When you are totally mind-centered, it is impossible to take a course of action, trust the process you have initiated, and then let go, confident that you will reap the harvest of what you have sown. Instead, you worry—and with worry the need to control escalates.

Ironically, the worry itself can thwart the success you are seeking. As the Law of Mind Action states, we get more of whatever we focus our attention on. When you do what you can on the material plane to achieve a result—and that means doing *everything* your inner guidance suggests you do—you then optimize your chances of success if you let go of the result and let the action you've put into motion unfold in its own order. Remaining attached to the result will cause you to continue to worry about possible dire outcomes, and you will expend energy attempting to think up ways of heading off those imagined disasters. The more you understand about the Law of Mind Action the more you will see that worrying is equivalent to praying for what you *don't* want to have happen.

When you are being authentic, it is easy to let go because you have open access to creativity, innovation, and intuition. The Authentic Self will tell you when it is necessary to take additional action on the physical plane, if any additional action is necessary. At the same time, letting go itself actually pulls us along toward greater and greater authenticity, releasing us from the more confining Corporate Self, whose focus on the material plane provides little or no space for letting go and therefore little space for creativity, innovation, and intuition. Think of letting go as a tool giving you access to your authenticity.

Make a list of all the items you have not yet let go of. Review each one and determine what it is that is preventing you from truly letting that item go. You may find that your failure to let go of many of the items on your list is simply a function of habit. Highlight the ones you are now willing to let go and do it!

There is no trick to learning to let go. You simply do it. In your work environment, begin by looking for opportunities to practice letting go. These will include opportunities to delegate to others in the truest sense of the word. These will include times when you focus on what you need to do, and after having done that, you completely release the process from your mind, which you can best do by focusing your mind on something unrelated to that process instead of playing the "what if" tapes over and over.

Delegating is a skill that can be acquired and mastered; however, it does take practice, and along with practice it takes both *attention* and *intention*. It requires *attention* because, like many of the managers I have counseled in dozens of companies, we may think we know how to delegate, but the controlling aspects of our corporate personalities prevent us from doing so effectively, so we need to take extra care to ensure success. And it requires *intention* because the people to whom we generally delegate have become used to "delegations" that are not really delegations at all, and so it is necessary that we clearly and intentionally communicate our expectations regarding their new behavior as well as our own. Part of your new behavior would include letting go.

When you let go, it invariably is a signal to the person to whom you've delegated responsibility and authority that the ball is in his or her court and that you trust this person to take on the challenge and do the best that can be done. When any of us senses this, it generally releases us, and we start drawing from our own resources and our own creativity much more. As the one who is delegating (the "delegator"), you can also instruct people that you are open to them coming to talk with you any time they get stuck or have questions, but always attempt to keep the responsibility for decisions and actions in the purview of the person to whom you have delegated (the "delegate").

Learning to be a good delegator takes practice. It is important that the delegator clearly communicate to the delegate the preset parameters of the delegation. For example, it might include the responsibility for handling all matters up to a certain dollar amount or all matters with the exception of certain circumstances. Then, the delegator must trust the delegate to know when he has power to act and when he must return to the delegator for further instruction. Within those parameters, the delegator then lets go until the delegate returns with an issue outside his authority.

If you find that you are having trouble with the concepts of delegation, there are dozens of books available on the subject, any one of which could be useful to you. Whether by reading a book, taking a class, or some other method, learn proper delegation techniques and then, most importantly, practice them.

If you do find yourself in the throes of worry, either over an action you have taken yourself or over whether someone to whom you have delegated a task will be able to handle it, you might apply what I described in chapter 8,

"Manage Monkey Mind," as the "cancel command." When your mind begins presenting you with one calamitous vision of the future after another, simply say, "Cancel!" and the visions of disaster disappear immediately.

On the other hand, if you experience a gentle but strong urge to reconsider some course of action, particularly during times of quiet reflection, it may be worth paying attention to. A feeling or a single phrase that keeps inserting itself into your consciousness—such as "Check with Janet on the XYZ account"—that isn't overwrought with anxiety and dire predictions may be a clue from your inner guidance. You can count on calming messages from your intuitive and spiritually based inner self to give you advice that is useful on the material plane.

Learning to let go has other significant advantages: First, it will greatly reduce your personal stress levels. You do what is yours to do on the physical plane, and that means doing *everything* that is yours to the best of your abilities. Then you let go and allow the spiritual plane to make its unique contribution.

Second, when you let go, you are more productive and efficient. Every day you have just so much time for thought available to you. You can spend that time worrying about the things you can do nothing about, or you can spend that time in creative thought dealing with new issues which need your attention.

Getting in touch with your ability to truly let go will lead you into authenticity, because the two go hand in hand.

31

Refresh Your Screen

Not the power to remember, but its very opposite, the power to forget, is a necessary condition for our existence.

—Sholem Asch

If you use a computer, you are probably familiar with a function known as "refresh" or "refresh the screen." When you are working with complex software programs or going back and forth between multiple tasks, the screen gets cluttered because the computer doesn't always instruct the monitor to totally clear the screen when a particular task has been completed. That's when a "refresh the screen" function comes in handy, clearing the screen of extraneous information without erasing any of the work you have been doing. There is nothing "wrong" with the old data—it is just no longer relevant to the tasks at hand. Having that extra data on the screen is distracting at best and misleading at worst.

In some respects, the human mind is not so very different from our computers. We gather data about life and the people around us, and then we put it on our inner screens. Unlike our computer software, however, we have no function—whether automatic or manual—to refresh our screens, and so the old images stay with us—possibly all our lives. We continue to rely on them as if the information is current, relevant, and universally true.

We further complicate the problem of carrying around all this information with our natural inclination to categorize and pigeonhole people and situations. We take a first look at people and immediately catalog them in our minds: "Oh, that's the kind of person she is . . ." or "This is the same as when . . ." And then we complete those sentences from our memories, certain that what happened in the past is a perfect predictor of the future. These cataloging characterizations then become a part of the permanent images on the mind's screen.

Why do we catalog people and events like this? Why do we take each potentially fresh experience with another person and bend it, adjust it, twist it, viewing only so much of it and measuring it against something we already know?

For one thing, it makes the unfamiliar, well, familiar. It gives us a comforting though usually false sense of security to find something in our past experience that helps us make sense of every new encounter. It makes new situations and new people seem somehow less dangerous, somehow more controllable.

For another, it's a habit acquired during our early training in outer-centered reality. We learn that if we are to *fit in* we must agree with our parents, our families, our teachers, and the others with authority over us. We do this partially by accepting the judgments of people we are closest to. Without even thinking about it, we adopt the instant cataloging system of those from whom we are trying to win approval because it is a condition of our survival in that environment. By the time we are out on our own, assuming we actually achieve being on our own, it's too late—the insidious cataloging system has now become part of *us*. We may have changed some of the particulars, or we may have even swapped the entire set of "these are bad" categories so that we now label them "these are good," but the *system* of using the past to judge the present remains the same.

Most of us continue to use this system in our relationships with others throughout our lives and most particularly in the workplace. We make up our minds about people based on our observations of what we see them do or what we hear them say. We then categorize them according to our past experiences with people who acted or spoke or looked in ways that were similar to this present person. And there they will stay as long as we continue to project our images of them onto our inner monitors. Worse, because we actually filter what we see based on what we believe, the real person becomes frozen in time—insofar as our inner image of them is concerned. We only recognize that person's actions according to how they match up with the image we have of them in our minds. What we have decided is the truth about them remains static. Remember, the mind sees what it believes and then believes what it sees.

When we categorize people and events in these ways, we are actually creating miniature paradigms around them. In science, a paradigm is a set of rules that establishes boundaries and defines how we are observing a phenomenon. Those same rules can help us solve problems—at least within the boundaries we've established. Once a particular set of beliefs is accepted as valid, it becomes a filter that determines not only how we see but also *what* we see. A paradigm becomes our model of reality, whether for the entire universe or for just one of our co-workers. What science ultimately tells us, however, is that what we believe we are seeing tells us more about ourselves and our particular filters than it does about the individual or phenomenon we are observing.

This system of categorizing other people and creating miniature paradigms around them is really an invisible thief in the night. It is invisible, because as a paradigm, we do not know it is controlling how and what we see. It is a thief, because it robs us of experiencing a person or situation afresh. We simply cannot experience the new if it doesn't match the filters of the paradigm we have adopted, and most of the time that doesn't happen.

I discovered two ways of overcoming this phenomenon of putting people into categories and then keeping them there. The first method for refreshing my screen occurs whenever a tidal wave of change comes along. This is a process over which I have no control. Tidal waves come along when people act in a way that is so uncharacteristic and inconsistent with the way I've cataloged them that I am forced to look at them anew. For a brief moment my paradigm is shattered and I can see them accurately or at least differently. Usually I am open to them long enough to get some new data, and then I recategorize them. When this blessed opportunity presents itself, I frequently take it. When I keep my eyes—

and my inner self—open long enough to experience how things *really* are, I have the chance to transform my experience of the other person. At such times a proportionally matching transformation takes place in my own life. It's amazing what I can learn about people I think I know when I am able to set my personally constructed paradigms aside!

The second method for refreshing my screen is more voluntary. By this process I manually refresh my screen on a regular basis. This technique started when I began looking at the dynamics of the tidal-wave phenomenon, which, in scientific terms, actually amounts to a natural "paradigm shift." A paradigm shift occurs when we have a change in consciousness from one set of beliefs to another, often caused by incontrovertible evidence that is inconsistent with the old paradigm. When a new piece of evidence or a new experience occurs that causes us to change the paradigm, we are suddenly able to see with new eyes, that is, to see what we previously did not see. The change in the way we look at the world— our paradigm—usually results in an *expansion* of our experience of reality.

I discovered that the best way to force a paradigm shift is through a close examination of each individual paradigm. There is no reason we cannot be proactive in breaking down the miniature paradigms we inadvertently create without having to wait for some relationship crisis to occur first. The way to do this is to just sit quietly and focus on the person with whom you are having difficulty. Then allow your mind to present you with whatever images it is holding at that moment. Just allow the images to drift into your mind. Invariably you will experience thoughts about the person that you can identify as elements of your belief system about him or her. These may take the form of complete sentences, such as, "He has a problem working with women." They can take the form of single words, such as *intimidating, self-centered,* or *shy.* Images of that person may also come into your mind, such as a frown or a smile or body posture that suggests a certain character trait or attitude. Any or all of these will help define the elements of the miniature paradigm you have created around this person.

You may find that writing these elements down *exactly* as they are presented to you gives you an excellent opportunity to examine them. Sometimes it helps to write them down in two separate columns—one column for the characteristics you consider positive and another for the characteristics you consider negative. Once you have identified these elements, simply remind yourself that these are elements of the paradigm which you have created around this person. While you cannot say for certain that they are accurate depictions of this person, you *can* say that they are your filters, your paradigm. Try to fully own what you are seeing.

Identifying the paradigm you have created around the individual and then examining all of its elements permits you to step outside your perceptions of this person. Having done that, you can begin to open up to the possibility that this paradigm is no longer relevant—indeed, may never have been relevant. It is an illusion that you have created. That thought alone may be enough to refresh your screen. What's interesting—even startling—to me at times is that after I have done this exercise, I will experience my next encounter with that person in a totally different way, one that would have been inconsistent with the paradigm I had been holding earlier. It's not that I am necessarily seeing new behaviors in the person; instead, I am seeing the person's behaviors in a new way. All this occurs simply because I have allowed for the possibility that my mind's screen may have been presenting me with data that is no longer relevant.

On occasion, it may take something a bit more concrete to refresh my screen. In those instances, I have found that some physical action is helpful. For example, I might take the paradigm list that I generated and ceremoniously burn it, envisioning at the same time my preconceived notions about the person going up in smoke. I might memorize an opening line to use when I next see the person which will remind me that I am no longer looking at him or her through the eyes of my old paradigm.

It doesn't matter what process you use to refresh your screen, because the value comes from your willingness and your intention to make the effort. Should you begin dealing with someone from the context of your old paradigm, you will notice what you are doing. You can then choose whether to continue to do so or make a change.

You can also engage in a valuable discipline of regular paradigm mainte- nance by developing a program of refreshing your screen with respect to the

people in your life on a regular basis, say once per week. Each week choose someone else in your life and apply the "refresh your screen" process to your relationship with that person. Then, stand back as the ground on which you have based
that relationship shifts and something new and wonderful begins to take shape.

By clinging to past experience and judging the future accordingly, we
lose our aliveness and authenticity. Remember that you created the paradigms
which control your relationships with each person in your life, and you have
the power to re-create those paradigms at will. In the process, you can expand
and enrich your relationships with them, more fully experiencing their authenticity and your own.

32

Employy
Conscious Visioning

Where there is no vision, the people perish.

—Proverbs 29:18

Many of us are familiar with the concept of *visioning*. It is also known as
"active imagination" and "creative visualization." It is a technique used by
famous sports figures, inventors, entrepreneurs, and motivational gurus. Few
of us consciously apply visioning to our everyday lives in the workplace. The
truth is that we all use visioning, for it is a normal, and usually automatic,
human function. The most common incidence of visioning in the workplace is
unconscious and tends to be negative, painting bleak and sometimes frightening pictures of the future, particularly during times of challenge or crisis.

    Our experience of work is, as often as not, based on cause and effect:
something happens (the cause) and we make the best of it (the effect). For many
people, the truth is that they live "at the effect" of the external environment,
both at work and at home. The concept that they could actively create an environment of success, one that nurtures their development and supports their
authenticity, seems an impossibility because they do not see themselves as a
potential "cause." They are, simply, living *at the effect* of their workplaces.

The Law of Mind Action is as active in our workplaces as it is in the rest of our lives. Your workplace is no less a reflection of your consciousness than is your bank account or the physical condition of your body. If your workplace is not giving you what you want from it—whether an abundant income, a sense of personal fulfillment, nourishing relationships, or the ability to be yourself— it becomes particularly difficult to accept that it is a reflection of your consciousness. Your only chance of getting more of what you say you want from your workplace is to accept the fact that you have created what you now have. Once you are able to take responsibility in this way, you gain the ability and the authority for changing your work conditions—to *anything* you desire.

Change always begins with visioning. When the Law of Mind Action is combined with a vision held in mind, that vision will become reality. Try using conscious visioning to help realize long-term goals for yourself and for your organization. Hold a vision of yourself sitting in that new office after your promotion, enjoying your new job responsibilities. Create a vision of yourself closing that important deal and getting the order. In your mind's eye see your boss and co-workers congratulating you or see yourself receiving and depositing that huge commission check. All of these are examples of visioning, and some of the most successful people in the business world consider it a basic tool for success.

Just as you can use visioning to effect fundamental changes in your workplace, you can also use it to assist you in performing the most mundane tasks at work, many of which can be quite stressful. For example, suppose one morning you look at your calendar and discover that today is the day for a meeting you have been dreading for nearly a month. Now that it is upon you, your immediate reaction is likely to be one of increased stress fueled by the negative images of what you think could happen at the meeting. Note here that the negative images are the products of your visioning—they may be based on past experience, but they are nevertheless your creations at this moment.

Instead of taking the route that is likely to lead to the disaster you are holding in your mind, you can replace your fears with a vision of the outcome that you *want* for the meeting. How? Start by sitting quietly for a few moments. Close your eyes, if you are comfortable doing so. See yourself at the meeting.

See everyone else who will be at the meeting and imagine the physical environment where you will be meeting. In your mind's eye go around the table of attendees, look each one in the face, and see them as human beings. Briefly imagine their lives away from work, their joys, their sorrows, and their challenges so that you can connect with their humanness. Lastly, envision a positive result for all concerned. If you don't know what the specifics of a positive result look like, envision the meeting concluding with everyone—including you—satisfied with the outcome, whatever that might be. It is most important to envision *yourself* coming out of the meeting satisfied with the outcome.

Are your visions of the future generally positive or generally negative? Are the visions of the future that your mind presents you in direct proportion to the "positive" or "negative" circumstances in which you find yourself? Start noticing how your mind presents you with visions of the future. This awareness will give you a starting place to change those automatic visions if you choose to do so.

Begin a program of visioning regarding your career and your workplace experience. Spend five to ten minutes on a regular basis—every day if possible, but no less frequently than once per week—envisioning your future. See yourself doing exactly what you want to be doing, enjoying it, and reaping great rewards from it. Be specific and embellish your vision with lots of details.

Visioning is as natural to us as breathing, yet few of us learn to use it consciously to actually direct the course of our lives. As a young child you held visions of the joy of the holiday season or an upcoming birthday for weeks and months before the actual event. Adults hold visions of what it will feel like to be on vacation or the anticipated happiness of what life will be like with a new spouse, a new child, a new home, or even a new car. Many of us envision how wonderful a new job will be, and we hold to that vision—at least until we get to the job and settle in.

While visioning comes naturally to all of us, conscious and deliberate visioning does not. For most of us, visioning is undirected and unconscious and occurs most often when we anticipate events that we fear. Our overly active minds automatically conjure up visions of the future that are usually based on worst-case scenarios. Memories of past experiences, or even of stories we've heard, filter into our minds and we latch onto them, making these dire predictions our own. It can take significant self-discipline to change our worst-case vision of disaster to one of opportunity and success. We can feel like we are fighting an uphill battle the whole way.

This is where direction and consciousness come in. It is possible to retrain our minds to immediately present us with positive visions of the future regardless of the circumstances in which we find ourselves. When we can hold those positive visions in our minds, we will create that future through the Law of Mind Action. This process begins with you consciously recognizing the vision you are presently holding in your mind and then activating your willingness and determination to change that vision, if necessary, and replace it with one which will help you shape the future that you truly desire.

When you find yourself having created a vision that does not look like the future you want, apply the "cancel command." Cancel that vision from your mind and immediately replace it with the vision you do want. Over time, your mind will get the message. It will begin to develop the habit of initially presenting you not with dire predictions but with visions of new possibilities. You may want to keep inspirational sayings in mind, such as, "The world turns, and what may seem like an end can also be seen as a beginning."

Use this technique in team environments. Share your own vision of the future that will result from the team's efforts, and ask others to share theirs. See if a common team vision can be articulated. Gauge the results of the efforts of a team united by a common vision or a set of visions with common elements.

Visioning allows you to change your experience of work and of life using just the power of your mind and your heart. You are doing visioning anyway, so you might as well employ it to your best advantage and have it work in your favor instead of against you.

33

Be Generosity

Real generosity is doing something nice for someone who will never find out.

—Frank A. Clark

The title of this chapter is not a typographical error. I am suggesting something beyond simply being generous. *Being generous* is when your favorite charity calls you on the phone and you give them a contribution or when you buy a lavish graduation gift for your nephew. Being generous is not unlike dressing up in a tuxedo or an evening dress—when the occasion is over you put it away again.

But to *be generosity* is entirely different. It is a significant shift from responding positively to a request, as with giving a contribution or a gift, to habitually finding opportunities to give all that you can in the course of everyday life. For the person who is *being generosity*, life is rich with opportunities to contribute to others without expecting anything in return.

Many people have trouble with this concept, particularly in the workplace, which is so often based on models akin to warfare or physical contests such as football or boxing. The belief is that competition in business is a zero-sum game, meaning that for every point I get, you must lose a point, and vice versa. In that paradigm an individual's success is dependent on others' *inability* to succeed. In other words, you can only get ahead at the expense of others. In this context, we should hardly be surprised to discover that we lose our humanness and heart.

The real tragedy is that when we operate from this point of view, we lose a great deal in terms of both our authenticity and our own personal success. Why is this a sacrifice of our authenticity? Because the essence of the Authentic Self, the inner self, *is* generosity. The Authentic Self will risk sacrificing itself to help another, such as when a person jumps into a freezing river to save the life of a person he doesn't even know. It is this generosity that moves us with compassion when we see suffering on the faces of starving children and make the choice to do something about it. It is through this generosity that we experience our connection with all beings, and it is this that allows us to see how by helping others we help ourselves. When we fail to live our lives from the place of *being generosity*, we have turned away from our own authenticity.

Being anything less than generosity personified in our relationships at work may actually cause us to fail to achieve our own goals and objectives. It is important to understand that we are building our *own* lives when we are supporting or not supporting others in building theirs. What we give to or withhold from others we also give to or withhold from ourselves.

I have been privileged to see how that works in my own life, as I am sure you have seen it work in yours. I cannot even recall the number of times that I have done something for someone with no intention of getting anything in return, only to discover later a *direct* connection between that act and something I wanted to achieve or have happen.

Indeed, my near decade of employment with Intel Corporation resulted from just such a set of circumstances. One summer, Steve, a lawyer friend of mine in Atlanta who has made a career of working in high-technology companies, called to tell me that he needed to leave his present position, which wasn't working for him. He was requesting my help as a resource and a sounding board for his process of seeking and obtaining a new job. Although I was in the middle of launching a subsidiary for another company at the time, I agreed to do it. I had absolutely no expectation that anything would come to me as a result of it other than the good feeling of helping out an old friend.

I spent the next several months talking frequently with Steve, reviewing and suggesting changes to his résumé, listening to his reports of job interviews, and assisting him in identifying his own feelings and reactions to each opportunity. Ultimately, I assisted him in making a decision about which job to accept of the three jobs that he had been offered. By late November, Steve had made his decision and was beginning the transition to his new job in Alabama.

On the very day that the moving van was sitting in the driveway of his home in Atlanta, the phone rang. It was Intel. Steve had sent them a résumé months earlier and had never received a response of any kind. Now Intel was pursuing him and asking him to come to California for an interview.

"You don't understand," he had to repeat over and over, "I have already accepted another position."

Nevertheless, the hiring manager on the other end of the phone continued to press Steve, finally asking him if he knew of anyone else with his expertise and experience. Steve gave Intel my name and phone number, although he thought I was content with my then-present job. As it turned out, just a few days before Intel called me in response to Steve's referral, I had made my own determination that it was time for me to move on. The rest, as they say, is history.

But recognize, too, that the universal principle of "what goes around comes around" doesn't necessarily mean that "what goes around" and "what comes around" must involve the same person or even the same context. Many times a willingness to be generosity will result in personal successes that have come through *indirect* connections you could never have foreseen.

Another of the great mysteries and limitless gifts of being generosity itself is that, despite having no intention of or putting any attention on getting anything in return, those who live from this shifted perspective simply cannot give away the bounty they receive into their lives as fast as it comes in. The truth is simply that the more you give away, the more you have. Every spiritual and religious tradition has something to say on the treasure that awaits those who participate in the dynamics of generosity. Luke 6:38 (RSV) tells us, "Give, and it will be given to you; a good measure, pressed down, shaken together, running over, will be put into your lap. For the measure you give will be the measure you get back." In the Buddhist tradition, the Theravadan discourse *Advice to Layman Tundila* says, "Without generosity, it would not be possible to become an enlightened one, a solitary enlightened one, or a worthy saint. Therefore, it is said that there are great profits and benefits from generosity."

One of the most important principles of Islam is that all things belong to God and that all wealth is therefore held by human beings in trust. One of the "Five Pillars of Islam" is *zakat*, or "required expenditure." *Zakat* means both purification and growth, and a Muslim's possessions are purified by setting aside a proportion for those in need, and like the pruning of plants, this cutting back balances and encourages new growth. Each Muslim calculates his or her own *zakat* individually. For most purposes this involves the payment each year of 2½ percent of the capital in excess of one's basic needs.

Indeed, some traditions so clearly understood the concept of generosity that their economies were to some extent based on it. In many tribal traditions a gift was meant to be currency rather than "owned" property. In such a tradition, it was imperative that a gift be circulated. Harriet Rubin writes that the old phrase of shame, "Indian giver," actually labels a tradition based in generosity and not one based in greed:

> *When Indians gave white settlers a gift, they expected one in return. Instead of keeping gifts in circulation, the settlers would put their peace pipes, which they had received from the Indians as gifts, on their mantles. The Indians believed that gifts were meant to be kept in circulation, so when they didn't get something in return, they asked for their gifts back. This shocked the settlers and their traditional notions of property. The whites faulted the Indians for their bad manners, but to the Indians, it was just good economics.*[1]

You can make generosity the basis for your success in the workplace and at the same time open the way for your Authentic Self to take center stage. The areas where one can be generosity in the workplace are limitless. If you are the owner of the business or a boss with overall financial responsibility, consider giving generous raises or promotions *in anticipation of extraordinary performance* instead of simply in response to it. You will discover that, in general, your employees will not disappoint you, and you will get much more in return than you would expect.

In your dealings with other organizations and individuals, always go for the win-win. You may gain something in the short term by negotiating a win-lose arrangement, but that benefit will be short-lived and will almost certainly come back to haunt you in the long run. Remember, what goes around comes around.

No matter who you are or what position you hold in an organization, you have the ability to be lavish with gifts of generosity. You can give praise to someone for doing a good job or even in response to their being generous to you. Praise is too frequently sparse in work organizations, and it is always appreciated. You can provide understanding and feelings of empathy or sympathy to someone who is having trouble dealing with work or personal issues. You can provide information, job-task assistance, or counseling with respect to someone's career. You can mentor someone or take someone out to lunch.

Practice generosity outside your workplace as well. If you see someone dining alone in a restaurant, consider secretly paying for his or her meal. Simply inform your server that you wish to pay the other person's check but that the other diner should only be told that his or her check has been taken care of—that you are not to be identified. Or, if there are toll roads or bridges where you travel, occasionally pay for the person behind you. What is your personal response to these acts of generosity? See how they make you feel the rest of the day.

Always be on the lookout for ways that you can demonstrate generosity in your life and in the workplace. The point is not *what* you do; rather, what matters is the intention and attention you bring to the opportunities you find where you can be of assistance. You need only keep your eyes open for the opportunities and your heart open to the willingness that is already an integral part of your Authentic Self.

Every day you weave and reweave the tapestries of relationships in your workplace. You can choose to weave those tapestries in a miserly fashion, giving only so much of yourself as you believe you must, or you can weave tapestries using skeins that represent the finest and most generous parts of yourself. When you do the latter, you invite the best part of yourself to participate—your Authentic Self—at the same time that you are helping to create an environment in which your personal success is assured.

34

Reintroduce Compassion

You may call God love, you may call God goodness. But the best name for God is compassion.

—Meister Eckhart

Several years ago the CEO of a small precision metal-fabrication company asked me to help him with some challenges he was having with his senior management staff. The company had grown incredibly fast and its senior executives had risen through the ranks of blue-collar workers. None of them had been prepared to run a company, but they found themselves with the responsibility for doing so nonetheless.

My task was to get them working together, enhance their managerial skills, and build a functioning, high-performing team. Twice each week for several months I attended a two-hour-long morning staff meeting. One morning I arrived on time only to discover the team already deep in discussion. After I sat down, they filled me in on the details.

In most blue-collar industries, particularly those where unions are part of the employment mix, rules are fairly black-and-white. One reason for this is that black-and-white rules are easier to apply when determining whether or not someone has stepped over the line. Another is that the ease of applying those rules reduces the possibility of someone claiming that he or she was treated unfairly.

One of the rules at this metalworking company was that after a person failed to show up for work three times and also failed to call in, that person was fired. Period. As I walked into the room that day, the senior management team was discussing just such an incident. As I listened to this discussion, my thoughts shifted from interest to horror at what I was hearing.

As it turned out, an employee had failed to report to work for the third time because he had been involved in a serious car accident on his way to work. His failure to call was possibly due to the fact that he was still unconscious and maybe in a coma! While I would have found *any* discussion of the possibility of his dismissal pursuant to the rule disturbing, what I found appalling was that the discussion did not revolve around *whether* the employee was to be terminated but instead *when* he would be terminated! Could he be terminated while he was still unconscious or did they have to wait until he regained consciousness? What would be the impact on his medical benefits if he was terminated while in the hospital? These sorts of questions were the grist of the mill of the discussion I walked in on that day.

Don't jump to the conclusion that these guys were a bunch of evil taskmasters, because they weren't. I have rarely met a nicer group of people. The problem was that they were operating in an environment where the rules were of paramount importance, and they had become so jaded with this concept that they ultimately let the rules override their hearts. Given the circumstances, it is difficult to imagine how they could have gotten so bound up with the rules that any sense of compassion was totally missing.

Thankfully, good sense and compassion prevailed, and the group began a discussion of what was appropriate in the circumstances, which did not include terminating the employee for failing to comply with the shop rules.

While this case may be an extreme, as a consultant to many leading companies in the country, I have to say that I've noticed a marked reduction in the level of compassion in our workplaces. This is a significant problem and represents a major challenge to those of us who want to express more authenticity with our co-workers. Just as with generosity, the Authentic Self is the seat of compassion. It knows no other way to be but compassionate. Conversely, when the Authentic Self finds itself in an environment where compassion is discouraged, it takes to hiding. It simply cannot be fully present in any situation where it is being asked to be less than what it really is. To do so would be a total contradiction.

This creates quite a conundrum for many of us. The Authentic Self within us wants to do the right thing in any given situation. We want to make the right decision and not have to worry about being taken to task for it. What has happened in our attempts to deal with these issues is that we have reduced our workplaces, and the decisions we make in them, to the lowest common denominator.

This might work in a fully automated society, but we humans are not machines, and putting the rules before all else costs us much of our humanity. Lou Gerstner, the CEO of IBM for many years, spoke directly to this concept when he said, "No machine can replace the human spark: spirit, compassion, love and understanding."

Indeed, the lack of compassion in our workplaces may result from what Alan Briskin, in his book, *The Stirring of Soul in the Workplace*, calls "the mechanization of work," which began in the last decade of the eighteenth century. The mechanized model of the workplace, and our individual roles in it, has us both seen and seeing ourselves as cogs in a machine. We know our tasks, and we are expected to perform them without any emotional involvement.

However, this is not the way we humans are designed to operate. When we come to work we do not automatically detach from the personal problems we may be dealing with in our lives outside work. Many of these issues are almost debilitating in their severity: the terminal illness of a loved one or a major health threat to ourselves, divorces with or without vicious custody battles over children, staggering debt, and addictions ranging from cigarettes and drugs to overeating and gambling. Every one of us has issues that we are dealing with at any given time. For many, these issues can be complicated, crippling, and devastating in both consequence and emotional impact.

Even the more commonly accepted elements of work life in the twenty-first century take their emotional toll on each of us. For example, if you are a parent who must leave your preschooler at day care so that you can go to work—a common enough reality in today's world—you know what I am talking about. If you have not had to deal with that emotionally charged daily event, stop for a minute and think how it would feel to hand the care of your young child over to another person for what amounts to the vast majority of his or her waking hours. Now, imagine showing up for work each day after dropping your kids off and feeling compelled to act as though you aren't carrying any of those feelings into the workplace because, after all, it might have an impact on your job performance. Certainly, people can and do get used to it, which only means that they numb themselves to their emotions, much as patients with long-term pain learn to numb themselves to their discomfort. Consider, though, that by numbing ourselves to pain and discomfort, we are numbing ourselves to life in a much broader way. Certainly, this numbing of one's self is inconsistent with personal authenticity!

The prevailing attitude in the modern workplace is that when we arrive at work each day we are to leave our private lives behind: put your concerns for your children aside, forget the fact that your spouse is going into the hospital for an operation or that your aging parent is ill, put on hold your concern over conflicts in a friendship you treasure—just focus on doing your job in the most efficient and cost-effective way possible. And through all of it, know that if you are distracted at work or don't produce as expected because of your personal issues, it will be reflected in your next performance review. Additionally, any emotional behavior is usually treated as out of the ordinary, and co-workers frequently judge a person harshly who carries personal problems to work. Certainly, each of us can recall some time during our careers when we watched in stunned silence as a co-worker simply "lost it" at work and we were unable to step in to help for fear that we might be ostracized for "not tending to our job."

Clearly, from the perspective of living life as a full human being, there is something seriously wrong with this picture—more so when viewed from the perspective of a man or woman attempting to live life from his or her authentic source. What's authentic about hiding your emotions and stuffing your feelings all day when you are being torn apart by those same emotions and feelings?

I am not suggesting that we turn the work force into daily therapy groups. What I am suggesting, however, is that we must start reintroducing compassion into our workplaces, and we can do this individually. We don't have to wait for the organization we work for to initiate a program. If we don't exercise individual initiative in this matter, we will soon find ourselves sitting around the table discussing rules instead of human issues, like my friends in that metal-fabrication company.

The reintroduction of compassion is more important than ever as we begin this new century. Employee and workplace demographics have shifted so quickly and so dramatically over the last forty years that neither we as individuals nor the companies for which we work have been prepared for the changes these shifts have brought. If we had prepared, perhaps ideas like on-site child-care would have progressed beyond the discussion stage and would have already become the norm rather than interesting but rare curiosities.

Beyond two-income households and children in day care, the character and meaning of work have also changed. We all work longer hours and are increasingly connected to work during our "off times" through pagers, cell phones, facsimile machines, mobile computers, two-way radios, or by simply having work on our minds. If compassion is removed from the workplace, where do we have space for it since our lives are increasingly involved with work and work issues? The answer is we won't. If we don't integrate compassion into our work lives, another piece of our humanity vanishes, along with access to our Authentic Selves.

Reintroducing compassion into the workplace is not difficult, and it can take an infinite number of forms. Start with yourself. Look to see where you are being less than authentic in your workplace, that is, where you may be denying your feelings about something that is happening in your own life. Having compassion for yourself expands your ability to have compassion for your co-workers.

Next, focus on those you encounter in your workplace. No one needs to give you permission to make yourself available to listen to a fellow employee with empathy; indeed, empathy is a fundamental people skill that will serve you well throughout your entire life. You need no special authorization to care about and ask how someone is holding up under the strain of pressures such as the serious illness of a loved one, a divorce, or other life-changing events.

Of course, if you are in management and have the ability to do so, you can give that single mother some extra time off once in a while to spend an unhurried day with her children. You can cut some slack to one of your workers who regularly comes in a few minutes late because you know that every morning he is dealing with getting the kids ready for school or dropping them off at day care. Perhaps you can arrange a more flexible work schedule for an employee whose situation would be eased by such a concession. Consider each of your employees or co-workers one by one. Identify what, if anything, you can do to assist each of them in dealing with the various life issues with which they must contend. Sometimes all that is needed is a brief acknowledgment that you know that she or he is going through a difficult time and that you care. Of if a family member is ill, it might involve seeking funding or community resources that could ease pressure at home. Be creative in your approaches. Gauge the impact of your efforts on workplace morale and levels of performance. You may be surprised to discover that the time taken to show compassion pays off in less absenteeism, greater loyalty, and highly motivated work teams.

Arthur H. Stainback says, "The value of compassion cannot be over-emphasized. Anyone can criticize. It takes a true believer to be compassionate. No greater burden can be borne by an individual than to know no one cares or understands." This is no less true in the workplace than elsewhere in our lives.

Of course, with the practice of compassion, you must also learn to be discerning so that people do not take advantage of your caring, but be careful that you do not replace discernment with inflexibility in an effort to protect yourself from that possibility. If someone is taking advantage of you, you'll know it soon enough, and you can respond accordingly. The Dalai Lama had it right when he said that we must have compassion for all people but at the same time be careful about who we spend our time with.

The key element to understand is that compassion in the workplace starts with *you*. You have the power to create a 360-Degree Arc of Compassion around you. That arc will draw to you others who value the same things you do. Conversely, each of us also has the power to keep things moving in the direction they have been for the last several decades, which is away from compassion and toward a rule-bound environment where everyone and every situation is forced into a single mold. We know that the one-size-fits-all way of organizing human beings doesn't work, and it doesn't even create the efficiency it is intended to produce. Surely it is time to take a long, careful look at this issue and act to improve our workplaces.

The practice of compassion is an art, not a science, but it takes intention and practice to make it a living presence. When you are practicing the art of compassion, you are being your Authentic Self.

35

Consciously
· · · · · · · Create Community

The pathos of man is that he hungers for personal fulfillment and for a sense of community with others.

—J. Saunders Redding

Most of us tend to think that communities are organized groups which have come together for some stated purpose or goal, and to some extent that is true. The city or town you live in as well as your church, social clubs, and committees all fit this definition.

While it is true that we create communities to accomplish common goals, we also create communities when there appears to be no common goal or unifying trait. We humans are, by our very nature, social beings, so the impulse to create community is literally programmed into our genes. Some of the communities we create are short-lived and some last for decades. Even standing in line at the supermarket or warehouse store, grumbling "ain't it awful" and commiserating with those around you, is a form of community building. If you examine the dynamics of these groups closely, you will see that the group exists because everyone is in the same place at the same time for the same purpose, whether that's waiting at a checkout counter or for the Space Mountain ride at Disney World.

Some of our short-lived communities are so common that we have standardized expectations of behavior when we engage in them. Consider the elevator. In an elevator we create a community with its own rules of decorum. No one discusses these rules—they certainly have never been explained to me— yet we all learned them by example, and we continue to train others by example. For instance, you know that when you are standing alone in an elevator that stops to let in another passenger, you automatically move to one of the back corners to allow the newcomer and you to stand facing the doors. Rarely do we talk in elevators, and everyone looks at the indicator lights above the door. If perchance you do not believe that there are community rules of behavior for the elevator, check it out the next time you enter one. Try standing with your back to the doors facing the other people on the elevator!

There are dozens of other examples of instant communities. Your morning and evening commutes are communities of sorts; indeed, if you made a study of them, you would discover that there are similarities to most of your evening commutes that your morning commutes do not share. After several years of commuting, I discovered that one route in particular worked best going to work in the morning while an entirely different route was best for the evening commute. Each of these routes had completely different community "personalities."

As you can see, you are *always* in a community-creating mode. Just as with communicating, you really have no choice any more than you have a choice about whether your hair will grow. As I've said, it's in the genes.

All communities fall into two categories: those that are *consciously* created and those that are *unconsciously* created. For the most part, the communities we have made an effort to actively participate in, such as church groups, charitable organizations, social clubs, and so on, have been consciously created. Unconsciously created communities are the ones that we join when we step into an elevator or slide in behind the steering wheel of a car for the commute home. There's not a lot of deliberate effort to create a sense of community in these instances. More and more, however, these communities not only are enduring but have been unconsciously created without a sense of commitment to the concept of community, and that is where we start having problems.

Consider the changing face of our neighborhoods for a moment. Few would disagree that there has been a dramatic shift in the sense of community in today's neighborhoods when we compare them to neighborhoods of even thirty years ago. When I was growing up in suburban New York, we knew just about everyone who lived in a two-block radius around our house. That was so because there was a conscious effort to connect with the people around us. There were block parties, pool parties, and other opportunities to get together. That is not the case today. My wife, daughter, and I have lived in the same house in Silicon Valley now for over thirteen years. We know *two* families fairly well, but few others, and it has not been for lack of trying. For many of us, our homes have become fortresses—some quite literally—and those fortresses serve to keep us isolated as well as protected. Our neighborhoods are still communities—as the product of human endeavor they can be nothing else—but, for the most part, they are communities devoid of humanity and a sense of focus on something greater than any of their individual parts.

For some, the family itself has become an unconscious community in which people sleep under the same roof but live totally separate lives. For many young people, the lack of any sense of conscious community in their homes causes them to seek it elsewhere, and one result is an upsurge in youth groups and even gangs where the codes of a community are based on childhood fantasies. In the most basic terms, gangs are *consciously* created communities, although many would argue with the communal focus that gang members share. That, however, does not change the fact that gangs are communities and that they have been consciously created as communities.

For the most part, our workplaces are communities that we have created *unconsciously*. Our experience of the workplace is not unlike riding in an elevator with strangers, except that the ride can last for years or even decades. In general, we know the rules of behavior, and we abide by them. We may even have a shared focus or mission, whether on an organizational or team level, but there is little consciousness of the workplace as community, and we do little if anything about learning who our fellow travelers are and what is in their hearts.

Developing consciousness about the workplace as community can make a huge difference for everyone concerned. By definition, consciously created communities have a well-thought-out focus. And while the workplace itself has a focus—usually a very sharply defined one, such as making widgets, providing services, making a profit, creating lucrative returns for shareholders, even providing employment for its employees—that focus is not necessarily in and of itself conducive to building a functioning community.

What is necessary *and* sufficient for building a sense of community is a group of people who have come together with a particular focus which is aimed at the individual well-being of each member of that group. This is as essential as having a way to determine if the group's goals have been accomplished.

Margaret Wheatley writes,

> *The engineering image we carry of ourselves has led to organizational lives where we believe we can ignore the deep realities of human existence. We can ignore that people carry spiritual questions and quests into their work; we can ignore that people need love and acknowledgment; we can pretend that emotions are not part of our work lives; we can pretend we don't have families, or health crises, or deep worries. In essence, we take the complexity of human life and organize it away. It is not part of the story we want to believe. We want a story of simple dimensions: people can be viewed as machines and controlled to perform with the same efficiency and predictability. . . . In our machine-organizations, we try to extinguish individuality in order to reach our goal of certainty. We trade uniqueness for control, and barter our humanness for petty performance measures.*[1]

In other words, our work lives tend to be totally bottom-line-oriented, determined by the organization's economic goals, and that orientation is killing us. It contributes to the kind of statistics detailed in this book's introduction, such as 80 percent of workers suffering from stress-related illnesses and injuries, insomnia, exhaustion, ulcers, and depression.

Work can and should be more than this! We can create workplaces that take on the elements of a community that consciously cares about its members. We are building community in the workplace anyway, though more by default than by design. The results of those efforts, or non-efforts, as the case may be, have been destructive to our sense of well-being and have led most of us to hide our true selves, our authenticity. This condition is only exacerbated by the fact that most of us are spending more and more time at work or in work mode and are taking our non-authentic selves into our homes.

Why do we not build conscious communities in the workplace, ones that will support each of us in our well-being? Good question—and a lot of organizations are looking for answers to that question these days. This partially accounts for the focus on developing teams and teaming over the last decade, since that is one way to tap into the vitality of community. Some companies hire consultants and trainers and spend hundreds of thousands of dollars and countless hours on employee orientations and trainings, all in the hope of developing a healthy and productive community consciousness in the organization. All too frequently, a month or two after the consultants leave, most people agree that things have really not changed much.

In most of these efforts, what happens is that the members of the organization understand that a change is expected, so they start giving management what they believe management wants. People start saying the right things and doing everything that the consultants have suggested, but in truth everyone is just following what they believe are the "new rules." There is no real shift in consciousness, and the core community isn't working any better than it did before the consultants arrived because organizations can't be made to change. Only *people* change. And when people change, organizations reflect those changes.

Change literally takes place one person at a time. What this means for you is that the shift in your workplace, from unconsciously creating community to consciously creating community, is up to you. You must make the changes at a personal level—just as each person in your workplace will have to make the change at a personal level. M. Scott Peck tells us, "The human race is in the midst of making an evolutionary leap. Whether or not we succeed in that leap is *your* personal responsibility." You are probably reading this and thinking something like, "OK. I agree, and these are certainly noble thoughts. But how do I apply this practice at next Tuesday's staff meeting?"

Well, there is no single way. Consciously creating community in your workplace is not a thing that you do or even a set of things that you do; it is a way of being. It is not a destination *to* which you walk but a path *on* which you walk. That path can lead you to any destination. The journey is one of caring, self-awareness, self-fulfillment, satisfaction, and joy.

The good news is that you do not need to change the organization to completely transform your experience of your workplace. Part of your 360-Degree Arc of Authenticity is to consciously create, at the same time, a 360-Degree Arc of Community around you. Just around *you*. If you do that, you will have changed *everything* about your experience of your workplace. It works. I know because I've done it, and I've helped many others do it successfully.

Your goal must be to consciously develop and strengthen the sense of community in your workplace, to create the environment that you want to have in your work and in your life. The Golden Rule, which appears in some form in every major religion on this planet, is a good place to start: "Do unto others as you would have them do unto you."

The key ingredient for consciously creating community is learning to be fully present to the people and events around you. Understand that *every* interaction you have with another person is building community. Your awareness and choices in light of that fact will determine whether the community you are building is one you want or one you don't want. The old saying that you get back what you give is certainly applicable here.

Learn to be fully committed to your workplace as a community. I cannot repeat often enough that everything you do or say will have an impact on the community which is your workplace. Consciously focus on this basic truth and it will assist you in making choices about your actions and your words. Rely on your intuition and your inner guidance to know how to respond to people and events in a manner that will contribute to the kind of community you want. The knowledge is within you. It is within each of us. Trust it.

Become aware of your approach to community. At the end of the workday, sit quietly and review your interactions with others in your workplace. Look carefully at your responses to the events and conversations that made up your day. For each one, determine whether you believe your response contributed to the sense of community you want to create or detracted from it.

Make a conscious effort to identify the kind of community you want to create in your workplace. Take the time to make a list of the attributes of that community. That list can operate as a road map to help you create the community you want by being conscious of your interactions with others in the workplace.

As soon as you can, start consciously creating community in whatever way works best for you. Begin by reminding yourself as you walk in the door to your place of work that you are there to consciously create the community you want around you. Several times during the day remind yourself of your mission. Place some special object in your office that, when you see it, will remind you of your commitment.

As you increasingly focus on consciously creating community, your own authenticity will come out of hiding and will begin to guide you in every action and deed. As your focus expands, everything you say or do contributes to your sense of community, unlocking the doors to your authenticity as if by magic and doing the same for others. You cannot be in this awareness without your Authentic Self being present because the information you need to effectively make choices about your actions and words is available solely through your creativity, innovation, and intuition. Increasingly, you will come to recognize and trust your own inner guidance, and those attributes are the province of authenticity alone. Every time you are consciously creating community, you are being your Authentic Self, because your Corporate Self is simply not equipped to perform the functions that will be required of you.

If you approach your workplace with a full-time commitment to consciously create community, you will discover that authenticity becomes your stock in trade.

36

Build a Personal
Support System

A pilgrimage, after all, is a strenuous undertaking, one in which companionship and support may be pivotal.

—Julie Cameron

Taking the initiative to be authentic in the workplace can be a challenging and lonely undertaking. At first glance there doesn't seem to be much support from upper management, and it is difficult to tell if your peers and subordinates are warmed or threatened by you being yourself. To some extent, all of that is true, but my personal experience of bringing my Authentic Self to the workplace has been filled with surprises that, for the most part, have allowed me to take this conventional wisdom with a grain of salt.

First of all, I discovered that there are many people looking for the same thing I am. They would like to be able to be more themselves in the workplace, although they don't know how to do that. For one thing, many people do not realize it is even an option. These are often the folks who are so entrenched in outer-centered reality that they may have begun to believe that their Corporate Self is their true identity. Others have an inkling that it might be possible to have a greater sense of personal fulfillment from their experiences at work, but they are unable to articulate what is wrong and have no idea what it would take to make it right. There are those who know they don't have what they want and understand what it would take for them to achieve it, but they are immobilized by the fear of change.

There are those people who have at least a tiny hunch that things are not optimal in their present work situation, and on the basis of that hunch, that intuition, they are asking questions of themselves and others. With each step they take, they are able to see farther down the road, and because they like what they see, they take more steps and start making changes. And then there are those who are already fully engaged with interpersonal, metaphysical, and spiritual dynamics and feel compelled to bring these concepts into the workplace. Moreover, they are willing to take the risks necessary to bring those dynamics into play at work in a meaningful way.

You may not believe it, but you will find that there are people in your workplace *right now* who think as you do, and they are looking for others, like you, to share their dreams and their knowledge about workplace authenticity. In fact, they're looking for *you* because of the special perspective and gifts that you bring. Finding these people is simply a matter of intention; you need not *do* anything. These people will begin to make themselves known to you as the natural result of you becoming more authentic in the workplace. This really does work. As you begin to use some of the tools and techniques in this book to create a 360-Degree Arc of Authenticity around you, others of like mind will be drawn to you. Your Authentic Self will act as a natural magnet to attract other Authentic Selves to you. Trust that it will happen.

While you do not need to look for these people, you do need to act when your paths cross. This will require that you be open to the possibility of being supported and to supporting others. You need to be part of the group that is ready and willing to risk putting themselves out there and letting others get to know them. If you find just one person who is thinking along the same lines that you are, your support group may consist of only that single person, but that will be enough.

In my own life, I have had several situations in which my support was only one person, but that relationship became invaluable for both of us. That person became my work-buddy, and a work-buddy can be an invaluable resource and support when things get difficult. You know the situation: It's been a particularly tough morning. Your desk has been on fire with emergencies since before you even arrived. A project you promised your boss is due today, and you can't see your way clear to even think about it, much less do it. You find yourself trapped in a whirlpool of thoughts, emotions, conflicting priorities, demands on your time, and possibly fear. When that happens, it's the time to call on your work-buddy.

It is not your work-buddy's job to do your work or to tell you what to do first or how to do it. It is not his or her job even to give you advice; you already know that the answers to the questions about your job are in you, not anyone else. Your work-buddy's sole purpose is to help you get out of that whirlpool you are in by being immediately available and by just listening to your issues, your concerns, and even your fears. The goal is to get you back to being centered. That allows you to focus on the one thing you can do immediately and perhaps determine what, if anything, can be done about the rest, which is generally all you need to do to get yourself back on track. Without that, you may find yourself spinning your wheels all day or possibly for several days. As I said, work-buddies can be invaluable.

Be on the lookout for a work-buddy who can give you immediate support whenever you find your efforts to be authentic are being challenged. Then call on your work-buddy for support, recognizing that when things get tough your natural inclination will most likely be to *not* want to call someone for help. Do it anyway! And remember to reciprocate and make yourself available to your work-buddy.

If you are fortunate enough to find yourself surrounded by a support group of more than one person, immediately begin to think of it as a community within the community of your workplace. Consider what kinds of things would contribute to the concept of successful support for every member of the group. Perhaps it's a regularly scheduled lunch for all, which would give everyone the opportunity to be with like-minded people, all of whom have similar experiences because they work in the same organization. It could be as simple as each of you knowing who the others are or as complex as creating a formal group with stated intentions of bringing about changes in the organization's work environment.

Some enlightened corporations and organizations already have support groups of one sort or another. If you work in one of those organizations, see if what already exists will meet your needs. If it doesn't, do whatever you need to do to create the support system you envision. Your support group need not be people who work with you in the same company. The most important element of your support group is that it supports *you* in whatever way *you* want to be supported. There are no rules. There is no handbook.

If you find that you need something to do to get started pulling together your support group, consider a regular program of networking, which can bring you immediate results. Look through your Rolodex or telephone list for the names of like-minded people you have met and whose cards you have collected but whom you may not have contacted on a regular basis. These can be people either inside your organization or outside it. Spend just fifteen minutes every day calling one or more of these folks just to keep in touch. Note that there is no purpose to these calls except to connect and say hello and discuss whatever comes up to discuss. In a short time, you will discover you have developed friendships and special connections with many of these people, and if you follow your intuition and inner guidance in deciding whom you will contact, over time you will have also created an extensive support group.

Finally, there is a global movement of people and organizations that are supportive of an authentic approach to work and the workplace. Just by virtue of your interest in this book, you are already part of that movement. Part of your program for personal support might be to develop contacts with others in that movement, which is easy enough to do in the Internet Age. There are several national and international conferences held each year that deal with this subject and related topics. Attending just one of those conferences will greatly expand your horizons and your contacts in the movement, which will also expand your support group.

If you are looking for a great place to start, try the Spirit at Work Web site, put together by my good friend Judi Neal at the University of New Haven. Many of us consider Judi to be the hub in the great wheel of information that helps keep us all connected. You can access the Web site at *www.spiritatwork.com*. There you will find links to other related Web sites (including my own), a list of upcoming conferences, and an extensive bibliography on the subject of our interpersonal, metaphysical, and spiritual relationships to work and the workplace. You can also sign up to be on the Spirit at Work e-mail distribution list, which will give you ongoing information about relevant books, events, and stories of real-life workplace heroes.

A support group is a symbiotic relationship of the purest kind. It is a gift that you give to yourself at the very same time that you are gifting others. It is an exchange for mutual benefit, in which the giving of support to others immediately gives back to you in kind.

PART III

Authenticity and Higher Powers

37

See Yourself on a Spiritual Path

Two roads diverged in a wood, and I—
I took the one less traveled by,
And that has made all the difference.

—Robert Frost

In the preceding chapters we have explored methods that can—when combined with intention, commitment, and mindfulness—help you bring spirit into your workplace. But nothing will change your perspective about your work, or any other part of your life, faster or more permanently than your realization, acknowledgment, and acceptance that you are on a spiritual path—*right here, right now*. Everything that you have done and everything that has happened to you in the course of your life has been part of that spiritual path.

It is easy to get caught up in the minutiae of daily life and to delude ourselves into thinking that spirituality is only for special people—those who are presumably selected by God or who have given their lives entirely to spirit, such as priests and saffron-robed monks. But this is not the case. Our lives are imbued with spirit, and its reflection can be found in every human relationship, every human activity, and every human choice—including those occurring in the workplace.

One way to develop the understanding that you are on a spiritual path is to begin seeing your life in the context of its greater purpose. How does it serve you, those around you, your community, and as the Navajos call it, the "sacred geography"? One sure way to answer these questions is to discover your life purpose.

Discovering your life purpose is not unlike the "connect-the-dots" puzzles we used to do as kids. If you look at your life up to this point, you may begin to find themes and patterns that, when connected in the context of seeking your life purpose, will give you a clear idea about what your life has been and can be about.

It has been several decades since I first saw patterns that showed me how my life fits into the higher purpose of things. Ultimately, I began seeing my own story—the challenges and crises, the failures and successes, in fact, all the events of my life—as the evidence I needed to prove that my life has had purpose from the beginning, although during much of that time I may have found little purpose in those events.

For example, I never felt that I fit in with the "guys" at work. Even as one of several vice presidents running a large international software company, I always had the feeling that the other executives were "over there" and that I stood alone "over here." I was fully involved in the operation and success of the company, but somehow I had a strong sense of being separate, perhaps not fully accepted, and this was a source of anguish for me. Sadly, this feeling had plagued me through my early school years, during my time at the university, in the military, when working as a practicing attorney, and finally, in my business career. I frequently felt isolated, and it was painful. But then I began asking a different kind of question. I started asking in what way this circumstance might be contributing to a higher purpose in my life.

The truth was, I *was* different. I didn't fit in with the other males rising to the top of organizations. My approach was atypical for a man, albeit also a successful one. I was not fully in accord with the metaphors so many other men used, such as business as war or that a football game was all about winners and losers. My approach was more yin and less yang, less testosterone and more feminine in nature. No wonder the other men were as uncomfortable around me as I was around them!

Like an anthropologist, I discovered a pattern in the kinds of relationships I have created with the world around me. And this pattern gave me clues about a major piece of my life purpose, which is to do what I can to bring a spiritually based and authentic human face to business organizations. From this vantage point, everything now makes sense to me. As I contemplate the future, looking back over a half century, I can follow the line from any event in my life all the way to the place where I stand today.

Try it yourself. Imagine yourself standing on the threshold of your life. Turn around. Look back over your life and search for major life events of a similar nature. Those events undoubtedly contained valuable lessons for you. Connect those events with events in the present and look for patterns and clues. If you connect enough dots, you will find an image that provides you with valuable information about your life and its purpose. Once you identify another element of your life purpose, it becomes ridiculously easy to look back and see how your life events have been giving you clues about your life purpose all along.

Every event in your life, no matter how seemingly significant or insignificant, negative or positive, is a clue to your life purpose. Certainly, we all want our experiences to be joyful, but most of us know that life isn't always going to be like that. The smartest among us also know that all experiences, no matter how painful and apparently joyless, represent at least one more step along the path of finding and living our life purpose. Seen in that light, every event is an occasion for joy. Paying close attention to the experiences in your life from the perspective of discovering more about your life purpose transforms the direst situation into one of promise and opportunity.

Our goal is to view work as an integral part of our spiritual path, not as an interruption of it. Too often we see work as a time when we put aside our pursuit of spiritual wisdom, seeing the latter as an off-work activity. Seeing your hours at work as integral to your spiritual path will change your relationship to your work and the people in your workplace. More important, it will change *how* you do your work. Indeed, it will cause you to make different choices. Richard Leider, author of *The Power of Purpose*, says,

Purpose is that deepest dimension within us—our central core or essence—where we have a profound sense of who we are, where we came from, and where we are going. Purpose is the quality we choose to shape our lives around. Purpose is a source of energy and direction. . . . Working on purpose gives us a sense of direction. Without purpose, we eventually lose our way. We live without the true joy in life and work. . . . Purpose is a way of life— a discipline to be practiced day in and day out.[1]

Practice mindfulness about being on your spiritual path at work. Stay alert for any and all clues that would suggest to you the potential ways that your day's activities and issues contribute to your spiritual path. *Be in the world but not of it.* Consider making notes about the impact of the day's challenges and opportunities. Notice how it feels to be in this particular state of awareness and gauge the responses of others.

Choosing your battles wisely is important in your quest for personal growth and spirituality. If you have a sense that taking a particular course of action will not help you on your spiritual path but is rather a diversion, then do not take it. Contrariwise, if you see something in your workplace that looks as though it is directly on your personal spiritual path, take it on no matter how difficult or even impossible it may appear at the outset. When we are faced with one option that looks difficult and another that appears somewhat easier, our natural proclivity as humans is to do what is easy, because the easier path is the one with which we are already familiar. But if we are living according to our life purpose, we may choose the options that we feel will make the greatest contribution to our movement along that path.

At the same time, we may be challenged by our inner guidance to make a choice that is right from a spiritual perspective but which appears, on the surface, to be illogical or even foolhardy. Under those circumstances, we must rely on faith, which is another major element in the game of living life on a spiritual path. At such times, we are best advised to take the seemingly more difficult option. Traveling that road will clearly provide lessons that will move you forward on your individual spiritual path. The easier option may be more comfortable, but it won't move you forward in spiritual development.

Remember, too, that if you fail to take on a life task at the time it is first presented to you, you will end up running into that same issue again some time in the future. The way it works is that you will be presented with that issue in various forms until you decide to handle it and then do so effectively. You may have noticed that when you choose to just walk away from some difficult situation such as a job or a relationship, you think you are leaving it behind you, but then you find yourself in the exact same circumstances sometime later, perhaps with different specifics of place and people. This is no accident. The principle is simple: Handle it now or handle it later. Don't understand this to mean that, having handled a particular situation, it will go away forever. You may see it again, but it does get easier each time it comes around, assuming that you have at last handled it effectively. At some point, it is almost as though the universe understands that this particular issue doesn't bother you anymore. You no longer fall into the same trap, and the universe stops presenting it to you as an option.

One of the nice things about seeing your life as a spiritual path is that what is true about paths and roads in the physical world is also true about your personal spiritual path: The farther along the path you travel, the farther down the path you can see. Take some quiet time to cast your thoughts onto your evolving spiritual path. What does your life look like in five years? In ten years? In twenty years? Look into those futures to see the person you have become, and looking back from the perspective of that future, see how your life purpose and spiritual path will have unfolded between now and then.

Seeing yourself on a spiritual path that includes everything which happens in your life—even work—will dramatically shift your perspective of your life in its entirety. In truth, it may be inaccurate to call ourselves human beings living on a spiritual path; perhaps it is more accurate to say, as did Teilhard de Chardin, that we are spiritual beings on a human path.

38

Discover the
Power of Prayer

Prayer is less about changing the world than it is about changing ourselves.

—David J. Wolpe

Prayer works. Period.

In the field of healthcare, there have been many studies which have shown that prayer has a positive effect on patients' immune systems, general states of health, and recovery from illness and surgery. In some cases these positive effects have been not only significant but also extraordinary. Since the 1950s, studies have demonstrated that prayer can ease asthma, high blood pressure, gastrointestinal disorders, and anxiety. In laboratory experiments, prayer has been shown to affect the growth rate of fungi, yeast, and plants.

In 1988, Randolph C. Byrd, M.D., a former cardiologist at San Francisco General Hospital, conducted a fascinating study on the effects of intercessory prayer—praying on someone else's behalf. The study involved 393 individuals admitted to the coronary care unit. Patients were randomly placed in either control or experimental groups. The control group received only medical care, while five to seven individuals prayed for each patient in the experimental group. Those who prayed were given only the patients' first names and their diagnoses. This was a carefully controlled, double-blind study, meaning that neither the subjects nor their caregivers (physicians, nurses, and aides) knew which group each patient was in. After ten months, the groups were compared, and a number of statistically significant findings surfaced. The prayed-for group had one-fifth the number of infections requiring antibiotics as the control group. They were also three times less likely to develop pulmonary edema (a buildup of fluid in the lungs due to heart failure). Twelve members of the control group required endotracheal intubations (the placement of a tube in the windpipe for connection to a breathing machine), while none of the prayed-for group needed the procedure. Despite the fact that these findings have been under attack for failure to control all possible variables—clearly an impossibility when dealing with human subjects—Byrd's research opened the eyes of many skeptical physicians.[1]

Notwithstanding the documented and generally held beliefs about the power of prayer to change conditions in our lives—even our health—I am continually amazed by the number of my friends and associates who will immediately turn to prayer in the face of any health, relationship, or financial crisis but who don't even consider the possibility of prayer as a tool to be used in the workplace. I believe there are two reasons why prayer has not come into wider usage as a transformational force for positive change in the workplace.

First, there seems to be general—although unspoken—agreement that work and prayer do not mix. Somehow, we have all been formally or informally indoctrinated with the notion that the workplace is not the proper venue for prayer and that, worse, even if we tried it, prayer would have no effect there. After all, it is only Wall Street, the CEO, and our immediate supervisor who are in charge in that arena, and there is nothing that you or God can do about it!

For Americans, in particular, this concept may be rooted in our constitutional doctrine concerning the separation of church and state. On a more global basis, it appears to have arisen from a perhaps legitimate effort to keep religion out of the workplace. Whatever the origin, the result has been that the use of prayer as a personal resource for dealing with work-related issues has become almost nonexistent.

I am not suggesting that we round up all employees to participate in a company-sponsored program to bring prayer into the work setting, but I am also not denying that there is both the need and the desire to do just that. A few years ago, a friend of mine was having a conversation with one of her colleagues about affirming positive outcomes. During the conversation, Susie mentioned something that came across as far more "spiritual" and "metaphysical" than she usually expressed in the workplace. There followed a few moments of awkward silence. But Susie was then surprised to discover that her colleague took her comment as an invitation for him to talk about his own spiritual needs in the workplace, and one thing led to another. In short order, the two of them discovered they had parallel interests and needs, and they cooked up a scheme to provide a forum for a weekly half-hour employee "Affirmations Meeting" before regular work hours. Their idea was to create an opportunity for employees to bring their difficult work issues into an environment where others would speak and think affirming thoughts to help bring about resolutions to those problems. In short, it was a meeting focused on affirmative prayer.

The first meeting was advertised strictly by word of mouth. Only eight people attended that first week. But the following week those eight people brought others, and forty people showed up for the second meeting. By the fourth meeting, two hundred people showed up! For months thereafter, hundreds of people from all over the company regularly attended the meeting held before work on Thursday mornings. There was no effort to advertise these meetings— every one of those attending was there as a result of having heard about the meeting through fellow employees. People began referring to these meetings as the weekly "prayer meeting."

While stories like this clearly illustrate a deep hunger for prayer in the workplace, my main point is that if you are not consciously using intentional prayer to help you resolve your work issues, you are overlooking a powerful resource that can help you accomplish the results you want in your workplace.

Look to your own experience and become aware of the times in your workplace when prayer would be very much an appropriate response for you. Place a "Remember Prayer" reminder on your desk that you will be likely to see when you are dealing with difficult work issues. Notice your thoughts, your emotions, and the way your physical body feels as you contemplate prayer as an option. What judgments, if any, do you have around the idea of using prayer in your workplace?

Don't be put off by the fact that you may be surrounded by people who say that prayer is either inappropriate or ineffective in the workplace. You can quietly make your own choices and carry them out. No one need ever know that you are praying at work. When things are going crazy around you—yes, right in the middle of that meeting with people yelling and screaming—you can be silently uttering affirmative prayers for a positive outcome, regardless of how it might appear at the time. The manner in which one approaches prayer is extremely important, and our general failure to use prayer in the right way is largely responsible for it not having the recognition it so richly deserves.

The second reason that prayer isn't more common in the workplace is that most of us simply do not know *how* to pray. Most of us were never taught to pray. The lessons on how to pray successfully are there for us to read, but somehow organized religion has missed the mark on this and has trained people to pray incorrectly—in an almost anxious, fearful, hand-wringing, pleading sort of way.

What works is *affirmative* prayer, which begins with acceptance of the concept that the will of God/Spirit/Higher Power is totally good. As James Dillet Freeman says, "Prayer affirms our faith that God is, that God is Good, that God is within us, that God is one with us, and God is bringing us to fulfillment." Affirmative prayer is really an acceptance of God's will as good and an affirmation of our acceptance of that goodness with expectation, gratitude, and joy.

Affirmative prayer does not seek to change God's mind or to bend God's will to align with our own. It seeks only to change *us* through acts of affirmation rather than acts of solicitation, and in the realm of prayer, this is where the rubber meets the road.

The Hindus speak of *maya*, which means the mirror of illusion. And by this they are talking about all of our "perceptual reality." Their spiritual tradition is based on the premise that we believe our perceptions about the external world and take those perceptions to be the truth about our lives. Within that framework, it is important not to let external conditions—particularly adverse conditions—deceive us. The conditions of our lives—including our lives at work—are merely reflections and projections of our consciousness. If you want to change your life conditions, you must work on the underlying consciousness that is bringing these conditions into reality. This is one of the reasons that the anguished, hand-wringing brand of prayer does not work: it focuses our consciousness on the adverse condition. In this way, it reinforces the process of making the source of our distress more real than ever. It is, in fact, another negative application of the Law of Mind Action.

If you are in a movie theater and you do not like what is appearing on the screen, it will do you no good whatsoever to go up to the screen and attempt to change what is being projected there. The projection on the screen is only the effect; the film and the projector are the cause. If you want to change what is appearing on the screen, it is necessary to make changes either in the film being projected or in the projector. When we attempt to change the external circumstances of our lives rather than changing ourselves, it's like trying to change the projection on the screen. The circumstances in our lives are effects—reflections of our thoughts, ideas, and consciousness. They can be changed, but only by changing the underlying cause. Hold only the thoughts you want mirrored back to you in your life and you can change the reflections being projected. This is the essence of effective, affirmative prayer. Changing ourselves—and therefore our consciousness—will invariably result in changed circumstances.

Do not interpret this to mean that you have no role in moving the pieces of your life in order to get them more in line with your changed consciousness as you transform it through prayer. The Quakers say, "Pray and move your feet," meaning that while nothing happens without prayer, it is just as important for you to do the things that are yours to do. In prayer, what is yours to do is always made clear, particularly if you regularly practice some of the other disciplines suggested by this book, such as meditation, using intuition, telling your truth, and harnessing the power of your dreams.

I once heard a story masquerading as a joke that has some relevance here. A man was praying hard about his unfavorable financial situation. He realized that his prosperity consciousness was not all it could be. So he began to pray that he would be more accepting of God's bounty, which he knew to be all around him and available, but the state of his consciousness was preventing him from receiving it. Almost in response, he began having a recurring dream that God was answering his prayer in the form of his winning the lottery. At first, the man patiently waited, but he was never informed that he had won. As the weeks and then months went by, the dream continued. But still the man received no news of his winning the lottery. His frustration level grew until there was little he could think about except winning the lottery. Finally, his emotions at the extreme, he went into a church and screamed at God, "You told me I would win the lottery, and absolutely nothing has happened! I don't understand. Why are you tormenting me this way?" Suddenly there was a tremendous rumble that shook the building, and a voice—*The Voice*—boomed out, "Buy a ticket, stupid!"

Well, the moral of this story should be clear: Make sure that while you are praying you are also moving your feet, buying your lottery ticket, or doing the infinite number of other things that will come to you as silent urgings, gentle nudges, intuitive suggestions, and good ideas from listening to your inner guidance while you pray.

Start getting the benefit of the little-known truth that there is definitely an important role for prayer in your workplace—at least for you.

Practice praying correctly. Occasionally observe yourself while in prayer. Do you find yourself pleading for what you want, or do you have a firm grasp on the concept that your outer life is a reflection of your consciousness and that to change this outer life you must change your consciousness? Develop a habit of prayer that addresses the need for changed consciousness, not changed circumstances. Then, practice. *Practice a lot.*

39

Become a
Channel for Good

One way or another, we all have to find what best fosters the
flowering of our humanity in this contemporary life, and dedicate
ourselves to that.

—Joseph Campbell

As you come to understand that you are a spiritual being living a human life and that you are creating the reality you experience, you also begin to recognize that your work life is an integral part of your spirituality. This awareness expands as you come to understand your life purpose and the part it can play in your work life.

It is no accident that you have chosen the work you have. It is no accident that you are working in your present organization or that you are working with and for the people you do. All of this has been arranged by you—by your Higher Self—to give you as many opportunities as possible to learn and to grow spiritually. At the same time, all the lessons of your present circumstances give you the ability to express more of your Authentic Self.

The more we realize that our work is a valuable source of life lessons and learning opportunities, the more we begin to operate from the perspective that work is an ideal conduit for the expression of good. If you come to understand that your work—regardless of *what* it is, *where* it is, or *who* it is with—is exactly what you have created, with the assistance of Spirit, for the purpose of having the opportunity to do good in the world, doors of opportunity will open to you for exactly that purpose. As you develop and grow spiritually, you will start to identify opportunities to do a tremendous amount of good for yourself and for others. And all of this can occur within the context of your job. By being open to those opportunities and seizing them, you create a channel that allows good to pour through you, from your Spirit through your Authentic Self to the world around you. This is what becoming a *channel for good* is all about.

You begin channeling good by seeing your job as a means to an end—but by that I do not mean getting your paycheck into the bank in time to pay the rent. The end I'm talking about is the ability to see your job as a means for achieving your life purpose. See your work as a natural expression of your spiritually based Authentic Self. Start asking difficult questions about your work and its role in your life: Is your job supporting you in your spiritual growth and development? How is your work contributing to the fulfillment of your life purpose? Are you aggressively seeking and seizing opportunities to do good in your job?

It is easy to assume that we have no right to ask these kinds of questions about our work or to expect our work or our employers to satisfy our spiritual needs. Most of us have bought into the philosophy that since our employers pay us for our time at work we must do almost anything we are asked to do, regardless of how it impacts our spiritual development or our authenticity.

Let's examine the premise that your employer is the source of your income. If you are ready to accept the fact that your life is a reflection of your consciousness, created by your spiritual self, then your job, as a major part of that life, is also a reflection of your consciousness created by your spiritual self. I would submit that your income does not come from your employer but rather that Spirit/God/Higher Power uses your employer to provide you with the income you need to do the work—the "good" work in the metaphysical sense—that you have come to do. In other words, the source of your income is Spirit, and that income comes to you not *from* but *through* your employer. Another way to think of it is that you have chosen this particular employer to act as a conduit to pass through to you the income that Spirit is giving you. When you know this, you understand that you can easily choose another conduit. As I have pointed out, however, many of us believe in the illusion that our paychecks come *from* our employers, and in that context, we feel compelled to do whatever it takes to ensure continuation of those checks—even if it means sacrificing our life purpose and our Authentic Selves during the workday.

Let's say that you accept the notion that your income comes *through* your employer rather than *from* your employer. You then start asking the questions—and you don't like the answers at all. Not one bit. What do you do then? The answer is that you make some changes.

When I say this in my workshops, many people think I am suggesting that they quit their jobs and go in search of employment more in alignment with their Authentic Selves and their individual life purposes. Quitting your job may be one answer, but there are others. Remember that you are in your job—this *particular* job—for spiritually based reasons. It is conceivable that one of those reasons is to have you discover Spirit in every area of your life, including that seemingly banal position you may hold, or with tasks you may find boring, or with people you may find difficult or commonplace. If part of the plan is for you to learn to find the sacred in the ordinary, abandoning your efforts where you are now in order to seek a "better" place will only likely cause you to re-create the same circumstances and relationships at a different location. Remember, your job, like everything else in your life, is simply a reflection of your consciousness. Choose carefully before deciding to bail out of one job situation to pursue the Holy Grail elsewhere.

This brings me to a discussion of the one place where you *can* make changes to transform your relationship with your job: Change begins in your consciousness.

Just as with prayer, any attempt to change the outer circumstances without making a change within the consciousness is pointless. In fact, to do so might be compared to believing it possible to change the configuration of a room by rearranging the reflections of that same room in a mirror. It won't work—you cannot move the reflected objects in the mirror, quite simply because they are only reflections. What will work is making an honest evaluation of how you are holding your job and the people in it in your consciousness and the extent to which you have either made use of or ignored opportunities to use your job as a channel for good.

Recognize that this "good" may have absolutely nothing whatsoever to do with your specific job responsibilities, although it certainly can be related to them. The good you are able to do through your job is your *work*.

I was an employee at Intel for nearly nine years. At various times during that period my job responsibilities included practicing software, contract, antitrust, trademark, and general business law. At other times my job responsibilities included staff administration and development, corporate branding, employee recruitment and retention, training and organizational development, and the creation of new products and lines of business. Those were my official job responsibilities; none of those was my *work*. My job responsibilities were clearly delineated by the company, my manager, or myself; nowhere was there a written description of my work—indeed, my employer would very likely have been shocked to know what I considered my work responsibilities to have been. Within job categories, my duties stayed fairly much the same from day to day, and in time I was able to perform them pretty much by rote. Meanwhile, my work changed minute-by-minute and required me to be very much in the moment or risk losing opportunities to do some good. There was a sense of structure and orderliness around the completion of responsibilities with my job; there was a sense of wide-eyed wonder, as well as a bit of uncertainty, about my work. My job existed within the confines of a clearly defined space with precise boundaries; my work was living on the edge.

I don't think it will come as a surprise for me to say that spirituality is not exactly the highest priority at Intel. As someone recently remarked to me, Intel is not Ben and Jerry's—nor should it be. Nevertheless, I did spiritual work at Intel, bringing my 360-Degree Arc of Authenticity to bear wherever and whenever I could. Interestingly, everyone from outside Intel who touched that arc came to believe that Intel was a spiritual place, and to the extent that I created my own experience there, for me it was.

What would have to change for you in your employment environment to enable you to start thinking more in terms of your work versus your job? What would have to change within you? Using your life purpose as a starting point, make a list of the kinds of activities that are in alignment with your life purpose and through which you would consider yourself channeling good into your workplace. Be open to opportunities to take action and be that channel for good.

One way to start your own transition is to stop thinking about your place of employment as the *place* where you report to work. Instead, think of the place you report to work as an internal process. As you arrive at your employment facility, make a heartfelt statement of work intention: "I'm reporting to *work* now. I will do my job to the best of my abilities, but most importantly, I will seize opportunities to do good. *This* is my work."

Write your own statement of work intention. Consider putting your statement of work intention someplace where you will see it frequently. Then, for one week without interruption, recite your statement of work intention to yourself immediately prior to beginning your job responsibilities. Be aware and stay open to opportunities to put your intention into action and to channel good. If you like what happens, continue the practice.

No matter what your job and where you perform your duties, whether in a high-tech company, a bank, a medical facility, a bus, a manufacturing plant, a law firm, a theater, a government office, a pizza-delivery truck, a school, a ditch, or a restaurant, your true employer is always Spirit. Consequently, part and parcel of your job responsibilities is to do Spirit's work—to do good. If you start holding your relationship with your job that way, you will experience a major shift in everything that you do in the workplace.

Most of us would agree that taking bridge tolls qualifies as one of the most repetitive and boring jobs available. In his book, *Work as a Spiritual Practice*, Lewis Richmond tells the story of someone he calls the "Existential

Toll-taker on the Golden Gate Bridge" who discovered the truth about his work versus his job and clearly made a conscious decision to operate on the work side of the ledger:

> There was one toll-taker who met every car with a cheery grin and the greeting, "Howdy, big spender!" as he took our two dollars. He didn't just do it occasionally. Invariably, when I drove through his booth, his greeting and his smile were the same. I found myself looking ahead as I approached the toll plaza, to see if I could move into his lane. Once I joined in by saying, "What makes you think I'm a big spender?"
>
> "I can see it in your eyes," he replied, raising and lowering his eyebrows like Groucho Marx. That greeting was his way of getting through the day, using humor to enliven his repetitive job. Since of course we all paid the same two dollars, there was something about the way he greeted me every day as a "big spender" that made me feel a bit better about myself. I still remember that feeling now many years later. . . .
>
> "Howdy, big spender!" This tag line has more in it than meets the eye. It says, "I'm not going to just do the job. I'm going to create the job." It expresses a clear intention to reach past the limits of the job description with laughter and good humor. How many toll-takers do you know who have the energy and perseverance to do that? Most of them don't say anything, they just take our money. . . .
>
> Is "Howdy, big spender!" a spiritual practice? Done once or twice, it's just a funny remark. But to keep it up, day after day, the way he did, with that cheery grin on his face, is much more than humor. The Existential

Toll-taker was giving something of himself to each driver who passed through and engaging the world at a spiritual rather than a material level.[1]

Your job is a manifestation of your spirit in the physical world. You can pretend that this is not the case—basically ignore it—or you can consciously claim it.

You get to choose.

40

Employ Angels

See, I am sending an angel ahead of you to guard you along the way and to bring you to the place I have prepared.

—Exodus 23:20

It was a particularly dreary winter day in Silicon Valley. While the rain had not yet started, the streets were already wet from the mist hanging heavy in the air. It would certainly be raining—probably hard—by mid-afternoon, and that was likely to make the afternoon commute a complete nightmare.

I had started for the office at about seven o'clock in the morning, which was a bit later than usual, but I knew I would arrive by 7:45, well within the acceptable limits. As I drove north on Bascom Avenue through San Jose and stopped for the red light at Fruitdale Avenue, which was approximately the halfway point in my commute, my car phone rang. I expected it would be one of two possible callers who were the only people who had the car-phone number: my wife or Phyllis, my administrative assistant.

"Good morning. This is Ric," I answered, expecting to hear the friendly voice of either Betsy or Phyllis. The voice on the other end of the phone was neither one of theirs, and that voice was anything but friendly!

"Goddamn it! What the hell is going on? Where the hell are you?" It was my boss, Todd, and he sounded angrier than I ever remembered him being.

"I'm on my way in. I'll be there in about fifteen to twenty minutes," I said. "What's the problem?" I cautiously ventured, as anxiety rose in my body, mind, spirit, and certainly my voice.

"I don't want to discuss this on a cell phone," he countered, the glare and derision evident in his voice at my apparently idiotic suggestion. "You just make sure you get in here and see me the *minute* you get to the office."

He hung up. Loudly.

The light changed from red to green, and with it, the last of my mood that had not turned gray with the day now turned black and ominous. My spirits sank. My future with the company—if I had one at all—looked bleak. And, bizarrely, I had absolutely no idea what the problem might be. What had I done or not done? Whatever it was, I wondered, could I fix it, or was today going to end with me leaving the company with a final paycheck and a few weeks' severance?

As I continued north on Bascom Avenue, I felt alternately outraged by my boss's conduct and panicked that, despite his penchant for flying off the handle at the slightest provocation, this time his upset and anger at me were warranted. Clearly, I had done something very bad indeed in his eyes, and I still had about twenty minutes before I would even find out what it was. That was plenty of time to work myself up into quite a state before I got to the office. Maybe, just maybe, I thought, I would walk right into Todd's office and quit before he even had the chance to fire me. Yes, that's what I'd do. I'd quit!

Then, in the midst of all this mental mayhem, a funny and serendipitous thing happened. I remembered a conversation I'd had a few days earlier with an elderly woman friend from our church. Alice had told me that when she was heading toward some potential problem she would send angels ahead of her to help ease the situation before she even got there. For example, if she was having a meeting that was causing her some anxiety, she would sit quietly for a few moments and imagine herself sending angels to that meeting and to the other people who were to attend the meeting. She told me that when she arrived later herself, the overall situation and the relationships with the others were always better than she could have imagined. The angels, she said, had done their advance work.

I had listened politely. My logical and judgmental cognitive mind characterized her story as the quaint ramblings of a septuagenarian's faith in the unseen. I had thought no more about it until the moments after Todd's call.

Now, in my seemingly desperate circumstances, the entire conversation came back to me. Indeed, I almost felt Alice's gentle presence in the car with me telling me—reminding me—to visualize myself summoning angels and sending them ahead of me to deal with the issue in my office even before I got there. As I drove along I reweighed the words she had offered me just a few days before.

Despite everything I knew about Spirit's willingness to make my path straight and easy, I was having my doubts about this. My friend's technique just seemed too simplistic, too easy. It didn't require more than asking, and there was a big part of me still tethered to the concept that we always need to struggle with life's issues. Angels? Really, Ric, get a grip on yourself! Then, in a flash, I realized that I had nothing to lose and possibly everything to gain. After all, I really was feeling desperate!

So at the next red light and at every red light on my way to the office, I imagined myself sending angels ahead of me to deal with whatever the issue was that had made Todd so angry. At first, it only felt like a sputter, and I was also having a hard time getting a visual on sending angels before me. Then, quite suddenly, the perfect vision appeared. I knew it immediately because it felt right, and it also came along with a healthy dose of Spirit's sense of humor.

In my mind's eye, I suddenly remembered a scene from *The Wizard of Oz* in which the Wicked Witch of the West, after spying Dorothy and her friends in her crystal ball, calls the commanders of her army of flying monkeys and tells them to bring back the girl and her dog and to do what they want with the others. As the hordes of flying monkeys fly by her open window, the wicked witch steps up onto the windowsill to orchestrate their evil advance like some mad symphonic conductor. As they fly off after Dorothy and her friends, the witch waves her arms and screeches, "Fly! Fly! Fly!"

As ridiculous as the image seemed to be in the circumstances, I decided to accept it and run with it. Dressed in white robes, rather than the wicked witch's familiar black vestments, I stepped up to the wide, open window and out onto a terrace—*my* castle has a terrace!—from which I could see an almost infinite distance. Standing there and orchestrating their movement, much as the wicked witch had done, I called forth angels of light and sent them before me, telling them to "Fly! Fly! Fly!" In my mind's eye, at least, thousands upon thousands of angels responded, and the sky was soon filled with them. I stood on the terrace while the brilliant light of these emissaries radiated down upon me and lifted my spirits.

The final traffic light changed to green, and I turned in to the parking lot, parked the car, and walked to the building through the light drizzle that had now begun. My feelings of dread returned, and any expectation that my army of angels would have any effect at all disappeared. Indeed, in those moments of fear, I forgot about the imagery. I had no expectations other than what would likely result when I had to face Todd and his wrath.

I showed up outside Todd's office in my damp coat, clutching my briefcase in one hand and my car keys in the other. Before going in, I stopped by the desk of Todd's administrative assistant, Fiona, an Irish woman with whom I had a great relationship. "How's he doing?" I mouthed silently, motioning my head to Todd's office. Fiona didn't say a word; instead, she rolled her eyes with a painful grimace and a look of understanding and sympathy that bordered on outright pity. Clearly, this was not a good omen, and I was in for a tough time.

I took a deep breath in an attempt to calm myself and walked into Todd's office. He was pecking away at his computer, his back to the entrance.

"Todd," I said, and hoping to sound upbeat, I quickly added, "What's up?"

He didn't even look up. "Never mind," he said, "it's taken care of."

And that was it! I mean that was *really* the *end* of it! I never found out what the issue was, why Todd was so upset, what I had done or not done—nothing! That was the end of it, and despite a burning curiosity, I had the good sense not to ask any questions.

But it was just the beginning of my employment of angels. From that time forward, whenever I had a meeting or a task about which I had even the mildest case of anxiety, I would go inside my consciousness and stand out on the terrace, directing my angels to "Fly! Fly! Fly!" ahead of me to resolve all that could be resolved even before I got there.

Within months, things had changed around the office—for me, at least. I had made a concerted effort to send angels ahead to any meeting Todd would be attending. Our meetings were more productive, and I seemed to have developed greater insight into his thinking processes, which had been quite an enigma to me prior to this. The truth was that few, if any, of the members of Todd's staff got along with him, and as my relationship with him got better over time, others began to notice the shift.

"What are you doing?" Jerry, one of my colleagues, asked me one day when we were talking about yet another distressing managerial decision Todd had made.

"What do you mean?" I asked.

"You must be doing something," he said, "because it's obvious that Todd is treating you better than most of the rest of us."

I had mixed feelings about telling Jerry my secret. Jerry had a reputation for having fundamentalist religious beliefs, and I didn't know how this angel thing was going to go over with him.

"You sure you want to know?" I asked, "It's a bit 'out there' in terms of New Age metaphysical concepts."

Jerry said that he did, so I told him. He listened silently and politely while I told him the entire story, beginning with the phone call Todd had made to me months earlier through my continuing employment of angels in my interactions with Todd since then, as well as expanding the concept to include other areas of my life that needed special attention.

Jerry didn't say much, and since I felt uncomfortable putting him on the spot by asking him what he thought about it, I simply gave him the information he had asked for and left it at that.

A few months later, Jerry sidled over to me during a break in a meeting with a big grin on his face.

"You know that angel thing you told me about?" he said. "It works."

We never talked about it again, but I watched over the next few months as Jerry's relationship with Todd continued to improve much as mine had done. Whatever it was that Jerry needed to learn on a spiritual level from his relationship with Todd had been accomplished quickly.

How willing are you to believe that something inexplicable by human standards—a metaphysical mystery—can work for you? Ask yourself if you are willing to use a tool the workings of which you do not understand and are likely never to understand? Be honest about your thoughts and prejudices around the concept of employing angels to do advance work for you to smooth your work issues.

"That angel thing," as Jerry called it, really does work. I have used it with incredible albeit unexplained success in any number of situations: preparing to meet with difficult people, clearing expected traffic from my planned auto route, preparing an audience to be open and receptive to my keynote address—just about anything where a bit of advance work by angels could come in handy.

Try employing angels. Create your own visual such as my parallel image of the Wicked Witch of the West sending forth her army of flying monkeys. Make it fun and playful. Use it the next time a situation arises over which you seem to have no control whatsoever. You may need to post some kind of reminder to yourself. In the heat of upset and worry, it is not easy to remember to call on and employ angels on your behalf. Gauge the results. If it works, by all means, *do not forget* to use it in the future. (*Note*: You are most likely to forget about it when you most need it!)

I do not fully understand how or why calling on and employing angels works the way it does. I just know that it does work. Undoubtedly, it has something to do with acknowledging our connection with Spirit's realm. That acknowledgment alone could work wonders in terms of transforming one's experience of life if it is held in an appropriate frame of heart and mind. As I've said before, recognizing and honoring our connection with Spirit also allows us to be more authentic in life, because we *are* spiritual beings having a human experience. Remembering that fact is frequently difficult in a work world filled with rushing from this task to that, competitive advantages and disadvantages, big egos, difficult people wielding seemingly large amounts of power over us, and our own personal and societal training about how one is to function in the context of the world of work.

There is one thing I do know with absolute certainty about employing angels in the workplace, however: If you don't ask for help, you don't get any!

EPILOGUE

An adventure is going into the unknown. If you know exactly where you are going, exactly how you will get there, and exactly what you will see along the way, it is not an adventure. . . . Because they involve the unknown, adventures are inherently dangerous to a greater or lesser degree. Yet it is also only from adventures and their newness that we learn. If we know exactly where we're going, exactly how to get there, and exactly what we'll see along the way, we won't learn anything.

—M. Scott Peck

THE GREAT ADVENTURE

Helen Keller said, "Life is either a daring adventure, or it is nothing. To keep our faces toward change and behave like free spirits in the presence of fate is strength undefeatable." Hopefully, this book has helped you to discover that your life is your own daring adventure and, more particularly, that much of this daring adventure occurs in your workplace. Whether you choose to participate in your daring adventure consciously or unconsciously is what makes all the difference. That difference will be measured by the level of your results and successes, the extent of your happiness and contentment, your sense of professional and personal fulfillment, the degree to which you feel energized and excited rather than depleted and stressed, and the extent to which you and others are experiencing your authenticity in your workplace.

If authenticity provided no additional workplace benefits—and I assure you, it does—the mere fact that you no longer need to be someone other than who you are at your inner, spiritual core will save you a great amount of energy. Being who you are frees your attention and focus for other, more creative and fulfilling endeavors.

Change your thinking and your choices and you will change your life. Yes, this is another plug for the Law of Mind Action. If you comprehend the immense power of this simple concept, you will acquire the ability to change your life conditions, making new choices to have the life you truly want.

Every muscular movement you make takes into account the Law of Gravity—and whether you make that movement consciously or unconsciously is irrelevant. As soon as you make any attempt to ignore the Law of Gravity, you stumble or fall, or things do not remain where you have placed them. Just so, every thought you think and every choice you make should take into account the Law of Mind Action. When you do so, you can catapult the conditions in your life to heights you can only now imagine. The only alternative is futilely attempting to ignore the operation of this law, which you do at your peril. Plotting your life's course without consideration for the Law of Mind Action is about as foolhardy as planning to hike across the Grand Canyon with the intention of totally ignoring the Law of Gravity.

In the same way that the body's incorporation of the Law of Gravity is a combination of learned and inherent responses, so it is also with the Law of Mind Action. Some elements you inherit at birth while others need to be learned. You now have the tools to assist you with the latter.

UNDERSTANDING HABITS AND CHOICES

The conditions in your life result primarily from the choices you make. If you want different life conditions, you need to make different choices—pure and simple. That, however, may be difficult if you are making choices unconsciously—even if you are doing so only on occasion. Unconscious choices are more commonly called "habits."

You already have habits, and to a great degree they have dictated the choices you have made in your life situations. Those choices have, in turn, created the conditions you are presently living, which you may or may not be enjoying. By exercising *awareness* and becoming mindful of your habits and their results—and the results they are likely to continue to give you—you create a new opportunity to make a *choice* other than what your habit would normally dictate. In this state of greater awareness—and authenticity—you are likely to make choices that are consistent with your life purpose. In this way you maximize the chances of creating the conditions you *want* to have in your life. As you consistently choose life parameters from mindfulness and awareness, those choices eventually become your new habit, more in line with your life purpose and your Authentic Self, and you will see that area of your life transform.

You can kick-start this process by using any of the tools and techniques you have discovered in this book. Recognize, however, that to the extent that you practice any of them with *full* awareness, you will be creating for yourself the opportunity to put the Law of Mind Action to work for you in the creation of a better, more successful and fulfilling life.

WHEN ALL ELSE FAILS...

On occasion people approach me after one of my talks or programs to ask what they should do if the tools and techniques discussed in this book aren't working for them. Some of them tell me that they have tried some of these approaches, but to no avail. They have experienced no changes in their circumstances, in their feelings about those circumstances, or in their relationships with the people around them. These people all say the same thing: innately, they *know* that these principles work—indeed, many use them successfully in other areas of their lives—but in the workplace, well, they just don't seem to be functioning optimally. What, they say, do you do when all else fails?

There are two possible explanations for the seeming failure of these principles: The first is that the principles are not being used properly. That could mean a variety of different things. As I said earlier in this book, if you are not getting the results you want in some situation, check your level of commitment. You may lack the commitment to have the situation work in the first place. This can be somewhat insidious. You go through all the motions, but somewhere in the back of your mind you are holding thoughts like, "See, I'm doing this and I'm doing that, and it still isn't working," and the situation doesn't get any better. Often we will make a subconscious case that something cannot possibly get better than it is, and then we "prove" that case with the ineffectiveness of our attempts to change it. Think the Law of Mind Action.

If you find that you are, in fact, comfortable with the level of your commitment, check next to see if you are using a particular tool or technique in a way that makes sense in the circumstances, that you are using it consistently, and that you have been using it for a long enough period of time. While we certainly seem to *expect* miracles, most of us aren't quite ready to *accept* miracles, which means that changes in our consciousness may take some time to change our life's circumstances.

The second reason for apparent failure is somewhat more complex and deserves examination. It may be that success on your life's path requires seeming failure in the situation at hand. The histories and traditions of nations, science, art, business, and the affairs of people in all walks of life are filled with the stories of those who failed and failed and failed again only to see the seeds of those failures blossom into successes so overwhelming as to make them famous. If this has happened to others, why not you?

Also consider the possibility—particularly if these principles do not seem to be giving you the results you want—that you are simply in the wrong place or that you are there at the wrong time. We humans tend to be creatures of habit and will stay in a situation long after it ceases to be suitable for us. Indeed, we often become committed—not necessarily to the right or best path for ourselves but to staying in a situation *no matter what*. We may even turn to metaphysics to assist us in this hapless pursuit.

It is a blessing, albeit an uncomfortable one, that for each of us, our Higher or Inner Self, the God Presence Within, Spirit, the Universe—choose your favorite term—knows better. The result is that if staying in a situation will not bring about your highest good, no amount of metaphysical discipline or intention will make things work to keep you in that situation, because *you aren't supposed to be there!* In short, if things are not working for you despite your best efforts, the message may be, "So change already!"

ONE LAST NOTE

Authenticity—and its underlying spirituality—is not something that you can simply turn on. You will not wake up one day and discover that you are living fully in your Authentic Self whereas yesterday your Authentic Self was nowhere to be found.

Becoming authentic is a process. It is a process that *every* person on this planet is in right now. This includes those who do not know about the Authentic Self, those who deny the Authentic Self, those who know about the Authentic Self and are seeking the means to expand its presence in their lives, and those who know about the Authentic Self and believe they have already achieved complete authenticity. Each of those states of mind is . . . well, simply a part of that person's process.

It's no big deal to be in the process of becoming authentic, but at the same time it is *everything*. Authenticity is a game of awareness. The advantage you have, and which brought you to the place in your life that caused this book to come into your hands, is that you are *conscious* of your process of becoming authentic. That mindfulness is a priceless advantage.

The fact that your journey toward authenticity is just that—a journey—means that there will be times when you will feel as though you have fallen flat on your face. There will be times when you will wonder why you are even bothering. There may even be times when you will forget the process, forget authenticity, forget awareness, forget *everything*. Somehow, no matter how tough things seem to be when we are in one of the "dark spots" on this journey toward authenticity, it always seems to work out. *Always*.

And that, I think, is a key point to remember. It's the journey that counts and not the destination, because we are all going to arrive at that destination at some point or another.

If we were already at the destination of total awareness—Christ, Krishna, or cosmic consciousness, if you will—we would simply ascend, because our journey would have thus been completed. We would be, as it were, at the destination and no longer on the journey. At the same time, it's important to know that this could happen to you at any time.

Just watch your head on the ceiling!

NOTES

Introduction

1. Joel Levey and Michelle Levey, *Living in Balance* (Berkeley, Calif.: Conari Press, 1998), pp. 227 et seq.
2. Joel Levey and Michelle Levey, *Living in Balance*, p. 227.

Chapter 3

1. Oliver Wendell Holmes, *Lockner v New York*, 198 U.S. 45, 75 (1904).
2. Pentium is a registered trademark of Intel Corporation.
3. Intel Inside is a registered trademark of Intel Corporation.

Chapter 10

1. Joseph Murphy, *How to Attract Money* (Marina del Rey, Calif.: DeVorss & Co., 1955, 1998), p. 17.

Chapter 14

1. C. G. Jung, "The Practical Use of Dream-Analysis," in *Dreams* (Princeton, N.J.: Princeton University Press, 1974), p. 90.

Chapter 15

1. David Whyte, *The Heart Aroused: Poetry and the Preservation of the Soul in Corporate America* (New York: Currency-Doubleday, 1994), pp. 233–34. (Emphasis in original.)

Chapter 18

1. Joseph Lewis, *The Ten Commandments* (New York: Freethought Press, 1946), pp. 184–86.

Chapter 19

1. Kate Ludemann and Gay Hendricks, *The Corporate Mystic* (New York: Bantam Books, 1996), pp. 42–45.

Chapter 21

1. *Emoticon* is an Internet-spawned term from "emotion" + "icon" meaning those symbols many people use in e-mail messages, chat rooms, and bulletin boards to express emotions, such as ☺.

Chapter 23

1. Edward de Bono, *de Bono's Thinking Course* (New York: Facts on File Books, 1982, 1994), pp. 93–95.

Chapter 33

1. Harriet Rubin, "Only the Paranoid Survive," *Fast Company* 29 (November 1999), p. 330.

Chapter 35

1. Margaret Wheatley, "The New Story Is Ours to Tell," *Perspectives on Business and Global Change* (Ojai, Calif.: World Business Academy, June 1997).

Chapter 37

1. Richard J. Leider, *The Power of Purpose* (San Francisco: Berrett Koehler Publishers, 1997), p. 1 et seq.

Chapter 38

1. Randolph C. Byrd, "Positive Therapeutic Effects of Intercessory Prayer in a Coronary Care Unit Population," *Southern Medical Journal* 81 (July 7, 1988), pp. 826–29.

Chapter 39

1. Lewis Richmond, *Work as a Spiritual Practice* (New York: Broadway Books, 1999), pp. 97–98.

For more information about other books and tapes, or to invite Ric for a speaking engagement, consultation, or facilitation of a workshop, program, or retreat, please contact

The Spirit Employed Company
800-538-2001
or
408-264-9723
or e-mail
info@spiritemployed.com

You can access the Spirit Employed Web site at
www.spiritemployed.com

Other Books from Beyond Words Publishing, Inc.

PowerHunch!

Living an Intuitive Life

Author: Marcia Emery, Ph.D.; Foreword: Leland Kaiser, Ph.D.

$15.95, softcover

Whether it's relationships, career, balance and healing, or simple everyday decision-making, intuition gives everyone an edge. In *PowerHunch!* Dr. Emery is your personal trainer as you develop your intuitive muscle. She shows you how to consistently and accurately apply your hunches to any problem and offers countless examples of intuition in action, covering a wide spectrum of occupations and relationships. With its intriguing stories and expert advice, *PowerHunch!* gives you the necessary tools and principles to create an intuitive life for yourself.

The Intuitive Way

A Guide to Living from Inner Wisdom

Author: Penney Peirce; Foreword: Carol Adrienne

$16.95, softcover

When intuition is in full bloom, life takes on a magical, effortless quality; your world is suddenly full of synchronicities, creative insights, and abundant knowledge just for the asking. *The Intuitive Way* shows you how to enter that state of perceptual aliveness and integrate it into daily life to achieve greater natural flow through an easy-to-understand, ten-step course. Author Penney Peirce synthesizes teachings from psychology, East-West philosophy, religion, meta-physics, and business. In simple and direct language, Peirce describes the intuitive process as a new way of life and demonstrates many practical applications from speeding decision-making to expanding personal growth. Whether you're just beginning to search for a richer, fuller life experience or are looking for more subtle, sophisticated insights about your spiritual path, *The Intuitive Way* will be your companion as you progress through the stages of intuition development.

Know Your Truth, Speak Your Truth, Live Your Truth
Author: Eileen R. Hannegan, M.S.
$12.95, softcover

Know Your Truth, Speak Your Truth, Live Your Truth is a transformational guide for those seeking truth and authenticity in their personal and professional lives. This book provides inspiration, encouragement, and practical steps on the road to discovering and living one's own truth. It is filled with illustrative stories as well as exercises, affirmations, and questions for reflection that will enhance your personal and spiritual growth and light the way to owning, asserting, and honoring the power of the truth within.

Celebrating Time Alone
Stories of Splendid Solitude
Author: Lionel Fisher
$14.95, softcover

Celebrating Time Alone, with its profiles in solitude, shows us how to be magnificently alone through a celebration of our self: the self that can get buried under mountains of information, appointments, and activities. Lionel Fisher interviewed men and women across the country who have achieved great emotional clarity by savoring their individuality and solitude. In a writing style that is at once eloquent and down to earth, the author interweaves their real-life stories with his own insights and experiences to offer counsel, inspiration, and affirmation on living well alone.

Forgiveness

The Greatest Healer of All

Author: Gerald G. Jampolsky, M.D.; Foreword: Neale Donald Walsch

$12.95, softcover

Forgiveness: The Greatest Healer of All is written in simple, down-to-earth language. It explains why so many of us find it difficult to forgive and why holding on to grievances is really a decision to suffer. The book describes what causes us to be unforgiving and how our minds work to justify this. It goes on to point out the toxic side effects of being unforgiving and the havoc it can play on our bodies and on our lives. But above all, it leads us to the vast benefits of forgiving.

The author shares powerful stories that open our hearts to the miracles which can take place when we truly believe that no one needs to be excluded from our love. Sprinkled throughout the book are Forgiveness Reminders that may be used as daily affirmations supporting a new life free of past grievances.

The Great Wing

A Parable

Author: Louis A. Tartaglia, M.D.; Foreword: Father Angelo Scolozzi

$14.95, hardcover

The Great Wing transforms the timeless miracle of the migration of a flock of geese into a parable for the modern age. It recounts a young goose's own reluctant but steady transformation from gangly fledgling to Grand Goose and his triumph over the turmoils of his soul and the buffeting of a mighty Atlantic storm. In *The Great Wing*, our potential as individuals is affirmed, as is the power of group prayer, or the "Flock Mind." As we make the journey with this goose and his flock, we rediscover that we tie our own potential into the power of the common good by way of attributes such as honesty, hope, courage, trust, perseverance, spirituality, and service. The young goose's trials and tribulations, as well as his triumph, are our own.

Seeing Your Life Through New Eyes
InSights to Freedom from Your Past
Authors: Paul Brenner, M.D., Ph.D., and Donna Martin, M.A.
$14.95, softcover

Seeing Your Life Through New Eyes is in a hands-on workbook format that helps you create a diary of self-discovery and assists you in resolving any misunderstood relationships. You can learn how to uncover unconscious patterns that define how you love, what you value, and what unique gifts you have in life. This book reveals those obstacles that too often interfere with loving relationships and creative expression, and it includes diagrams to use for your personal exploration and growth.

Taming Your Inner Brat
A Guide for Transforming Self-Defeating Behavior
Author: Pauline Wallin, Ph.D.
$14.95, softcover

An inner brat?!! Who, me?? We've all got one: that force within us which compels us to sneak just one more cigarette or cookie, procrastinate on taxes, or throw a hissy fit when the store clerk takes too long. With humor and without scolding, *Taming Your Inner Brat* gives readers specific strategies and skills to bring bratty thoughts, feelings, and behaviors under control. The author explains the psychological sources of the inner brat and addresses social and cultural conditions that encourage the self-centeredness and sense of entitlement on which the inner brat thrives. By teaching us how to recognize our inner brat, *Taming Your Inner Brat* helps us bring problems into manageable perspective and make changes that last.

When Money Is Not Enough
Fulfillment in Work
Author: Eileen R. Hannegan, M.S.
$10.95, softcover

In an age when Americans spend more than half their waking hours either at work or performing a function related to work, it is important that the workplace be a healthy community rather than a chaotic battleground. *When Money Is Not Enough* offers the premise that when personality battles create stress and illness, no amount of money in the world is enough to justify continued employment. The book is neither pro-employer nor pro-employee in its approach. Instead, it encourages increasing interdependence among all staff members. Approaching the workplace as a community or family is the key to resolving problems. Drawing from her years of experience as a consultant and lecturer in family systems and organizational development, author Eileen R. Hannegan offers proven methods of transforming the workplace from toxic to healthy. Work can indeed enhance life as well as pay the bills.

You Can Have It All
Author: Arnold M. Patent
$16.95, hardcover

Joy, peace, abundance—these gifts of the Universe are available to each of us whenever we choose to play the real game of life: the game of mutual support. *You Can Have It All* is a guidebook that shows us how to move beyond our beliefs in struggle and shortage, open our hearts, and enjoy a life of true ecstasy. Arnold Patent first self-published *You Can Have It All* in 1984, and it became a classic with over 200,000 copies in print. This revised and expanded edition reflects his greater understanding of the principles and offers practical suggestions as well as simple exercises for improving the quality of our lives.

When God Winks

How the Power of Concidence Guides Your Life

Author: SQuire Rushnell

$16.95, hardcover

When God Winks confirms a belief secretly held by most readers: there is more to coincidences than meets the eye. Like winks from a loving grandparent, coincidences are messages from above that you are not alone and everything will be OK. The compelling theory of why coincidences exist is applied to fascinating stories in history, sports, the news, medicine, and relationships involving both everyday people and celebrities.

Conscious Seeing

Transforming Your Life Through Your Eyes

Author: Roberto Kaplan, O.D., M.Ed.

$14.95, softcover

In Conscious Seeing, the reader learns that no eye problem is independent from our experience and perceptions. It is the first book that explains in depth how the mind elaborates on the sense of sight. By being guided to look at their eyes beyond the diagnosis of a problem, readers will come to understand that their visual symptoms are valuable messages through which they can be more aware of their true nature. If an eye problem exists, a person can gain the skills to modify his or her perceptions. As the author asserts, looking is trainable when people see consciously.

The Infinite Thread

Healing Relationships beyond Loss

Author: Alexandra Kennedy

$14.95, softcover

The death of a loved one is often accompanied by regrets—for what we said or didn't say, what we did or didn't do. In our grief, our old resentments, regrets, and unexpressed love can hinder our emotional growth, creating wounds that affect all our other relationships. With exercises designed to re-create and heal past relationships, *The Infinite Thread* illustrates that keeping our loved one alive in our hearts—and in our minds—will enable us to make peace with the past and move freely into the future.

Midlife Clarity

Epiphanies from Grown-Up Girls

Editors: Cynthia Black and Laura Carlsmith

Contributing Editor: Jane Foley

$14.95, softcover

The wisdom of a woman is one of our earth's greatest natural resources. *Midlife Clarity* brings together the insights of thirty women from all over the country who have found clarity in midlife and have life lessons to share. Hear their thoughts on the duality of the female nature, vulnerability, body acceptance, freedom, self-discovery, men, the decision whether to have children, and mindfulness of the moment. The diverse entries include essays, humor, personal stories, opinion pieces, and short poetry. *Midlife Clarity* is a timely, touching, and often hilarious window into the hearts and souls of the treasured, yet often overlooked, gatekeepers of the human condition.

Rites of Passage

Celebrating Life's Changes

Authors: Kathleen Wall, Ph.D., and Gary Ferguson

$12.95, softcover

Every major transition in our lives—be it marriage, high-school graduation, the death of a parent or spouse, or the last child leaving home—brings with it opportunities for growth and self-actualization and for repositioning ourselves in the world. Personal ritual—the focus of *Rites of Passage*—allows us to use the energy held within the anxiety of change to nourish the new person that is forever struggling to be born. *Rites of Passage* begins by explaining to readers that human growth is not linear, as many of us assume, but rather occurs in a five-part cycle. After sharing the patterns of transition, the authors then show the reader how ritual can help him or her move through these specific life changes: work and career, intimate relationships, friends, divorce, changes within the family, adolescence, issues in the last half of life, and personal loss.

There's a Hole in My Sidewalk

The Romance of Self-Discovery

Author: Portia Nelson

$7.95, softcover

This classic, well-loved guide to life is warm, wise, and funny. Portia Nelson's book and her poem "Autobiography in Five Short Chapters" have been embraced by individuals, therapy groups, and self-help programs around the world.

To order or to request a catalog, contact
Beyond Words Publishing, Inc.
20827 N.W. Cornell Road, Suite 500
Hillsboro, OR 97124-9808
503-531-8700 or 1-800-284-9673

You can also visit our Web site at *www.beyondword.com*
or e-mail us at *info@beyondword.com*.

BEYOND WORDS PUBLISHING, INC.

OUR CORPORATE MISSION

Inspire to Integrity

OUR DECLARED VALUES

We give to all of life as life has given us.
We honor all relationships.
Trust and stewardship are integral to fulfilling dreams.
Collaboration is essential to create miracles.
Creativity and aesthetics nourish the soul.
Unlimited thinking is fundamental.
Living your passion is vital.
Joy and humor open our hearts to growth.
It is important to remind ourselves of love.